Austin Farrer for Today

Austin Farrer for Today

A Prophetic Agenda

Edited by

Richard Harries
and
Stephen Platten

scm press

Published in 2020 by SCM Press
Editorial office
3rd Floor, Invicta House,
108–114 Golden Lane,
London EC1Y 0TG, UK
www.scmpress.co.uk

SCM Press is an imprint of Hymns Ancient & Modern Ltd
(a registered charity)

Hymns Ancient & Modern® is a registered trademark of
Hymns Ancient & Modern Ltd
13A Hellesdon Park Road, Norwich,
Norfolk NR6 5DR, UK

978-0-334-05944-8

British Library Cataloguing in Publication data
A catalogue record for this book is available
from the British Library

Typeset by Regent Typesetting
Printed and bound by
CPI Group (UK) Ltd

For all those scholars inspired by Austin Farrer
as they build on his remarkable foundations.

Contents

Language and Symbolism

Doctrine

Prayer and Preaching

Farrer and the Future

Acknowledgements

Any essay collection of this sort requires much work from a host of people. Paramount here is Kay Norman who has helped us with typing, reformatting and organizing the digital files of all the manuscripts. Rob MacSwain has kindly allowed us to use his very thorough bibliography and Mark Goodacre has added to this in the area of biblical studies. Our families have been generous in allowing the editors the time to complete their work and in listening to countless references to Austin Farrer! Thanks too to all contributors for their work amid all else for which they are responsible. Many thanks to Rosslie Platten for her help in the unenviable tasks of producing both subject and author indexes, and thanks as ever to David Shervington and all the team at SCM Press.

List of Contributors

John Barton was Oriel and Laing Professor of the Interpretation of Holy Scripture in the University of Oxford, 1991–2014, and is now a Senior Research Fellow of Campion Hall. He studied Theology at Keble in the 1960s and was one of Austin Farrer's last students. He wrote his doctoral thesis on the eighth-century prophets under the supervision of John Austin Baker. A Londoner by birth, he lives in Abingdon near Oxford, where he is an honorary assistant priest in the parish of Abingdon-on-Thames. He has written 20 books, the most recent being *A History of the Bible: The Book and Its Faiths* (2019).

Paul J. DeHart is Professor of Theology at Vanderbilt University, where he has taught since 1997. Born in Memphis, Tennessee, he studied Theology at Yale University and the University of Chicago, where he obtained his PhD. He has published *Beyond the Necessary God* (1999), *The Trial of the Witnesses* (2006) and *Aquinas and Radical Orthodoxy* (2014), along with several journal articles and book chapters. His current research includes projects on incarnation and the historical Jesus, on the theology of divine infinity, and on the tension between Nicene and modern Protestant treatments of the Trinity.

Mark Goodacre is the Frances Hill Fox Professor of Religious Studies at Duke University, North Carolina. He earned his MA, MPhil and DPhil at the University of Oxford. His research interests include the Gospels, the Apocryphal New Testament, and the historical Jesus. Goodacre is the author of four books including *The Case Against Q: Studies in Markan Priority and the Synoptic Problem* (2002) and *Thomas and the Gospels: The Making of an Apocryphal Text* (2012). He is well known for creating web resources on the New Testament and Christian origins, including his podcast, the NT Pod. Goodacre has acted as consultant for several TV and radio programmes including *The Passion* (BBC/HBO, 2008), *Finding Jesus* (CNN, 2015–17), and *Jesus: His Life* (2019). Goodacre is currently working on a book on John's knowledge of the Synoptic Gospels.

Richard Harries, a former Bishop of Oxford (1987–2006), is an Honorary Professor of Theology at King's College, London. His main focus in recent years has been on the interface of Christian faith and wider culture, most recently in *Haunted by Christ: Modern Writers and the Struggle for Faith* (2018) and *Seeing God in Art: the Christian Faith in 30 Images* (2020). He is the author of an anthology of Farrer's writings, *The One Genius: Readings Through the Year with Austin Farrer* (1987).

Morwenna Ludlow is Professor of Christian History and Theology at the University of Exeter. She is author of *The Early Church* (2009), co-editor with Scot Douglass of *Reading the Church Fathers* (2011) and has written widely on Gregory of Nyssa. Her most recent book is *Art, Craft, and Theology in Fourth-Century Christian Authors*, published by Oxford University Press (2020). In this she explores the subtle interplay between theology and literary form in early Christianity. She argues that authors like John Chrysostom and the Cappadocians saw themselves as practitioners of a theological literary craft – they were wordsmiths who experimented with literary techniques, working alongside each other like members of a workshop.

Robert MacSwain is Associate Professor of Theology at the University of the South in Sewanee, Tennessee. He previously served as the Ramsey Fellow and Chaplain of St Chad's College, Durham University. A graduate of Princeton Theological Seminary, the University of Edinburgh, and Virginia Theological Seminary, he received his doctorate from the University of St Andrews. The author of *Solved by Sacrifice: Austin Farrer, Fideism, and the Evidence of Faith* (2013), he has edited or co-edited seven other volumes, including two on Austin Farrer. He is currently writing a monograph on the idea of holy lives as evidence for God.

Gregory Platten is Canon Chancellor of Lichfield Cathedral. Previously he was the Vicar of All Saints, Friern Barnet and Area Dean of Barnet, in the Diocese of London, and Chaplain to Lincoln College, Oxford. While at Lincoln, Gregory completed his DPhil in twentieth-century Russian religious thought, supervised by Professor George Pattison. His current theological focus is on modern doctrine and political ethics.

Stephen Platten taught Theology at Lincoln Theological College, moving later to become the Archbishop of Canterbury's Secretary for Ecumenical Affairs, then subsequently Dean of Norwich and Bishop of Wakefield. He is the author of a number of books including *Augustine's Legacy*, *Rebuilding Jerusalem* and *Animating Liturgy*; among the books he has edited is one other in collaboration with Richard Harries, *Reinhold Niebuhr and Contemporary Politics: God and Power*.

Jane Shaw is Principal of Harris Manchester College, Professor of the History of Religion, and Pro-Vice-Chancellor in the University of Oxford. Formerly, she was Dean for Religious Life and Professor of Religious

Studies at Stanford University; Dean of Grace Cathedral in San Francisco; and Reader in Church History, and Dean of Divinity and Fellow of New College, in the University of Oxford. She has also served as Canon Theologian of Salisbury Cathedral, where she is now Canon Emerita. Her books include *Miracles in Enlightenment England* (2006), *Octavia, Daughter of God: the Story of a Female Messiah and her Followers* (2011), *A Practical Christianity* (2012) and *Pioneers of Modern Spirituality* (2018).

Jenn Strawbridge is Associate Professor in New Testament Studies at Oxford and Caird Fellow in Theology at Mansfield College. She is a Wiccamical Prebendary (Honorary Canon Theologian) of Chichester Cathedral and Canon Theologian at Blackburn Cathedral. She is also an Associate Priest at St Andrew's, Headington. She has published on the letters of Paul in the early church, as well as early Christian inscriptions, teaching, education and doctrine, including her monograph *The Pauline Effect* and two edited volumes, *Love Makes No Sense: An Invitation to Christian Theology* (2019) and *The First Letter of Peter: A Global Commentary* (2020). Her current work is a study of sightlessness in the ancient world and especially the New Testament.

Leigh Vicens is an Associate Professor of Philosophy at Augustana University in Sioux Falls, South Dakota. Her research is mainly on free will, moral responsibility, and related topics in philosophy of religion such as divine providence and the problem of evil, and she has published articles in a number of philosophy journals and anthologies, as well as a recent book with Cambridge University Press, co-authored with Simon Kittle, called *God and Human Freedom* (2019). She is also a priest in the Episcopal Church.

Jeffrey Vogel is Professor of Christian Theology and Ethics at Hampden-Sydney College in Virginia. He has written numerous articles on prayer and ascetic practice in Christian spirituality, with essays appearing in such publications as *Pro Ecclesia*, the *Scottish Journal of Theology*, *Spiritus* and the *Anglican Theological Review*. He is currently finishing work on a book on suffering, death and eternal life in Christian theology and practice.

Rowan Williams grew up in South Wales and then studied Theology in Cambridge, moving to Oxford to do research on modern Russian Orthodox theology. He was Professor of Divinity at Oxford from 1986 to 1992, Bishop of Monmouth from 1992 to 2002, and also Archbishop of Wales from 1999 to 2002, when he was nominated as Archbishop of Canterbury. Since 2013 he has been Master of Magdalene College, Cambridge. He has written many books on theology, spirituality and culture, and his recent book on *Christ the Heart of Creation* includes a discussion of Austin Farrer's thought.

Margaret Yee is Senior Research Fellow by Special Election, Principles of Knowing: Science, Humanities and Theology, St Cross College, University of Oxford. Her primary research was the History and Philosophy of Science and Austin Farrer's Philosophical Theology. She tutored, lectured and examined Psychology of Religion and Science and Religion for the Faculty of Theology and Religion in Oxford, was Chaplain of Nuffield College Oxford (1989–2005), and Associate Director of the Ian Ramsey Centre, Oxford (1996–2008). Two published articles of importance on Farrer are 'Austin Farrer' in *Key Theological Thinkers, Part V: British & American Theologians* (2013) and 'Theological Studies' in *Questioning Causality* (2016).

Introduction

RICHARD HARRIES

Austin Farrer has been described as the one genius produced by the Church of England in the twentieth century. This book is the result of a shared conviction that Austin Farrer explored new depths in thinking about God and biblical revelation, whose implications have not yet been fully worked through by subsequent theologians and that there is work to be done by a new generation of scholars.

There were two highlights during my time studying at Cuddesdon Theological College from 1961 to 1963. One was a set of lectures by Bill Vanstone that in 1977 became the basis of his classic *Love's Endeavour, Love's Expense*. The other was the set of Holy Week lectures by Austin Farrer on the Atonement. Taking place in the parish church, Farrer walked quickly and quietly up the aisle, mounted the pulpit, spoke for an hour and went out as unobtrusively as he had come in. It was as though he was thinking aloud to God and we had the privilege of overhearing what he was saying. As I heard the lectures a series of clicks registered in my mind as one half-formulated question after another was addressed and answered.

Farrer left a vivid impression on those who knew him well, and very many who only heard him lecture or preach. First of all was the acuteness, quickness and depth of his mind. As has been written, 'His works exhibit a philosophical incisiveness and a breadth of imagination that are the equal of the most gifted thinkers of his generation.'[1]

Secondly, springing from the breadth of his imagination referred to there, was the literary quality of his writing and speaking. They are studded with fresh, arresting images and memorable aphorisms. As his fellow philosopher Basil Mitchell wrote: 'Given Farrer's originality and independence of fashion it is possible to celebrate his writings as exquisite works of art to be appreciated for their aesthetic qualities alone ... a sparkling clarity of expression is achieved which can have a certain intoxicating effect.'[2]

Thirdly, there was the impression he left on people of a self-forgetful holiness. C. S. Lewis, not an easy person to please, asked why books like Farrer's were so rare and answered in response that they were the distillation of the work of a lifetime. Then he added:

For another, they demand something like a total conquest of those ego-
isms which – however we try to mince the matter – play so large a part in
most impulses to authorship. To talk to us thus Dr Farrer makes himself
almost nothing, almost nobody. To be sure, in the event, his personality
stands out from the pages as clearly as that of any author, but this is one
of heaven's jokes – nothing makes a man so noticeable as vanishing.[3]

The word 'genius' usually brings to mind someone with one overwhelming
talent, say as mathematician or musician. Farrer's genius was different. It
was the total fusion in him of the intellectual, the aesthetic and the spiritual,
each area highly developed and refined in itself.[4] As Basil Mitchell put it:

There was no discernible difference of tone between preaching and
lecturing or between lecturing and everyday speech. Even the sustained
eloquence of his Bampton Lectures was no more than the natural and un-
affected expression of a unified intellectual and spiritual vision. Yet surely
St Mary's had heard and seen nothing like it since John Henry Newman
occupied the pulpit.[5]

Although Farrer was deeply revered by those who knew him and highly
appreciated by those who read his published writings, especially his
sermons, he was not, like a Barth or Rahner, a star in the theological firma-
ment. One reason is that he made contributions not in one discipline but
three: philosophical theology, biblical studies and Christian symbolism.
Secondly, in doing this he stood outside the intellectual fashions of the time
and thought independently from basic premises. Although widely read in
the literature he did not engage in debates with what other scholars had
written, and his work is notoriously free of all references and footnotes. A
good example of this is the paper on signification that he gave to the *Metaphysicals*, an informal group of philosophers, at a time when linguistic
analysis was beginning to make its way in philosophical circles. Farrer used
the occasion to go right back to first principles and explore how language
might have arisen in the first place.[6] In it we see the emergence of one of his
most fundamental ideas that mind is a social reality and that it is talking
that brings about that inner talking we call thinking.[7]

A third reason why his influence in professional theological circles has
been less than it might have been is that his genius had a special flower-
ing toward the end of his life in his more popular writings, not least his
sermons, and that much of this was published after his death. To properly
assess his legacy these have to be taken into account as much as his difficult
early writings like *Finite and Infinite*.[8] These later writings, and especially
his papers to small groups, contain remarkable distillations of his key ideas.
As C. S. Lewis commented about a collection of these shorter writings, 'In
each of them there is matter out of which some theologians would have
made a whole book.'[9]

To this might be added a fourth reason, mentioned by Rob MacSwain later in this book, that in both biblical studies and philosophical theology he was ahead of his time. Positions or approaches he took then came to the fore much later.

To some it was strange that Farrer was not appointed to one of the major Chairs at Oxford, but as he told one of his students when he congratulated him on his appointment to Keble:

> Well I don't know if it is a matter of congratulation. I decided I didn't want to be a Professor, and that wasn't sour grapes – for a godly and an ungodly reason. The first was I wanted a cure of souls, and the second was I don't like research students![10]

Farrer is a deceptive writer in a number of ways. Because he was such an obviously devout, even holy, person it is easy to overlook the fact that he had a highly questioning, sceptical mind. In the words of Basil Mitchell, Farrer was 'in all his writings an out-and-out rationalist'.[11] As John Barton writes later in this book, 'his "pious" language masks a steely scepticism. In tutorials with him I learned to be deeply suspicious of the accuracy of Acts precisely because of its typological elements, just at a time when Roman historians were praising its historical grounding'.

This scepticism, applied both to the views of some modern theologians and to the New Testament documents, went with a robust defence of Orthodoxy and was an arresting mix. However, when it went with his playful, teasing style and use of the vernacular, as in a reference to God who will 'smash' the universe, it must have left some audiences bemused.[12]

Farrer argued that your thinking had to be of a piece. You could not escape into a museum of scriptural or medieval images. The canons of rationality that were deployed in science or history or literary studies had to be used in Christian theology, where they were appropriate. The qualification is important for of course he did not believe that scientific reasoning was the only kind. This emphasis on reasonableness meant that the Christian thinker had to be in touch with the main intellectual currents of the day – not to be swept along by them, let alone accepting their assumptions, but to be aware of the questions they posed for anyone with religious faith. A rational faith was one which faced those questions head on. Those questions are not purely intellectual ones; some arise from a changing moral climate, so that ways of putting things acceptably in the past come to be seen as immoral.

One consequence of this is that in all his writings, not least his sermons, there was in fact a hidden dialogue going on with the main questions of the age – which is why of course they spoke to people then, and because many of the questions are the same now. The much-respected philosopher Donald MacKinnon, who was a major influence on a generation of students at Aberdeen and Cambridge, once remarked that apologetics was the lowest form of Christian life. In the light of that it might seem surprising to claim that Farrer was, for some, the supreme apologist of his time What MacKinnon had in mind no doubt were those apologists whose prime purpose was to secure intellectual victory for the Christian faith over its opponents. Farrer's apologetics was not like that. His own overriding concern, like that of MacKinnon, was, rather, the truth of things. He had a faith which he sought to relate to the world in all its aspects, but never at the expense of the truth as he saw it. The result is that at the end of a long argument he might say that what could be asserted from a rational point of view alone was minimal in the extreme. We might put the difference between the two kinds of apologetics this way. The one sees arguments against the Christian faith which they seek to refute. The other, aware of the prevailing intellectual questions of the time, seeks to relate their faith to those arguments which are experienced not in the form of attacks from opponents, but personal questions for the believers themselves. We hear or read Farrer addressing those questions and we have the privilege of listening in to the conversation going on in his mind. Because his mind was so remarkable and his faith so central to his being, what he wrote still carries conviction.

Against this background it is a pleasure for us to introduce Farrer to a new generation of scholars. We have focussed on the five main areas in which he contributed: biblical studies, philosophical theology, language and symbolism, doctrine, and prayer and preaching.

Although some contemporary scholars found Farrer's approach to the Bible irritating, John Barton argues in his chapter on 'Austin Farrer and Typology' that he was in fact ahead of his time. Farrer was thoroughly sceptical when it came to the historicity of particular events in the Bible. It was the scriptural text as a whole that mattered for him: "It provided the intellectual and imaginative universe which, no less than the real world, Christ died to transform". In his approach to this text Barton suggests that Farrer not only aroused the interest of literary scholars, he is thoroughly postmodern in seeing it as a tissue of reference and allusion. But, again anticipating modern developments, it was not the Hebrew Scriptures alone which provided the intellectual framework for the first Christians, but the intertestamental writings and their ideas from the Greek world. Barton concludes that Farrer's typological approach is his abiding legacy to biblical studies and one which deserves further development.

Mark Goodacre in 'Farrer on Q' argues that Farrer's willingness to dispense with Q, regarded as idiosyncratic at the time and relatively ignored, has in fact gained traction over the years. He assesses the evidence for and against Farrer's view that Luke only had Mark and Matthew before him, not Q. He concludes:

The ultimate legacy of Farrer's scholarship on Q is that a new generation of students has been enlivened by the way the evangelists come to life as inspired figures in a vision of Christian origins that is itself inspirational.

Jenn Strawbridge in her chapter on 'Farrer on Paul' points out that although no one has written on the relationship of Farrer and Paul, Paul was central to Farrer's whole understanding of the Christian faith. Strawbridge teases out why, for Farrer, he is essential reading. Often with a wry, dry humour Farrer managed to communicate a picture of Paul and his message in a way that broke down the barriers of student minds. He acknowledges the weaknesses Paul shared with all human beings but is clearly himself captivated by the wholehearted love he had for Christ and the congregations springing up under his care. Farrer corrects a popular misunderstanding about the relationship between faith and works in Paul, and argues for a close relationship between his understanding of Christ and that of the Gospels.

In 'Farrer's Relevance for Contemporary Philosophical Theology' Margaret Yee draws out Farrer's emphasis on our knowledge of God being a rational activity. She leads us through his major philosophical and theological writings to reveal two decisive changes in his thought. Firstly, showing that in our apprehension of God the mind works in two ways: logical deduction and symbolic realism. Both are necessary. The former can help us understand the difference between the finite and infinite but only the second can indicate how we might begin to grasp that infinite. Secondly, she shows how his thought came to take fully into account the empirical findings of science, and give it a theological perspective, especially in the way God does not just make the world but makes the world make itself. In all this the human will interacting with the divine will, definitively disclosed in Jesus, is fundamental to our knowing.

Leigh Vicens in her chapter on 'Providence and the Problem of Evil in Farrer's *Love Almighty and Ills Unlimited*' examines another huge contribution by Farrer to theological reasoning. *Love Almighty and Ills Unlimited*, though not the best known book on the subject of God and suffering, was arguably the most significant one during the twentieth century and is still indispensable reading for any serious student of the subject today. Based on Farrer's fundamental premise that to be created is to have a life of our own, whether as an atom or a complex multi-cellular structure, he explores the implications of this for a belief in divine providence in relation to both physical and intellectual existence. Leigh Vicens picks her way carefully through Farrer's arguments and relates them to the writings of Brian Hebblethwaite and Marilyn McCord Adams and others. She offers her own critique of Farrer but comes back in the end to what was so fundamental to him, the integral connection of philosophy, theology and spirituality. When we have said all we can say on the subject there remains the prayerful, practical task of 'engaging the will of God that we can only perceive by so doing'.

Robert MacSwain begins '"The Evidence of Faith": Austin Farrer, Diogenes Allen and Reformed Epistemology' by teasing out what is meant by Reformed epistemology and then shows how trends in epistemology in recent decades have tended to support its understanding of faith and the arguments which justify that understanding. He then goes on to maintain that many years before this Farrer had anticipated that modern approach, which takes seriously what is in fact the common experience of most believers, that they come to faith via a community of faith and are drawn into it because they find it nourishing. This requires a prior openness or receptivity of heart, but reasoning is also present at every stage both in setting out and explicating what it is that is believed. Furthermore it involves making sense of the evidence provided by the world about us, including those aspects that offer a challenge to faith. He ends by suggesting that this has implications for spirituality.

Paul DeHart in 'Farrer's Theism: *Finite and Infinite*' writes that Farrer's first book published in 1943 is one of the most penetrating and ambitious essays in philosophical theism to appear in the twentieth century. Although its reception was muted and its influence is hard to discern, he argues that it offers highly suggestive ways forward for philosophical theology today. This is not, following Farrer, to offer arguments of which God is the inescapable conclusion, but to indicate what might actually be meant by 'the Cosmological Idea': the notion that every finite action is dependent on the infinite and undifferentiated act of being itself. DeHart argues that Farrer's Cosmological Idea is indeed Thomist but properly modified by modern philosophical considerations. His argument is rooted in our understanding of ourselves as volitional beings, not just intellectual ones, and this gives us a clue to how we should think about God. DeHart writes:

> Farrer's brilliant accomplishment, his assimilation and extension of Aquinas's theism, remains undiminished ... a keen insight or startlingly suggestive formulation is to be found on virtually every page ... he deftly restates the analogy of being to usher us into the Thomist theory by way of its most natural yet surprising conclusion: that we are all already 'inside' the experience of God.

Stephen Platten in 'Through a glass? Farrer, Coleridge and Revelation' argues that Farrer rejected a sharp distinction between natural and revealed knowledge of God. Our rational minds are involved at every point, and all knowledge of God is in some sense revealed. Farrer's starting point is Christ, not a bare Christ, but a Christ who inherited a stock of fundamental images which he interpreted and lived out in a life of unbroken union with his Father. In him there is a co-inherence of the divine and the human. At this point Platten draws attention to the links with Charles Williams and the similarities (and possible influence?) of Coleridge. He then relates this to Farrer's concept of double agency, considering both critiques of this at the time and the recent work of Rowan Williams which draws significantly upon Farrer.

Morwenna Ludlow in 'Language and Symbolism: Austin Farrer Meets Gregory of Nazianzus' explores the relationship between the different kinds of inspiration: poetic, prophetic and apostolic. Farrer was keenly interested in the concept of poetic inspiration both because of his love of poetry and because, as is obvious to anyone who reads his sermons, they were the product of a creative spirit fully focussed. Certain sentences once read echo in the mind for a lifetime. At the same time as a theologian he had a distinctive understanding of revelation, not as a series of propositions or Jesus Christ *tout simple*, but through certain images. Christ used these major images to interpret the events of his life and those events in turn gave new meaning to the images. In the apostolic age, through the inspiration of the Holy Spirit, those key images gave birth to secondary ones. So 'The stuff of inspiration is living images'. In this exposition of Farrer Morwenna Ludlow examines and illuminates the connections and differences in approach of Gregory Nazianzus.

Rowan Williams in '"A society of two"? Austin Farrer on the Trinity' offers a rich exploration of the whole range of Farrer's writing, especially the sermons, on the Trinity. Those who have seen in Austin Farrer a sophisticated modern restatement of Christian orthodoxy have always been startled by his apparently binary view of the Trinity. Taking only the relation of the Father to the Son, into which we are adopted, and in which we participate through prayer, as the revealed parable of the Trinity as Farrer often does, we ask: what has happened to the Holy Spirit? Rowan Williams shows that there is much more on the Holy Spirit than the binary model itself seemed to allow. God is not just the generator of the Son, he bestows on the Son the capacity to love and live for the other. The Son is able to make a perfect filial response to the Father because of this gift. But is this gift really a hypostasis, or just a dimension of the Divine Being? Williams suggests there is more work to be done here, and he himself looks to Vladimir Lossky's insight that the Holy Spirit is a genuine hypostasis proceeding from the Father but one who in an act of kenosis empties himself into the Son, enabling him to live for the other. He/She enables the Son to be the Son, both in relation to the Father and the world, but because of this emptying remains hidden to us.

In 'Farrer on the Atonement' Richard Harries brings out how Farrer cuts through the debate between those who see the efficacy of the atonement solely in terms of a change of heart on the part of believers and those who stress that something objective was achieved for all time. Harries shows how Farrer, while having nothing to do with any idea that God has somehow to be propitiated, nevertheless argued that something was achieved in history with eternal consequences. He shows how Farrer, while stressing that salvation comes only through Christ, brings that salvation to all humanity. This is because, for Farrer, that work of salvation went on through the church, and in heaven all will have a chance to see Christ in those who are his. When Christ is seen in glory, he is seen 'with his saints' as the New Testament states. In heaven they see not a solitary Christ but Christ in and through all those who are incorporated in him, who are part of his body. In this way Christ's salvation is made efficacious for those who do not know him in this life.

Gregory Platten in 'Theosis, Godmanhood and Double Agency: Berdyaev, Farrer and the Divine-Human Relationship' explores the contrasts and similarities between the once popular Nicholas Berdyaev and Austin Farrer. Both emphasize the centrality of human choice, and how through our choices we can allow the free creativity of God to work in and through us. For Berdyaev this stress is on the creativity of those choices in shaping the future both of ourselves and the world. For Farrer it is above all a free submission of our will to the divine will which leads to union with, and participation in the life of, God. In this process of *theosis* Christ is central for both thinkers as the one in whom that union is perfect and through whom our union with God can come about.

In 'Farrer, the Oxford Preacher' Jane Shaw paints a vivid picture of Farrer in his Oxford context as priest, preacher and scholar. So unified was his life that each of these epithets was equally true, but such were his personal priorities that the first suffused and shaped the other two. Similarly his preaching arose out of both his prayer and his wrestling with fundamental issues of faith. Jane Shaw shows in particular how his preaching is most intimately related to the concerns of students and the issues that arose in college life. With a lightness of touch, and flashes of humour, he spoke very directly to what was on their minds and hearts. So these sermons, very much of their time and place, an Oxford which is now long gone, could have passed into obscurity. But they continue to live. As Jane Shaw writes, it is, 'paradoxically, the very particularity of those examples that enables the reader to transcend their context and grasp the spiritual and theological wisdom that Farrer lived, preached and taught'.

Jeffrey Vogel in 'Until Their Hunger Is Their Mind: Farrer's Theology of the Eucharist' shows how the essential elements in Farrer's theology find powerful expression in his understanding of the Eucharist. Here Farrer anticipates a trend in modern theology by his emphasis on bodiliness. Christ is present with us first of all as a body, and he gives himself to us in the physical form of bread and wine, which we take into ourselves as we are physically present at the Eucharist. This bodily receiving unites us to the body of Christ and his sacrifice for the world, and this in turn enables us to seek the will of the father for our lives. Time and again we fail but these failures break down our self-dependence. They lead us to receive Christ again, that once again we might try to do the will of the Father in sharing his love for the world.

It has been a pleasure to immerse ourselves in Farrer again, and to read new responses to his work. Our hope is that this book will arouse fresh interest and stimulate people to rediscover Farrer's writings, or discover them for the first time. We believe that his work was prophetic and his legacy a lasting one which has yet to be fully explored.

Notes

1 Jeffrey C. Eaton and Ann Loades (eds), *For God and Clarity: New Essays in Honor of Austin Farrer*, Allison Park, PA, Pickwick, 1983, pp. xii–xiii.

2 Basil Mitchell, in *The Human Person in God's World: Studies to Commemorate the Austin Farrer Centenary*, ed. Brian Hebblethwaite and Douglas Hedley, London, SCM Press, 1988, p. 3. This is the best short introduction to Austin Farrer in the Oxford of his time by a friend and colleague.

3 C. S. Lewis, in Austin Farrer, *A Faith of Our Own*, Cleveland, OH, World Publishing, 1960, p. 10.

4 See Richard Harries, 'We Know on Our Knees', in Brian Hebblethwaite and Edward Henderson (eds), *Divine Action: Studies Inspired by the Philosophical Theology of Austin Farrer*, London, T & T Clark, 1990, pp. 21–33.

5 Basil Mitchell, *A Celebration of Faith: Communications, Mostly to Students*, London, Hodder and Stoughton, 1972, p.16.

6 A. Farrer 'Signification', in *Reflective Faith*, ed. Charles C. Conti, London, SPCK, 1972, p. 149.

7 A. Farrer, *Saving Belief*, London, Hodder and Stoughton, 1967, p. 61.

8 A. Farrer, *Finite and Infinite*, 2nd edn., London, Dacre Press, 1959. In this regard we can only lament the fact that the original DNB entry on Farrer seems to consider only these early writings.

9 C. S. Lewis, in Austin Farrer, *A Faith of Our Own*, 1960, p. 9.

10 Christopher Hall, who studied ancient philosophy with Farrer, in a private communication. I know that those who were in fact among his few research students will not take this personally, for to them, especially those from the USA a great deal is owed in keeping Farrer's flame alive. It is simply that Farrer's approach to scholarship was so different from the average research project. He used to sit and think for a very long time, then jump up and say 'I think I will write that one down.'

11 Basil Mitchell, 1988, *The Human Person*, p. 5.

12 For example the American audiences he lectured to in 1966. See the previously unpublished lectures in *Austin Farrer: Oxford Warden, Scholar, Preacher*, ed. Markus Bockmuehl and Stephen Platten with Nevsky Everett, London, SCM Press, 2020.

Biblical Theology

I

Austin Farrer and Typology

JOHN BARTON

We thank you, almighty God, for the gift of water
to sustain, refresh and cleanse all life.
Over water the Holy Spirit moved in the beginning of creation.
Through water you led the children of Israel
from slavery in Egypt to freedom in the Promised Land.
In water your Son Jesus received the baptism of John
and was anointed by the Holy Spirit as the Messiah, the Christ,
to lead us from the death of sin to newness of life.[1]

This prayer over the water of baptism in the Church of England's 2000 liturgical collection *Common Worship* illustrates very simply what is meant by typology. It is the correspondence of a past event as described in an earlier text to a later event, in such a way that the later event can be seen as prefigured in the earlier one (not necessarily explicitly foretold). Here it works by linking together places in the Bible where creation or salvation comes through water, so as to create a background for the use of water in Christian baptism. It is a phenomenon to which Austin Farrer devoted a great deal of controversial attention in his biblical exegesis and, as we shall see, it was crucial to his theory of scriptural inspiration.

Farrer gives a clear example of how typology works in his reply to Helen Gardner's criticism of *The Glass of Vision*:

St Paul writes thus: 'I was alive once, without any law incumbent upon me. But when the commandment came, sin came to life, and I fell into death.' ... it is very generally supposed by interpreters that the choice of expressions is dictated by St Paul's seeing himself in Adam, or in the type of Adam. ... [After the Fall,] though he continued to drag his mortal body, it was dead to goodness; though he might now approve of God's law in his mind, he found an anti-law in his body, preventing it from being alive to God. And so St Paul, as a child of Adam, exclaims, 'Who shall deliver me from the body of this death?' That is, of the death Adam died on the day he ate; and he replies, 'I thank God, through Jesus Christ our Lord' – through union, that is, with his death and resurrection, the 'body of death' is abolished, and true life regained.[2]

Rather than providing an analysis of his own psychology,[3] Paul is here describing his theological state as a human being by analogy with Adam: he is the antitype to the type of Adam. Adam foreshadows the plight of humanity in general, and Christ, whom Paul elsewhere describes as 'the last Adam' (1 Cor. 15.45) restores the original state of humankind. More elaborate forms of this kind of typology are to be found all over the Fathers, as in this example from John Chrysostom, the fourth-century bishop of Constantinople (349–407 CE), in one of his homilies:

> If you reflect upon the Scriptures and the story of our redemption, you will recall that a virgin, a tree and a death were the symbols of our defeat. The virgin's name was Eve: she knew not a man. The tree was the tree of the knowledge of good and evil. The death was Adam's penalty. But now those very symbols of our defeat – a virgin, a tree and a death – have become symbols of Christ's victory. In place of Eve there is Mary; in place of the tree of the knowledge of good and evil, there is the tree of the cross; and in place of the death of Adam, there is the death of Christ.

Now there are two questions about this, which tended to get elided in the generally hostile reception Farrer experienced from other New Testament scholars when he argued that such typologies were common in the New Testament itself. One is a factual or empirical question: is typology as common in the New Testament as Farrer supposed? The other is an evaluative question: is such typology wholesome and important in understanding Scripture, and even in understanding the *inspiration* of Scripture and God's providential guidance of it? Is typology a good thing? Most scholars saw the promotion of it as inimical to a historical-critical reading of the Bible and therefore as undesirable. But in the process they tended to reject the empirical evidence that the New Testament writers shared in many ways the same sort of mindset as their patristic successors, and thus they emptied out the baby with the bathwater.

On the empirical question Farrer surely had much more evidence on his side than many scholars of his day were prepared to allow, and the atmosphere in biblical studies is now much less hostile to acceptance of this claim. The use of the Old Testament in the New is a major area of research, which even has an annual conference, held at Gladstone's Library at Hawarden in North Wales, and the detailed work of Richard B. Hays and others[4] has demonstrated even more references to the Old Testament in the Gospels and Paul than Farrer himself ever proposed.

It is, in fact, not only the New Testament's use of the Old that provides evidence for typology. There is typology already in the Old Testament itself, in what is now often referred to as inner-biblical exegesis. One of the clearest examples can be found in the text usually called Deutero-Isaiah (Isaiah 40–55):

This is like the days of Noah to me:
  Just as I swore that the waters of Noah
  would never again go over the earth,
so I have sworn that I will not be angry with you
  and will not rebuke you.

(Isaiah 54.9)

This is a prophecy to Judaeans suffering during the period of the Babylonian exile, and it promises God's steadfast love by drawing an analogy with his promise after the Flood that there would never again be such a cataclysmic destruction. The promise after the Flood is the type; the restoration after the exile is the antitype. Any biblical scholar would accept this interpretation. It is thus not strange if the New Testament writers inherited such a way of thinking.

Farrer argued that prefiguration also occurred within the New Testament, and this was certainly more controversial. The mysterious young man in a linen garment (Greek *sindon*) in the garden of Gethsemane in Mark 14:51–52, who was captured but 'left the linen cloth and ran off naked' is an antitype of Joseph in Genesis 39.12 – and not all would accept that – but is in turn a type of the young man in a white robe (*sindon*) who greets the women at Jesus' empty tomb in Mark 16.5. 'Coming events cast their shadows before' within the New Testament itself.

It is important that prefiguration or typology is often signalled not only in the substance of the parallel incidents but in how they are described, that is, in the actual vocabulary or construction used. Farrer argued that the ending of Mark, with its abrupt 'for they were afraid' (*ephobounto gar*), also paralleled the story of Joseph, in which Genesis 45.1–3 tells how Joseph's brothers could not answer him when he revealed his identity to them, 'for they were dismayed'.[5] This can easily become fanciful or exaggerated, and Farrer probably did his position no favours by emphasizing rather slight similarities of wording. Nevertheless we know that the New Testament writers were sensitive to the detailed words of the Old Testament, and there is nothing in principle unreasonable in Farrer's approach.

But apart from the factual question of how far typology actually occurs in the New Testament, there remains the theoretical or theological question of whether or not it is a good thing. Traditional critical scholars of the Old Testament tend to be resistant to New Testament, let alone patristic, 'rereadings' of the text to bring out Christological or ecclesiastical meanings. It is quite clear that for Farrer on the contrary such readings were highly desirable. This was in part because he saw prefiguration as more than a merely literary feature. For him, the way historical people and events were described by the biblical writers really did prefigure the events of the life, death and resurrection of Jesus Christ: that is, there was a divine providence in the fact that they were so described. It is not an accident that the story of Joseph parallels in significant ways the story of the passion of

Jesus, for the scriptural writers were inspired by God to write in the ways they did.

At this point the patience of many biblical scholars runs out. Did God actually guide the pen of the author of Genesis and the pen of St Mark so that they produced texts that exhibit these parallels? Surely that is going too far.

Farrer's theory of inspiration is, however, more subtle than that and deserves fuller elaboration. He does not think of the types and their anti-types as random images provided by God in a casual or unordered way, but as forming a coherent set, which took shape in the mind of Jesus Christ himself:

> He spoke of the Kingdom of God, which is the image of God's enthroned majesty ... Again, he spoke of the Son of Man, thereby proposing the image of the dominion of a true Adam, begotten in the similitude of God, and made God's regent over all the works of his hands. ... He set forth the image of Israel, the human family of God, somehow mystically contained in the person of Jacob, its patriarch. He was himself Israel, and appointed 12 men to be his typical 'sons'. He applied to himself the prophecies of a redemptive suffering for mankind attributed to Israel by Isaiah and Jewish tradition. He displayed, in the action of the supper, the infinitely complex and fertile image of sacrifice and communion, of expiation and covenant.[6]

Thus there are five 'master' types that together constitute an interpretative framework for grasping the nature and work of Christ: David and his kingdom; Adam, type of the Son of Man; Jacob and his sons, the foundation stones of Israel; the suffering servant; and the sacrificial system of the Old Testament. These types Farrer describes as 'images', and in his study of the book of Revelation, *A Rebirth of Images*,[7] he seeks to show how they worked on the imagination of the seer of the Apocalypse. There are other types too, on which Farrer has less to say: Melchizedek, in Hebrews; Joshua, who as Farrer points out shares in Greek the name Jesus; the ram slaughtered in the place of Isaac; and the new heaven and earth foreseen in such passages as Isaiah 65.17–25, fulfilled in the city coming down from heaven in Revelation 21. Thus the Old Testament provides matrices through which the events of the New can be seen to have a meaning and to contribute to a coherent story.

That story begins with the creation of Adam in the image of God, and continues with the creation of Israel through Jacob and the patriarchs and its consolidation through the reign of David. The institution of the temple cult provides a setting in which the covenant with God can be reaffirmed, and the idea of the suffering servant emerges from reflection on atonement and expiation in that context. Thus the *praeparatio evangelica* in the Old Testament is not merely a matter of words, or images in a purely literary sense, but is instantiated in actions and institutions that actually existed, and in reflection on them by inspired minds. The type-antitype pattern is not adventitious or merely conventional, but reflects the actual development of ancient Israel.

Or so at least Farrer thought. How far the relation of Old Testament to New exists at a historical level, and how far only or principally at a literary one, remains the question that anyone who enjoys the typological imagination is bound to be confronted with. Was the kingdom of David, say, *really* a type of the kingdom to be exercised by Christ – and what does that mean anyway? Or was it that the descriptions of David's kingdom attractively illustrate, in very human and this-worldly terms, the sublime kingship to be exercised by Jesus in eternity? To return to a much more minor type or image, when the young man in the garden leaves his *sindon* and runs away naked he is an antitype to Joseph with Potiphar's wife: but does that imply that the story of Joseph, or even, more extremely, the actual events of Joseph's life, existed simply so that they could serve as an illustration of the events in the garden? That seems a considerable stretch.

On the whole Farrer in practice treats typology chiefly as a literary phenomenon. Although it is grounded in real events and in the development of the history of Israel, it is the Old Testament as a book that seems uppermost in his mind. A good indication of this can be found in a place where he is not discussing typological issues at all, in the Introduction to his *A Short Bible*, a cleverly abridged Bible that deserves to be more widely known.[8] He there distinguishes an 'apostolic' from a 'historical' way of reading the Old Testament:

> On the one hand it is a body of writings which existed for Christ and his Apostles much as it does for us. It provided the intellectual and imaginative universe which, no less than the real world, Christ died to transform. I can read it over the shoulders of St Paul or St John, I can listen to it in synagogue with the child Jesus. On the other hand it is evidence for the reconstruction of two thousand Israelite years: not a fresco on one plane, but a series of fragmentary pictures, of inscriptions half defaced, set back one behind another into a haze of distance.[9]

Of these two approaches Farrer commends the first to the ordinary reader. In it the Old Testament is read as a single work: not, indeed, 'flat', but still as a book in which all the parts contribute to the understanding of the whole. It constitutes the 'intellectual and imaginative world' of first-century Jews, who were not concerned, as the modern biblical scholar may be, with the underlying events and literary developments that formed it, but with the shape that it finally acquired. Within that overall shape, one text can play off another, and images can take on a life that breaks out of the original historical matrix in which they were generated.

Already in this formulation Farrer claims that Christ died to transform not just the real world, but the world of the imagination: one can see parallels here with Lewis and Tolkien, perhaps especially the latter. The fixing of the canonical text of the Old Testament was not simply an accident: it was a providential act by which these texts came to be made available to provide the basis for an imaginative grasp of the ways of God. The underlying history that the Old Testament scholar reconstructs is not, for Farrer, the beating heart of biblical study. That heart beats in the sacred *text*, which provides the images with which it became possible to interpret Christ and his saving work, in such a way that that work was comprehensible, not merely a brute fact. The images or types give us the vocabulary of faith, almost one could say its grammar. It was in working and reworking them that the apostles made sense of their experience of the living Christ.

It is not surprising, therefore, that Farrer's work has been of interest to some literary critics. His literary reception got off to a bad start in the reactions of Helen Gardner, who found the typology fanciful and forced,[10] but more recently such musings on 'intertextuality' have become much more acceptable in literary circles. Frank Kermode already picked up Farrer's ideas about the boy in the *sindon*, and the abrupt ending of Mark with its arguable allusion to Joseph and his brothers, in *The Genesis of Secrecy*.[11] But in a world of postmodern readings the idea that one text may draw on another is almost *de rigueur*, and not seen as in any way improbable or odd, rather as normal and to be expected. That the seer of Revelation reads Jesus through Ezekiel is just what one might expect, and the master images or types simply illustrate the interplay between old texts and new. Indeed, it need not be a question of old and new. Even though Farrer, with a historical awareness, thought in terms of New Testament texts drawing on pre-existing Old Testament ones, from a postmodern perspective one could see texts as interrelated irrespective of their relative dates. Thus Revelation can illuminate Ezekiel as much as Ezekiel Revelation. Already for Farrer himself the antitypes give us the true meaning of the types, and from a postmodern literary perspective this is completely normal.

Indeed, some postmodern readings have close analogies with Jewish midrash. Farrer was well ahead of his time in seeing that literary 'close' readings are not unlike what we find in the New Testament's use of the Old, which in turn is similar to some rabbinic use of the Hebrew Bible. The analysis of individual words as clues to the meaning and structure of passages of Scripture that Farrer practises is quite 'rabbinic' at times. A standard principle of rabbinic exegesis is that 'there is no before and after [or, earlier and later] in Scripture', meaning that younger passages, or passages later in the text, can be used to illuminate earlier ones, without regard to the fact that the earlier author could not possibly have read the later one. Thus the prophets can offer illumination on the Pentateuch even though, from a traditional Jewish perspective, they came later. Themes, like leitmotifs, can crop up in passages of very different date. Robert Alter, for example, points to the use of the 'type scene' of the woman at the well,[12] which occurs in Genesis 24.15–21 and in Exodus 2.16–22 (and indeed in John 4). There are, he suggests, interconnections among the different examples, irrespective of whether their authors knew each other's work.

Scripture thus forms an interconnected tissue of allusion and cross-reference when it is read in what Farrer calls the 'apostolic' mode, that is, not historically but as a finished product. There are even analogies with the (theologically very differently grounded) proposals for 'canonical reading' that we find in the work of Brevard S. Childs.[13] Contemporary biblical scholars were probably not wrong to see in Farrer's work a certain 'pre-' or 'post-critical' tendency that undercut 'normal' historical criticism, though Farrer (like Childs) was perfectly capable of practising historical criticism when he chose.

Typology is not quite so readily acceptable within the discourse of Jewish-Christian dialogue as its Jewish analogues might suggest. The types – fulfilled in Christ and his new revelation – seem in many ways annulled or sidelined by these antitypes. If Jesus is a new Moses, then the old Moses is superseded. For Farrer I think it was obvious that Christianity superseded Judaism, despite his great respect for Jewish learning and indeed for Jewish interpretation of the Bible, about which he knew far more than most New Testament scholars of his day. '[For St Paul,] if we look carefully at the Law, we see that it carries in it the mark of its own provisional character and the promise of what will supersede it.'[14] If John the Baptist is a new Elijah, then the historical Elijah fades into a mere literary prefigurement of John. If Jesus is our new Joshua, then Joshua son of Nun need not really have existed at all. And so on. This is the line taken in the second-century *Epistle of Barnabas*, where even the Old Testament's description of the creation of the world matters only because it is to be seen as an oblique description of the new creation of Christians.

For Farrer, Christianity, though arising within Judaism, was quite simply a new religion. It was anchored to the old religion by the interplay of types and antitypes in such a way that Judaism could not be simply ignored: Jesus could not be understood without the types that pointed to him. But 'old things have passed away; behold, all things have become new'. This sounds a rather harsh note in a more contemporary phase of Jewish-Christian dialogue.

The tension between old and new can however be mitigated by taking a somewhat more historical, or at least less ahistorical, approach. The 'images' or types, especially the five main ones that Farrer identifies (see above), do not exist only within the text considered as an entity in its own right. They were ideas that were very much in the air in the first century CE, and did not derive directly from the Old Testament. Indeed, reading the Old Testament alone will not prepare one for the thought-world encountered in the New. Many features in early Christianity, and in the varieties of Judaism from which it sprang, cannot be found there. Heaven and hell, the doctrine of Adam's Fall and of original sin, the existence of the devil, the hosts of angels that surround the human race, and speculation on the origins of suffering, are all central to the world of the New Testament, yet marginal or even non-existent in the Old. In so far as they are 'Old Testament' themes, this is because they are part of how the Old Testament was *read and received* at the turn of the era, rather than because they belong to its natural meaning. The Davidic promises and the importance of the covenant and its rituals are important to both the Old Testament in its own right and to the period in which Jesus lived, but the Adamic theme (and the consequent image of the Son of Man) and the suffering servant are much more matters of reception than of the Old Testament text taken straight.

To discover this reception history we need to read not simply the Old Testament itself, but other Jewish works from the third and second centuries BC that for the most part are not now part of Scripture at all: books attributed to Enoch, Ezra, the patriarchs such as Abraham and Joseph, Moses, and Solomon, even Adam and Eve. We also need to be aware of what was being thought in the wider Hellenistic world, of which Judaism was perforce a part. Farrer himself made much of the *Testaments of the Twelve Patriarchs*, though passages he cited from them as Jewish are widely regarded as later Christian interpolations. This is true, for example, of the line 'For him the heavens will be opened, and there will descend hallowing upon him, with the Father's voice as from Abraham to Isaac', which Farrer quotes in lecture II of *The Glass of Vision*.[15] The point stands, however, that it is Jewish traditions of thought, and not simply the Old Testament as a text, that provided the matrix for nascent Christianity, a point that Farrer himself acknowledges. The great images derive from the Scriptures with different degrees of intensity, and in some cases (such as the Adam theme) are barely scriptural at all – very little indeed is made of Adam in the Old Testament, read on its own terms. In any case, the very point Farrer is making is that Christianity involves a *rebirth* of the great images: the Old Testament is realigned and read as pointing toward Jesus Christ and the church, by a recombination and purification of images that may be quite marginal to the Old Testament itself.

A recent work that helps to remind us about the lack of identity between the Old Testament and its reception in the first century is the important *Crucible of Faith*[16] by Philip Jenkins. Identifying the period in which the New Testament was produced and the preceding century (that is, from roughly 100 BCE to 100 CE) as 'the crucible age', he shows how the distinctive ideas of what would become Judaism and Christianity were formed through a reinterpretation of the Old Testament and other scriptural or quasi-scriptural books, to yield new horizons on the relationship between God and the human race. In the process parts of the Old Testament that are marginal to any historical investigation of it are foregrounded – consider for example the importance in the New Testament of the desperately obscure Zechariah 9–14 – while central elements, such as the moral invective of the prophets, fall into the background. The Old Testament as read by early

Jews and Christians is a different book from the one studied by critical scholars. What irritated such scholars was Farrer's apparent belief that this reread Old Testament was superior to the one they studied; but in the process of rejecting this, they often rejected also the empirical evidence that such a rereading did in fact take place, as Jenkins shows in detail that it did. Farrer was again ahead of his time, though the mystical way in which he described much the same developments as Jenkins outlines was sure to alienate scholars who, like hobbits, 'liked to have books filled with things that they already knew, set out fair and square with no contradictions'.

Typology is in many ways a feature of what would nowadays be called the reception history of the Old Testament. People in New Testament times, both Jews and Christians, though in different ways, read the great events described in the Hebrew Bible as prefiguring events of their own day. Farrer was not yet familiar with the bulk of the Dead Sea Scrolls, where the *pesher* genre consists precisely of the interpretation of old prophecies as coming true in the history of the Qumran community, much as Paul saw them fulfilled in the life and ministry of Jesus and in the development of the church. But we can now see that the Dead Sea sect operated with Scripture in many ways much as did another Jewish sect, the Christian community. Both received the biblical text as a tissue of ciphers pointing to the times in which they were now living. Farrer's Jewish parallels to Christian typological reading were mostly taken from later, rabbinic Judaism, but if he could have read all the Dead Sea Scrolls that have now been published and translated he would have only seen his approach confirmed, I think. To take just one example: the place of Melchizedek as a type of Christ in Hebrews now proves to belong in a wider context in which this figure was seen as having heavenly features, and as a type of the coming Messiah.[17]

The time is ripe for a rediscovery of Farrer's typological exegesis of the New Testament. For too long he has been seen as pre-eminently a great philosophical theologian to be taken very seriously when writing on metaphysics, and a profound preacher and Christian apologist, but as an eccentric oddity in the world of biblical studies. He provoked, and provokes, many scholars with his mannerisms, always referring to the New Testament writers as 'Saint' Mark or Paul or John, and coining irritating neologisms such as 'Luke-pleasingness' in his notorious attack on the Q hypothesis (which however is also experiencing something of a renaissance).[18] There was a suspicion that his exegesis was tainted with too much piety; though in fact his emphasis on the creativity of the evangelists tended, if thought through, to lead to much greater scepticism about the historicity of the events recorded in the Gospels than many more 'traditional' scholars could accept. Farrer did not found a 'school', but Oxford under his influence had students less conservative on matters of historicity than did Cambridge with C. F. D. Moule. Farrer thought form criticism was mistaken, not because it led to doubt about the historicity of the Gospel stories, but because it diminished the creative role of the evangelists. But that in turn produced an even more sceptical approach to the historicity especially of events that had a strong typological component, since one could easily argue that the evangelists had composed them on the basis of the underlying types. Farrer never denies the truth of the birth stories, for example, but it is hard to see that much is left of their historical veracity once the typological elements have been subtracted. His 'pious' language masks a steely scepticism. In tutorials with him I learned to be deeply suspicious of the accuracy of Acts precisely because of its typological elements, just at a time when Roman historians were praising its historical grounding.[19]

The immediate legacy of Farrer's typological studies is to be seen in the work on the lectionary basis of New Testament narrative by Aileen Guilding and Michael Goulder. Farrer himself found their work persuasive but did not follow lectionary schemes himself, though in *A Rebirth of Images* he certainly suggested that the book of Revelation followed the order of the Jewish liturgical year. This he modified in his later commentary on the book, much as he modified the schematic arrangement he found in Mark in *A Study of St Mark* when he came to write the sequel, *St Matthew and St Mark*. Over time he became less convinced of grand schemes and more inclined to see informal allusions.

But the typological approach as such is a significant contribution to understanding the use of the Old Testament in the New, and it is Farrer's abiding legacy to biblical studies: not indeed as important as his philosophical work, but deserving to be developed further as the reception history of the Hebrew Bible burgeons.

Notes

1 'Holy Baptism', *Common Worship: Services and Prayers for the Church of England*, London, Church House Publishing, 2000, p. 355.

2 Austin Farrer, 'On Looking below the Surface', *Interpretation and Belief*, ed. Charles C. Conti, London, SPCK, 1976, pp. 54–65, p. 61.

3 Farrer here anticipates the anti-psychological reading of Paul defended by Krister Stendahl in his famous article 'The Apostle Paul and the Introspective Conscience of the West', *Harvard Theological Review* 56, 1963, pp. 199–215.

4 See Richard B. Hays, *Echoes of Scripture in the Gospels*, Waco, TX, Baylor University Press, 2016 and *Reading Backwards: Figural Christology and the Fourfold Gospel Witness*, Waco, TX, Baylor University Press, 2014. Compare also Craig A. Evans (ed.), *Paul and the Scriptures of Israel*, London, Bloomsbury, 2015.

5 Farrer later recanted his theory that Mark was intended to end with these words, arguing that there was at least one further sentence, but it was his defence of the abrupt ending that established itself in what may be called the Farrer tradition, and which Helen Gardner (1959) and later Frank Kermode (1979) discussed.

6 *The Glass of Vision*, lecture III. The easiest access to this work is in Robert MacSwain (ed.), *Scripture, Metaphysics, and Poetry: Austin Farrer's The Glass of Vision with Critical Commentary*, London and New York, Routledge, 2016. The passage quoted is on p. 42 in this edition.

7 Austin Farrer, *A Rebirth of Images: The Making of St John's Apocalypse*, Westminster, Dace Press, 1949.

8 Austin Farrer, *A Short Bible*, Glasgow, Collins, 1956.

9 'Introduction: from *A Short Bible*', *The Truth-Seeking Heart: Austin Farrer and His Writings*, ed. Ann Loades and Robert MacSwain, London, Canterbury Press, 2006, pp. 3–13.

10 Helen Gardner, *The Business of Criticism*, Oxford, Clarendon Press, 1959.

11 Frank Kermode, *The Genesis of Secrecy: On the Interpretation of Narrative*, Cambridge, MA and London, Harvard University Press, 1979.

12 Robert Alter, *The Art of Biblical Narrative*, London, George Allen & Unwin, 1981.

13 See Brevard S. Childs, *Biblical Theology of the Old and New Testaments*, London, SCM Press, 1992.

14 'Introduction: from *A Short Bible*', p. 12.

15 See MacSwain, *Scripture, Metaphysics, and Poetry*, p. 47.

16 Philip Jenkins, *Crucible of Faith: The Ancient Revolution That Made Our Modern Religious World*, New York, Basic Books, 2017.

17 See John J. Collins and Adela Yarbro Collins, *King and Messiah as Son of God: Divine, Human, and Angelic Messianic Figures in Biblical and Related Literature*, Grand Rapids, MI, Eerdmans, 2008.

18 Austin Farrer, 'On Dispensing with Q', D. E. Nineham (ed.), *Studies in the Gospels in Memory of R. H. Lightfoot*, Oxford, Blackwell, 1955, pp. 55–88.

19 See A. N. Sherwin-White, *Roman Society and Roman Law in the New Testament*, Oxford, Clarendon Press, 1963.

2

Farrer on Q

MARK GOODACRE

Introduction

Austin Farrer's 1955 essay 'On Dispensing with Q'[1] is easy to underestimate. Like a lot of his biblical scholarship, it can appear cheeky, quixotic, impish, even impudent. The sheer brass of trying to overturn a decades-old consensus in a few suggestive pages, waving away objections with rhetorical flourishes, is sometimes perceived as infuriating rather than inspiring. Does Farrer appreciate the sheer complexity of the Synoptic Problem, and the careful work done by generations of scholars? Is so much insight so easily abandoned? R. H. Fuller was typical of those who thought that Farrer's article was an essay in impertinence. 'It is hard to think that the patient work over many years', he said, 'can be blithely dismissed in a few pages.'[2] When Stephen Neill was reflecting on a century of New Testament scholarship, he depicted Farrer's article as no more than a blip. 'I think that Q has come to stay,' he asserted.[3]

But scholarly consensus is a fickle phenomenon, and it now seems clear that Farrer's contemporaries greatly underestimated his potential contribution. Even though Farrer only wrote 'a few pages' on the topic, his post-mortem influence on the discussion of the Synoptic Problem is immense, so much so that the scholarly acceptance of the Q hypothesis has eroded to a point where scepticism is widespread. How did this happen, and what is it about Farrer's argument that changed the debate about the Gospels? This chapter takes a careful look at Farrer's views on Q, the strengths and weaknesses of his argument, and the legacy of his attempt to dispense with Q.

'On Dispensing with Q'

Farrer was already flirting with the idea of a world without Q in the early 1950s. In *A Study in St Mark*, published in 1951, he writes:

> Q is, in fact, very like the electron in developed physical theory. You think the appearances demand that you should postulate it, and you can

describe it quite well in terms of the phenomena to which it gives rise, and you may carry a vague imaginative model of it in your head. But when you try to define its existence in itself by where, when, and what, you fall into contradictions.[4]

Farrer's enthusiasm for the idea was nurtured by his reading of B. C. Butler's *The Originality of St. Matthew*, which he reviewed for the *Journal of Theological Studies* in 1952. Although baulking at Butler's rejection of the priority of Mark, he celebrates his attack on Q. 'Here is a writer who demolishes the Q hypothesis,' he says. 'For the Q hypothesis is nothing but a learned construction, and if we show the construction to be faulty, the hypothesis withers away.'[5] His full questioning of Q comes to fruition, though, in his article for a volume that was intended as a Festschrift for R. H. Lightfoot, who had been Dean Ireland Professor of the Exegesis of Holy Scripture in Oxford from 1934 to 1949, but who died in 1953,[6] so that the volume, edited by Farrer's successor as Warden of Keble, Dennis Nineham, became a memorial.

Like many great articles, its thesis is in the title. Farrer's point is that Q is unnecessary. It can be dispensed with as soon as it becomes clear that Luke had knowledge of Matthew's Gospel:

> The Q hypothesis is not, of itself, a probable hypothesis. It is simply the sole alternative to the supposition that St. Luke had read St. Matthew (or *vice versa*). It needs no refutation except the demonstration that its alternative is possible. It hangs on a single thread; cut that, and it falls by its own weight.[7]

The inference that Luke cannot have known Matthew is what leads to the generation of Q, and Farrer sets out to demonstrate that Luke's knowledge of Matthew is actually highly plausible, and that objections to the theory are weak. This is the key point of the article, and it is underlined repeatedly. It is an application of Occam's Razor, an insistence that since good sense can be made of Luke's use of Matthew, their non-Marcan agreements do not require the postulation of an extra, hypothetical document:

> The point we are making is that the hypothesis of St. Luke's using St. Matthew, and the hypothesis of their both drawing independently from a common source, do not compete on equal terms. The first hypothesis must be conclusively exploded before we obtain the right to consider the second at all.[8]

Farrer's process for establishing this is essentially twofold. First, he considers what would count as a plausible argument for the Q hypothesis and concludes that the only viable argument is the independence of Luke from Matthew. Second, he proceeds to argue that Luke did know Matthew, and that the arguments against this are weak. Let us look at these in turn.

How could one argue for Q?

It is a mark of Farrer's argumentative skill that he does not simply assert Occam's Razor and move straight to the case for Luke's use of Matthew. He first carefully considers what kind of arguments for Q could in principle be persuasive. He asks whether the double tradition (the non-Marcan material shared by Matthew and Luke), once extracted, shows signs of a cohesive, distinctive structure and flavour. Do they make up a 'satisfyingly complete little book, with beginning, middle and end'? Do the materials have a 'strong distinctive flavour'?[9] Farrer's questions are prescient given that Q scholars decades later did try to formulate this kind of argument, albeit with limited success.[10] Farrer concedes, in one of his amusing turns of phrase, that the reader should expect the Q material to have a kind of 'Luke-pleasing' profile, but this is quite different from what the Q theory requires:

> Can we say that the Q sections of St. Matthew's Gospel have a strong distinctive flavour, marking them off from the rest of his writing? We cannot. They have a special character of a sort, but a character which can be plausibly enough described as Luke-pleasingness. It seems a sufficient account of them to say that they are those parts of St. Matthew's non-Marcan material which were likely to attract St. Luke, in view of what we know about the general character of his Gospel, or can conjecture about his aims in writing it.[11]

Farrer adds that the double tradition material does not resolve itself into the kind of literary structure that could make an argument for the existence of a discrete document embedded in Matthew and Luke. '[T]here is no independent evidence for anything like Q,' he says. 'To postulate Q is to postulate the unevidenced and the unique.'[12] Farrer's point is that the Q required by the Gospel facts has a 'strongly narrative exordium, not to mention narrative incidents elsewhere interspersed'.[13] It begins with John's preaching, goes on to Jesus' baptism and temptations, continues with the sermon, and on to the centurion's boy. 'Not only is the narrative character of such an opening strongly marked,' Farrer says; 'it further betrays a vigorous symbolical interest in the order of the events.'[14]

Arguments for Luke's use of Matthew

The heart of Farrer's piece is the argument that Luke's use of Matthew is plausible, and that objections to it are without merit. He pursues the case by isolating B. H. Streeter's classic arguments against Luke's use of Matthew,[15] showing their weaknesses, and replacing them with an account of the data that makes better sense on the assumption that Luke knew

Matthew. He notes, for example, that Streeter was fully aware of the difficult evidence of the minor agreements between Matthew and Luke against Mark:

> The difficulty Dr. Streeter has to face is that St. Luke, in a fairly large number of places, makes small alterations in the wording of his Marcan original which St. Matthew also makes. Now this is just what one would expect, on the supposition that St. Luke had read St. Matthew, but decided to work direct upon the more ancient narrative of St. Mark for himself. He does his own work of adaptation, but small Matthaean echoes keep appearing, because St. Luke is after all acquainted with St. Matthew.[16]

Farrer notes that Streeter's approach to these minor agreements is to divide and conquer, citing textual assimilation, the influence of Q, coincidence and so on. 'Thus the forces of evidence,' Farrer says, 'are divided by the advocate, and defeated in detail,'[17] and so evidence for a direct connection between Matthew and Luke is diluted and ignored.[18]

Farrer goes on to isolate several objections to Luke's use of Matthew. They boil down to three essential complaints. First, Luke would not have omitted key passages from Matthew (the argument from omission). Second, sometimes Matthew, sometimes Luke gives the more primitive wording of a saying (the argument from 'alternating primitivity'). And third, Luke's order seems incomprehensible given what we know of his use of Mark (the argument from order). On each of these, Farrer attempts to show that his own theory explains the data as well as, or better than the Q theory. On the question of omissions, Farrer stresses that Luke is not an archivist but an author:

> No one has ever attached decisive importance to St. Luke's unexplained neglect of certain Matthaean texts, and whatever importance it ever had derived from an antiquated view of St. Luke's attitude to his work. If we regard him as essentially a collector of Christ's sayings, then the omission of some particularly striking blossom from his anthology may seem incompatible with his having known it. But if he was not making a collection but building an edifice, then he may have omitted what he omitted because it did not seem serviceable to his architecture nor come ready to his hand in the building of it.[19]

On the argument from alternating primitivity,[20] Farrer suggests that 'There is scarcely an instance in which we can determine priority of form without invoking questionable assumptions.'[21] He has no problem, for example, imagining Luke changing Matthew's 'If I by the Spirit of God cast out demons ...' (Matt. 12.28) to 'If I by the finger of God cast out demons ...' (Luke 11.20) because the latter features a 'forcible allusion which St Matthew lacks' (Exod. 8.19).

The question that Farrer spends most time on, though, is Luke's re-ordering of Matthew's materials, the question that Streeter had stressed, and the question that Q scholars continue to raise to this day. The reason that this question looms so large is that the Two-Source Theory explains Luke's ordering of the double tradition by simply projecting it onto Q, so that Luke becomes a largely unimaginative author who reproduces his sources in large, continuous chunks, copying now from Mark for a stretch, and now from Q for a stretch. To dispense with Q is to enhance Luke's own editorial intervention in his source material, and the imaginative leap is simply too great for those who are used to thinking differently. Farrer's Luke takes a far more active role in the structuring of his materials than does Streeter's Luke. Moreover, the complaint is often expressed by means of a value judgement, one that denigrates Luke's order in comparison with Matthew's. Q is effectively allowed to take the hit for Luke. Farrer responds with characteristic eloquence:

> We are not bound to show that what St. Luke did to St. Matthew turned out to be a literary improvement on St. Matthew. All we have to show is that St. Luke's plan was capable of attracting St. Luke. You do not like what I have done to the garden my predecessor left me. You are welcome to your opinion, but I did what I did because I thought I should prefer the new arrangement. And if you want to enjoy whatever special merit my gardening has, you must forget my predecessor's ideas and try to appreciate mine.[22]

Streeter had said that anyone behaving in the way Luke would have done had he known Matthew would be a 'crank'.[23] Farrer partially concedes an element in what he calls 'Streeter's *boutade*',[24] and agrees that Luke's rearrangement of Matthew's teaching material is 'not so complete a literary success as St. Matthew's great discourses',[25] but he goes on to illustrate that good sense can be made of what Luke has done. Thus in Luke 11.1–13, for example, Farrer argues that Luke has juxtaposed the Lord's Prayer (Matt. 6.9–15) with the 'Ask, seek, knock' (Matt. 7.7–11) teaching, adding his own parable of the friend at midnight (Luke 11.5–8), to create a persuasive unit on prayer. 'And who will hesitate to say,' Farrer asks, 'that in the episode taken as a whole St. Luke has put an aspect of Christ's true teaching in a fresh and clear light, by means of the combination he has made?'[26]

Strengths and weaknesses

There are many things to admire about 'On Dispensing with Q'. Like all of Farrer's work, it is a delightful read – lucid, elegant, witty and full of brilliant observations. He is fearless in taking on the vested interests of New Testament scholarship, and challenging their assumptions. He does not attempt a line-by-line refutation of opponents' arguments but rather goes to the underlying logic of the Q hypothesis itself. But if the article is a diamond, it is an unpolished one. Farrer could not resist an unnecessary, speculative exposition of how Luke rewrote Matthew's 'Pentateuch', producing in his central section a kind of 'Christian Deuteronomy',[27] lending the impression that dispensing with Q involves problematic commitment to the kind of patterning that Farrer loved but his critics loathed. And for those unfamiliar with the joys of Farrer's prose, his rhetoric can come off as idiosyncrasy, even ignorance. One typical Farrer flourish, focussing on the hypothetical nature of Q, has proved an easy target:

> The Q hypothesis is a hypothesis, that is its weakness. To be rid of it we have no need of a contrary hypothesis, we merely have to make St. Luke's use of St. Matthew intelligible; and to understand what St. Luke made of St. Matthew we need no more than to consider what St. Luke made of his own book. Now St. Luke's book is not a hypothetical entity. Here is a copy of it on my desk.[28]

The copy of Luke's Gospel on Farrer's desk in Trinity College, Oxford, was not, of course, identical with the evangelist's autograph, and critics were quick to point out that scholarly reconstructions of the New Testament texts are themselves, in a sense, 'hypothetical'.[29] But to overinterpret the rhetoric misses the point of Farrer's contrast, which is between his observations about a book the existence of which is not in doubt, and a theory that solves the Synoptic Problem by invoking an additional, non-extant work ('a hypothetical entity'). His point is that we can look at Luke and consider it: 'Let us look at what kind of a book it is.'[30] We cannot do the same with Q.

Farrer's essay is vulnerable in another way. When he says 'We have no reason to suppose documents of the Q type to have been plentiful'[31] and 'in postulating Q we are postulating the unique',[32] he becomes susceptible to the charge that was later made, that the Gospel of Thomas provides evidence for a document of the Q type – a Sayings Gospel attested in antiquity.[33] Indeed, it is arguable that Farrer should have known about Thomas. Although the *editio princeps* was not published until 1959,[34] four years after 'On Dispensing with Q', the Oxyrhynchus fragments of what turned out to be Thomas (P.Oxy 1, 654 and 655) had been known for decades, though it was unclear what work they came from. Nevertheless, Farrer's point was actually a nuanced one: he is arguing that Q betrays its identity as the source-critically extracted material from Matthew and Luke, featuring a strong 'narrative exordium' with Matthew's symbolic patterning in the Exodus story. It is a hybrid, a mongrel.[35] But the quotability of the claim that 'To postulate Q is to postulate the unevidenced and the unique'[36] was a hostage to fortune, and a generation of Q scholars has delighted in repeating the myth that Q sceptics were silenced by the discovery of the Gospel of Thomas.[37]

Furthermore, there are aspects of Farrer's prose that can be disconcerting to those not used to it. Farrer's biblical scholarship is profoundly theological, and suffused with a doctrine of inspiration that sees each evangelist as acting under the Holy Spirit's guidance. Comments about what Luke was 'moved to do' are typical,[38] and he frequently appeals directly to inspiration to explain anomalies, as when he is looking at Luke's rearrangement of Matthew:

> He is not dividing and re-arranging existing material, he is presenting his vision of the gospel according to his inspiration. And inspiration works in such a field as this by novelty of combination. Every episode in these chapters puts together two texts at the least which had not been combined before, and the new combination reveals the point that St. Luke is specially inspired to make.[39]

For Farrer, the task of the biblical scholar is closely aligned with the task of the theologian, and to investigate Scripture is to interpret the divine. But for his critics, appeals to the inspiration seem like a refusal to argue a difficult point.[40] What problem could not be explained away by such an appeal? Although many fans of Farrer's writing will enjoy the integration of his theology with his biblical scholarship, it would be fair to say that appeals to inspiration are unlikely to be persuasive when one is arguing the merits of competing models in the discussion of the Synoptic Problem.

Another frustrating element of Farrer's biblical scholarship, which is on show as much in 'On Dispensing' as elsewhere, is his failure to engage in detail with any more than a handful of scholars. As Michael Goulder notes, 'Farrer contemned the footnote'.[41]Although he was widely read, and his learning exudes on page after page, Farrer limits his interaction with scholars to those he needed to mention, like Streeter, who is the effective dialogue partner in this piece, but the approach can be alienating in a field like Synoptic studies, where the thickets of detailed scholarship are especially dense, and detailed engagement with them is the norm.

Nor does Farrer provide any support for himself by citing potential allies. In his hands, dispensing with Q is a lonely affair, and he does not appeal to a single sympathetic voice, in spite of his enthusiasm for B. C. Butler, 'a writer who demolishes the Q hypothesis'.[42] It is not even clear whether Farrer was aware of other contemporary Q sceptics like James Hardy Ropes and Morton Scott Enslin, both of whom, unlike Butler, combined scepticism over Q with an acceptance of the priority of Mark, and whose logic is sometimes similar to Farrer's.[43] Ropes, for example, writes:

> The widespread idea of a common source, now lost, for these two gospels – the theory of the 'Logia' or 'Q' – has tended to be modified, refined, and complicated to such a degree as, for that reason if for no other, to arouse doubts of its validity. There is a simpler, competing possibility, namely

that Luke drew these sayings from our Gospel of Matthew, which has never been shown to be impossible. If this could be made a probability, the hypothesis of 'Q' would lose at least its main ground of support.[44]

Enslin similarly notes the elegance of a solution to the Synoptic Problem that takes seriously the possibility of a direct link between Matthew and Luke, building on the priority of Mark, and appreciating the evangelists as authors.[45] It is possible too that Farrer knew the work of E. W. Lummis, whose Q sceptical work was certainly known to Streeter,[46] but once again, it goes unmentioned.

The legacy of 'Dispensing'

Even with a handful of potential, uncited allies, Farrer's essay stands alone. It is ambitious, even reckless in its attitude to one of the crown jewels of New Testament scholarship, and it is not surprising that it seemed, at first, as if this seed had fallen on stony ground. Within months, *Theology* published an article by W. H. Blyth Martin declaring that Luke's knowledge of Matthew was 'impossible', appealing to the full weight of consensus:

> To question the existence of what has become definitely accepted as a new star in the Synoptic firmament is a bold venture. Its existence is accepted by the vast majority of scholars outside the Roman Church.[47]

For Blyth Martin, Farrer's article is an essay in implausibility:

> It is as certain as anything can be that Luke has not derived his versions from Matthew. Surely the verdict on all this must be that this tour de force has failed, leaving the main results of generations of patient scholars unimpaired.[48]

Within a decade, F. Gerald Downing countered Farrer in an article in *New Testament Studies*, the flagship journal in the field, that has been frequently cited in the last half century as providing a decisive critique of Farrer's theory. Downing's 'Towards the Rehabilitation of Q'[49] attempts a careful analysis of several pericopae that he argues only make sense on the Q hypothesis. Downing focusses specially on the Beelzebub Pericope (Matt. 12.22–32 // Mark 3.22–30 // Luke 11.14–22), and he argues that Luke's version can only be understood if the evangelist is working directly from Q, and if Matthew is conflating Mark with Q, a conclusion that is hugely at variance with Farrer's model. Since Farrer only treated this anomalous pericope in passing,[50] Downing's detailed analysis was often, in subsequent scholarship, thought persuasive.[51]

Yet if the Synoptic Problem elites sighed at Farrer and doubled down, and Q appeared to have emerged unscathed from his attack, a seed had been sown, and the damage was done. Farrer's colleagues in Oxford saw the challenge, and they began a series of 'Q Parties' to discuss the article,[52] and shortly afterwards, in 1959, E. L. Mascall wrote a delightful ditty, 'On Dispensing With Q':

Here lies poor Streeter, stiff and stark,
Whose corpse foul Farrer slew,
For, though in life he made his Mark,
In death he's lost his Q.

Let exorcists from far and wide
Placate his troubled spook,
Which else will range the Broad beside
The shade of Proto-Luke.

O base and disrespectful hand!
O thrice unhallowed rites!
To break such mossy coffins and
To quench such ancient lights![53]

Meanwhile, one of Farrer's students in Oxford in the 1950s, Michael Goulder,[54] picked up the baton and began running with it. In his view, Farrer's article was 'a vision, but the vision is for many days'.[55] In a series of books and articles over the next five decades, Goulder continued to press the case for his mentor's theory, to the extent that many began labelling it 'the Farrer-Goulder theory'. Like Farrer, Goulder was provocative, suggestive and inspiring, but unlike him, Goulder was patient, relentless and forensic. 'Q is not going to collapse,' he wrote in 1980, 25 years after the publication of Farrer's article. 'It has the highest vested interest of any New Testament hypothesis in that virtually every scholar has written a book assuming its truth.' His solution was that 'It will have to be hunted from the field',[56] and Goulder applied himself to the task.

Although others picked up Farrer's idea and ran with it,[57] they were almost all in the United Kingdom, and were themselves usually ignored. Wheels turn slowly on new paradigms, and it took many years before Farrer's theory even got a hearing in other centres of New Testament scholarship like Germany and the USA, where it was often assumed that any objection to Q must also be an objection to Marcan priority.[58] Yet eventually, with the dawn of a new millennium, Farrer's vision finally began to be realized, and a new generation of scholars and students became sceptical of their forefathers' and foremothers' certainty.[59] Recent years have seen a proliferation of new monographs and collections of essays that affirm Marcan priority while questioning Q.[60]

In spite of the brilliance of 'On Dispensing with Q', and in spite of the fact that it is now one of the things for which Farrer is most famous, the essay is in a sense incidental to Farrer's larger project. He wanted to dispense with Q not solely because he had never been persuaded of its existence, but also because he saw it as a serious impediment to appreciating the literary creativity of the evangelists, the inspiration of their Gospels and the interconnected nature of Scripture. 'The surrender of the Q hypothesis will not only clarify the exposition of St. Luke,' Farrer says. 'It will free the interpretation of St. Matthew from the contradiction into which it has fallen.' No longer would Matthew be seen as an 'artificial mosaic'. Instead it can be expounded as 'a living growth'.[61] At the end of 'On Dispensing with Q', Farrer lays out his vision for the future:

> The literary history of the Gospels will turn out to be a simpler matter than we had supposed. St. Matthew will be seen to be an amplified version of St. Mark, based on a decade of habitual preaching, and incorporating oral material, but presupposing no other literary source beside St. Mark himself. St. Luke, in turn, will be found to presuppose St. Matthew and St. Mark, and St. John to presuppose the three others. The whole literary history of the canonical Gospel tradition will be found to be contained in the fourfold canon itself, except in so far as it lies in the Old Testament, the Pseudepigrapha, and the other New Testament writings.[62]

Farrer is sometimes characterized as a saint,[63] less often as a prophet. Yet this prophecy,[64] this vision for many days, has at last been partially fulfilled. The ultimate legacy of Farrer's scholarship on Q is that a new generation of students has been enlivened by the way the evangelists come to life as inspired figures in a vision of Christian origins that is itself inspirational.

Notes

1 Austin Farrer, 'On Dispensing with Q' in D. E. Nineham (ed.), *Studies in the Gospels: Essays in Memory of R. H. Lightfoot*, Oxford, Blackwell, 1955, pp.55–88.

2 R. H. Fuller, *The New Testament in Current Study*, London, SCM Press, 1963, p.74 n. 1.

3 Stephen Neill and Tom Wright, *Interpretation of the New Testament: 1861–1986*, Oxford, Oxford University Press, 1986, p.136 n. 1.

4 Austin Farrer, *A Study in St Mark*, Westminster, Dacre, 1951, p. 210.

5 Austin Farrer, Review of B. C. Butler, *The Originality of St Matthew*, Cambridge, Cambridge University Press, 1951, *JTS* 3 (1952):102–6. Farrer's enthusiasm in this review is so marked that it may be that reading Butler's book was the catalyst for 'On Dispensing with Q'.

6 'Prof. R. H. Lightfoot – New Testament Studies' Obituary, *The Times*, 27 November 1953, p. 10.

7 Farrer, 'On Dispensing', p. 62.

8 Ibid., p. 56.

9 Ibid., p. 57.

10 See, for example, John S. Kloppenborg, 'Introduction' in John S. Kloppenborg (ed.),

The Shape of Q: Signal Essays on the Sayings Gospel, Minneapolis, Fortress, 1994, p. 2: 'For it is exceedingly unlikely that a subset of materials mechanically abstracted from two Gospels would display an inherent genre and structure unless in fact that subset substantially represented a discrete and independent Gospel.' For a critique of the argument, see Mark Goodacre, *The Case Against Q: Studies in Marcan Priority and the Synoptic Problem*, Harrisburg, Trinity Press International, 2002, pp. 66–75.

11 Farrer, 'On Dispensing', p. 57.

12 Ibid., p. 58. The rhetorical flourish makes Farrer vulnerable on this point in that later studies attempted to show the generic similarities between Q and other ancient literature, especially in John S. Kloppenborg, *The Formation of Q: Trajectories in Ancient Wisdom Collections*, Studies in Antiquity and Christianity, Philadelphia, Fortress, 1987. But Farrer's point is defensible. See further below.

13 Farrer, 'On Dispensing', p. 59.

14 Ibid.

15 B. H. Streeter, *The Four Gospels: A Study of Origins*, London, Macmillan, 1924.

16 Farrer, 'On Dispensing', p. 61.

17 Ibid., p. 62. Farrer lays the groundwork here for future discussions of the minor agreements. See especially Michael Goulder, 'Luke's Knowledge of Matthew' in G. Strecker (ed.), *Minor Agreements: Symposium Göttingen 1991*, Göttingen, Vandenhoeck & Ruprecht, 1993, pp. 143–60. See also M. Goodacre, 'Case Against Q', pp. 152–69, and literature cited there.

18 There is arguably a more important point that Farrer misses, that there are also many major agreements between Matthew and Luke against Mark, which Streeter and others sideline by recategorizing them as 'Mark–Q Overlaps'. See further Mark Goodacre, 'Taking our Leave of Mark-Q Overlaps: Major Agreements and the Farrer Theory', in Mogens Müller and Heike Omerzu, *Gospel Interpretation and the Q Hypothesis*, Library of New Testament Studies, London & New York, Bloomsbury, 2018, pp. 201–22.

19 Farrer, 'On Dispensing', p. 63.

20 Farrer himself does not use this term; for further discussion, see Goodacre, *Case Against Q*, pp. 61–6. In some respects, this is the least satisfactory aspect of Farrer's article because the problem is complex. Michael Goulder's analysis in *Luke: A New Paradigm*, JSNT Sup. 20, Sheffield, Sheffield Academic Press, 1989, pp. 11–22 is still essential reading, and still often neglected.

21 Farrer, 'On Dispensing', p. 64.

22 Ibid., p. 65.

23 Streeter, *Four Gospels*, p. 183.

24 Farrer, 'On Dispensing', p. 67.

25 Ibid.

26 Ibid., p. 70.

27 Ibid., pp. 73–82. The idea gains attractiveness by association with an article in the same volume: C. F. Evans, 'The Central Section of St Luke's Gospel' in Nineham (ed.), *Studies in the Gospels*, pp. 37–55; Farrer refers to Evans' article in 'On Dispensing', p. 79. Michael Goulder developed the idea in *The Evangelists' Calendar: A Lectionary Explanation of the Development of Scripture*, Speaker's Lectures in Biblical Studies, University of Oxford Faculty of Theology, 1972, London, SPCK, 1978, pp. 73–104.

28 Farrer, 'On Dispensing', p. 66.

29 See, for example, John S. Kloppenborg, 'On Dispensing with Q? Goodacre on the Relation of Luke to Matthew', NTS 49, 2003, pp. 210–36 and pp. 214–15 n.13; and 'Is There a New Paradigm?' in *Synoptic Problems: Collected Essays*, WUNT 329, Tübingen, Mohr Siebeck, 2014, pp. 39–61 (48). The suggestion that Farrer's argument is 'a sleight of hand' is unfair.

30 Farrer, 'On Dispensing', p. 66.

31 Ibid., p. 58.

32 Ibid.

33 See, for example, J. Fitzmyer, 'The Oxyrhynchus Logoi of Jesus and the Coptic Gospel

According to Thomas', reproduced in *The Semitic Background of the New Testament: A Combined Edition of Essays on the Semitic Background of the New Testament and A Wandering Aramean: Collected Aramaic Essays*, The Biblical Resource Series, Grand Rapids, Eerdmans, Michigan, Dove, 1997, pp. 355–433 (419).

34 A. Guillaumont, H.-Ch. Puech, G. Quispel, W. Till and Yassah 'Abd al Masih (eds), *The Gospel According to Thomas: Coptic Text Established and Translated*, Leiden, Brill, 1959.

35 For further development of Farrer's insight, see Goulder, *Luke*, pp. 50–51, and Goodacre, *Case Against Q*, pp. 170–85.

36 Farrer, 'On Dispensing', p. 58. A similar point is in fact made at an earlier point by Morton Scott Enslin, *Christian Beginnings*, New York, Harper and Brothers, 1938, pp. 431–2: 'We know that Matthew and Luke used Mark because we have Mark; the situation is utterly different in the case of Q, and all attempts to gauge its exact content – whether it was simply a catena of sayings, or whether the presence of the two narratives (the Temptation story and the Healing of the Servant of the Centurion in Capernaum) plus some material regarding John the Baptist suggest that it was in some sense a gospel or at least was provided with a modicum of narrative to hold the sayings together –and to debate with regard to the comparative fidelity of Matthew and Luke in the use of it appear to me precarious if not actually futile.'

37 See further Mark Goodacre, 'What does Thomas have to do with Q? The Afterlife of a Sayings Gospel' in Catherine Sider Hamilton with Joel Willitts (eds), *Writing the Gospels: A Dialogue with Francis Watson*, LNTS, 606, London & New York, Bloomsbury, 2019, pp. 81–9 (82–83).

38 Farrer, 'On Dispensing', p. 75.

39 Ibid., p. 68.

40 See Kloppenborg, 'On Dispensing', pp. 220–1.

41 Michael Goulder, 'Farrer as a Biblical Scholar', chap. 10 in Philip Curtis, *A Hawk Among Sparrows: A Biography of Austin Farrer*, London, SPCK, 1985, p. 193.

42 See above, Note 4.

43 Edward Hobbs, 'A Quarter Century without Q', *Perkins School of Theology Journal* 33/4 (1980): pp. 10–19 (12) helpfully discusses both Ropes and Enslin as precursors to Farrer, as well as Eduard Simons, *Hat der dritte Evangelist den kanonischen Matthäus benutzt?* Bonn, Universitäts-Buchdruckerei von Carl Georgi, 1880.

44 James Hardy Ropes, *The Synoptic Gospels*, 1934; second impression with new preface, London, Oxford University Press, 1960, p. 94.

45 See further note 35 above. As well as *Christian Beginnings*, which predates 'On Dispensing'; see also Morton Scott Enslin, 'Luke and Matthew', *JQR* 57 (1967), pp. 178–91, and the posthumously published expanded version, 'Luke and Matthew: Compilers or Authors?' *ANRW* II.25.3 (1985), pp. 2357–88.

46 E. W. Lummis, *How Luke Was Written*, Cambridge, Cambridge University Press, 1915, reviewed by B. H. Streeter in *JTS* 17 (1915–16), p. 125. See also E. W. Lummis, 'The Case Against 'Q', *Hibbert Journal* 24 (1925–26), pp. 755–65.

47 W. H. Blyth Martin, 'The Indispensability of Q', *Theology* 59 (1956), pp. 182–8 (182).

48 Ibid., p.188.

49 F. Gerald Downing, 'Towards the Rehabilitation of Q', *NTS* 11 (1964), pp. 169–81.

50 Farrer, 'On Dispensing', p. 83: 'He is perfectly ready to transcribe unused Marcan sentences embedded in Matthaean discourses, for example, in the Beelzebul controversy (Luke 11.15–22 and 12.10)'; see also 'On Dispensing', p. 72.

51 But see Ken Olson, 'Unpicking on the Farrer Theory', in Mark Goodacre and Nicholas Perrin (eds), *Questioning Q: A Collection of Essays*, London, SPCK, 2004, pp. 127–50, and E. Eve, 'The Devil in the Detail: Exorcising Q from the Beelzebul Controversy' in J. C. Poirier and J. Peterson (eds), *Marcan Priority without Q: Explorations in the Farrer Hypothesis*, LNTS 455, London and New York, Bloomsbury, 2015, pp. 16–43.

52 The parties are described in Hollis W. Huston, 'The "Q Parties" at Oxford', *The Journal of Bible and Religion* 25/2, April 1957, pp. 123–8. Huston was visiting Oxford from Ohio Wesleyan University in 1955–56. Huston clearly found the parties compelling: 'To one who

grew up on the Q hypothesis it is astonishing that there is so little decisive evidence to support it against an alternative view. For me, as a result, the synoptic problem is once more an open question' (p. 126).

53 E. L. Mascall, *Pi in the High*, London, The Faith Press, New York, Morehouse-Barlow Co., 1959, p. 48.

54 For the story of Farrer's influence on Goulder, see Michael Goulder, *Five Stones and a Sling: Memoirs of a Biblical Scholar*, Sheffield, Sheffield Phoenix Press, 2009, esp. pp. 17–19, 36–7, 56–9, but also throughout. The most important of Goulder's contributions is *Luke: A New Paradigm*, in which Goulder defends Luke's use of Matthew and Mark at length, including in a passage-by-passage commentary, but he made many other important contributions; for further bibliography and analysis, see Mark Goodacre, *Goulder and the Gospels: An Examination of a New Paradigm*, JSNT Sup. 133, Sheffield, Sheffield Academic Press, 1996.

55 M. Goulder, 'Farrer as a Biblical Scholar', p. 197.

56 M. Goulder, Farrer on Q, *Theology* 83 (1980), pp. 190–5 (194).

57 See especially John Drury, *Tradition and Design in Luke's Gospel*, London, Darton, Longman and Todd, 1976; Eric Franklin, 'Luke: Interpreter of Paul, Critic of Matthew', JSNT Sup. 92, Sheffield, Sheffield Academic Press, 1994; and H. B. Green, 'The Credibility of Luke's Transformation of Matthew' in C. M. Tuckett (ed.), *Synoptic Studies: The Ampleforth Conferences of 1982 and 1983*, JSNT Sup, 7, Sheffield, JSOT Press, 1984, pp. 131–56.

58 See M. Goodacre, 'Case Against Q', pp. 9–10.

59 Although I was only a year old when Austin Farrer died, I was inspired by his scholarship as a Theology student in Oxford in the 1980s and 1990s, where his legacy was alive. I learned a great deal, in particular, from my doctoral supervisor, John Muddiman, who had been one of Farrer's last students, along with John Barton.

60 Among recent publications, see Francis Watson, *Gospel Writing: A Canonical Perspective*, Grand Rapids, Eerdmans, 2013; Poirier and Peterson (eds), *Marcan Priority without Q*; Jesper Tang Nielsen and Mogens Müller (eds), *Luke's Literary Creativity*, LNTS 550, London & New York, Bloomsbury, 2016; Müller and Omerzu, *Gospel Interpretation*, and literature cited in these places.

61 Farrer, 'On Dispensing', p. 85.

62 Ibid.

63 M. D. Goulder, *Midrash and Lection in Matthew*, London, SPCK, 1974, xv – 'a genius as well as a saint'.

64 'Let us indulge ourselves a little here, and prophesy.' Farrer, 'On Dispensing', p. 85.

3

Farrer on Paul

JENNIFER R. STRAWBRIDGE

Studies of Austin Farrer and his writings rarely mention his thoughts about the Apostle Paul. Many a text focusses on Farrer's writings about the Gospels and how they pervade his thoughts, but rarely are more than a few pages devoted to the way Paul infuses Farrer's writings. While Farrer writes that the modern reader usually does not think he needs to read St Paul and concurs that 'it is difficult to refute him',[1] the words of the Apostle are essential to those of Austin Farrer.

Paul, for Farrer, is himself a preacher who 'wears his heart on his sleeve'.[2] Farrer argues that Paul's writings, with the Gospels, should be the starting point for all theology[3] and that 'It is through St Paul ... that our faith is rooted in history'.[4] For Farrer, Paul's writings ground the historical context of the Gospels and Paul, as a historical person, is embodied in numerous sermon illustrations. Paul's epistles are quoted time and again to support points that Farrer makes about philosophy, Mary, the Gospels, salvation, revelation, inspiration and faith. Moreover, Farrer does not shy away from engaging key issues drawn from Paul's writings such as justification, atonement, love, and the use of the Old Testament in the New. Those acquainted with the writings of Farrer will find it no surprise that he also holds a healthy sense of humour about Paul and his quirks, especially in his sermons. Thus, while some secondary reflections on Farrer tell us that he held Paul in high regard, only when we mine his writings for references to Paul can we grasp just how prominent and influential the Apostle is to Farrer's theology, preaching, and understanding of the New Testament. The ultimate hope is that this chapter opens up conversation on an oft-neglected topic: Austin Farrer and his Saint Paul.

Why read Paul?

'Why do I read St Paul?' is a question raised by Farrer in his writings. His answers to this question are both simple and manifold. In a section of *Interpretation and Belief*, Farrer focusses on the relation between the Old and New Testaments and the call to 'see God' within the words and works of both. He is especially keen to argue that Scripture is not given to prove God, but to see God. He writes that 'the primary purpose of the apostles, say of St Paul, when they looked into the Old Testament, was not to demonstrate Christ thence, but to see Christ there'. For, he continues, 'Certainly when they saw Christ in the Scripture it had the force of evidence, for seeing, after all, is believing; and they laboured to show him to others there, that they too might believe'.[5] One reason why Farrer reads the writings of Paul is that Paul 'gathered, or collected, Christ' so that those who read him might also see Christ and believe.

For Farrer, the primary revelation is always Christ and 'His life, words, passion, resurrection' and 'Providence was careful to provide fit witnesses of these events', one of the earliest being St Paul.[6] When Farrer speaks about Paul's writings, he does not deny the difficulty with understanding them for Paul 'used any sort of figure that came to hand: he picked up a rhetorical metaphor from a cynic preaching in the market; he turned a commonplace of the synagogue pulpit inside out. He would have been amazed to learn that subsequent generations would make such stuff the foundations of dogmas'.[7] Farrer writes that in Philemon, Paul expresses 'such a conflict of emotions that it's almost unintelligible'[8] while elsewhere in his letters, Paul 'is so tactful' at times 'that he falls over his words and is almost untranslatable'.[9] Nevertheless, 'tactful or clumsy, what St Paul says is both sincere and exact'[10] and one must persevere in reading Paul since 'at the very least we can safely conclude that Christ had for St Paul a supremely high numinous and ethical value; that he inspired him with new ideals, curing his bad habits, inhibitions, and worries'.[11]

Paul, therefore, points Farrer to Christ and this is at the heart of his understanding of Paul's writings: if Christ 'were not there, the rest would not concern me'. Therefore, Farrer can answer the question 'Why do I read St Paul?' in five words: 'Because he sets Christ forth'.[12]

However, Farrer also focusses on the inspired nature of Paul's writings as another reason that his works must be read. Farrer writes that 'Many students of scripture might incline to judge that the breath of high inspiration blows more unevenly in St Paul's true epistles than anywhere else in the New Testament'. And Farrer seems to agree to an extent for 'when it comes upon him, he achieves sublimities nowhere else found: when the mood or the subject is more pedestrian, so is the level of writing'.[13] Nevertheless, because some of Paul's writings are more 'pedestrian' does not mean they are uninspired.

Farrer gives the example of his great-aunt who reads Isaiah or Paul and says 'These are the words of God' as opposed to those who say 'These are the words of a couple of ancient Jews, giving their ideas about what God wants, warns against, or promises'.[14] Farrer wants to know which view is correct as he contemplates whether God 'put St Paul, or Isaiah for that matter, into a trance' and made them 'do automatic writing under his control'.[15] He concludes in one of many lengthy expositions on inspiration that no one believes that 'Bible writers were out of their ordinary senses when they composed', with God as 'no better than a puppet-master'. Rather, God's inspiration 'does not make us any less ourselves' but 'twice the men we were before. And St Paul does not cease to be St Paul, he is twice the Paul he was, when the Spirit of Jesus possesses his pen'.[16]

For Farrer, Paul was special because there is 'a great difference between the inspiration God gives us and the inspiration he gave to St Paul.' He continues:

> I do not merely mean that St Paul's inspiration was stronger than ours, or that he obeyed it more completely, though no doubt these things are true. I mean that what he was inspired to do was something different ... we are not inspired to speak to our fellow men the words of God, as St Paul was. We may be inspired to embrace what St Paul revealed ... we may be inspired to expound what he taught: but he was inspired to teach it. Inspired, not manipulated: he spoke for God and he remained himself.[17]

Of course, for Farrer, this means we get some of the 'Apostle's oddities' as well as his 'national prejudices or personal limitations' mixed in. But this doesn't mean Paul's text is not the word of God. On the contrary, Paul's writings call for reading and hearing his words with 'our spiritual ears'. As Farrer concludes, 'if we do not believe that the same God who moved St Paul can move us to understand what he moved St Paul to say, then (once again) it isn't much use bothering about St Paul's writings'.[18] Inspiration doesn't mean that Paul is beyond criticism. Paul and Luke and John all make some slips in dates, history and astronomy, but, for Farrer, 'it does not matter' because 'God can and does teach us the things necessary to our salvation in spite of these human imperfections in the texts'.[19]

Therefore, the teaching of Paul cannot be reduced to 'the fact of Christ', only telling us something about Jesus historically but saying nothing of revelation or inspiration. Rather, his words are 'the absolutely necessary guide to what I may recover of the Lord's own oracles'.[20] The writings and interpretation of Paul, therefore, are not simply his opinions and prejudices, but 'participation in the mind of Christ, through the Holy Ghost'[21] for 'in the apostolic mind ... the God-given images lived, not statically, but with an inexpressible creative force'.[22]

Ultimately, Paul's writings and his very person serve as an example of faith and of sharing the faith of Christ. As Farrer writes of those who want to engage with Paul:

> St Paul, having heard of the faith of the Roman Christians, as he says, wants to have a share in it; so he proposes the sensible method of walking down to the quayside at Corinth, and looking for a boat to Rome. We, similarly, have heard of the faith of St Paul; and though no ship will take us into his company, the fact of reading his letters will do almost as well. We can travel in time as well as in space; and I am aware that I might

profitably spend much more time than I do reading the words and the lives of the saints. I never return from such visits into the past without thankfulness and, as St Paul says, a share of encouragement.[23]

Paul and historical context

Throughout Farrer's writings, he is mindful of the historical contexts both of Scripture and of his audience. The historical context of Paul's letters is especially key since 'to understand St Paul it is essential to start in the right place, and not to put the cart before the horse'.[24] Farrer returns many times to the significance of the genre of Paul's writings as well as their early dating, seeing both as essential to understanding Paul's theology. Questions of Paul's theology, Farrer argues, are historical questions through which one can understand both 'what humanly happened in Christ' and what he understood 'to have happened divinely to him'.[25] Even so, while Paul might reveal things that are 'informative about saving facts' which contain 'historical matter' and which 'is of predominantly historical interest to us', unpacking this is not always possible.[26] Certainly, Paul's practical problems can be linked to a modern context, but then 'we, as we read, suddenly perceive that the apostle's feet have gone through the floor and his head through the roof, and that he is speaking in the large dimension of inspired vision' before he also 'returns to settle the matter in hand'.[27]

Issues arise, therefore, when Paul's words are 'studied through unhistorical spectacles' because such study has 'had a frightening effect'.[28] This is because 'Whatever St Paul does, he does with his might. When he rebukes, he rebukes; and when he comforts, he comforts'.[29] Paul's context is essential. One must know when he is rebuking and when he is comforting, and thus Farrer instructs his readers always to 'look at the context' because only then 'we can see that St Paul is speaking in a very special sense',[30] never disconnected from Christ.

Nevertheless, historical context is not only significant for how we read Paul, according to Farrer, but for how we read all of Scripture. He offers a close reading of Romans 7, examining how Paul describes his own situation 'with great intensity of language' and 'passion'.[31] While Farrer uses Romans to make a specific point about typology, symbolism and context in his exegesis, he also makes a wider contextual point: 'Now St Paul is writing an epistle, a mixed piece in which argument alternates with descriptive presentation, not to mention exhortation, laudation, and vituperation. And the argumentative passages are natural occasions for an explicit typology which is then available for allusive application'.[32] This, for Farrer, is essential to note because reading Paul is not the same exercise as reading a Gospel. As he writes, compared with Paul, 'St Mark's Gospel is a different sort of book. The evangelist is not going to come forward *in propria persona* and argue his typology; and so, perhaps, he has not such a natural occasion as St Paul has in Romans for putting the clue into our hands'.[33] Through the writings of Paul, Farrer draws out a point essential for all of his exegetical work: genre and context are essential for interpretation; one cannot handle 'an argumentative Epistle' and 'a perhaps wilfully enigmatic Gospel' in the same way.[34]

And yet, more clarification is needed for genre since even though Paul's writings are in the form of letters, 'to suggest that they were simply letters of the sort one writes every day, is grossly absurd'. Rather, returning to the theme of inspiration, 'they are at the very least instruments of sacred teaching and authoritative apostolic direction'.[35] As such, Farrer refers to Paul's own claims, writing that 'if St Paul invoked the spirit of prophecy when he spoke mighty and burning words in the congregation, so he might when he composed the letter which was to be read out as his voice's substitute'. Even Paul himself writes in II Corinthians that 'he was weightier with his pen than with his lips'.[36] Farrer cannot imagine, therefore, that 'the Corinthian or Philippian Church, after reading his inspired admonition, would toss it into the fire'. Rather, 'They would keep it by them (as they did) to be an enduring guide'.[37]

Paul and the Gospels

Paul's writings make a number of appearances as Farrer expounds Gospel tradition. For Farrer, 'St Paul alludes to, or quotes, part of' Gospel tradition throughout his letters, including 'Christ's teaching on marriage, his company of Twelve, his charge to missionary apostles, his last supper with his disciples, his death by Roman execution on Jewish initiative, his burial and resurrection, his prophecy of a second Advent to follow upon severe trials for his Church'.[38] Farrer refers specifically to 1 Corinthians 15 when he writes that 'St Paul, our earliest authority, gives us a piece of catechism which he had himself been taught and which he handed on to others. Christ died for our sins according to the scriptures, he was buried and rose according to the scriptures, he showed himself to Peter, then to the Twelve.'[39]

All this finds 'an echo in St Mark's pages', though whether Mark had 'before him much of what St Paul records' is one of many 'unverifiable conjectures' Farrer makes.[40] Nevertheless, this doesn't prevent Farrer from suggesting that the synoptic evangelists may be developing Paul's Gospel tradition. For example, Farrer writes of Matthew's Gospel that 'as though taking up St Paul's thoughts in Galatians and Romans, the evangelist begins his Gospel with a derivation of Christ from Abraham through David'.[41] And of Luke's Gospel, Farrer concludes that 'he too, as befits a good disciple of St Paul, takes up the inheritance of Pauline ideas and begins from Abraham'.[42] Parts of John's Gospel even can be 'best viewed as a balanced reflection on the previous tradition, a sort of synthesis of St Paul, St Luke, and St Mark'.[43]

Furthermore, Paul also offers historical context and a historical foundation to counter those who worry about the evangelists, their identity, and whether they say anything about this historical Christ. Farrer is clear that we cannot know exactly who St Mark or St Matthew were or when they wrote, but that this doesn't matter because 'the certainty of the Christian faith does not depend on the answering of these questions one way or another'.[44] Moreover, Paul comes to the rescue in questions about the historical Christ since 'our primary witness to a historical Christ is not any of the evangelists, but St Paul'. And here is where context of Paul and the Gospels is essential for 'with St Paul the case is quite different: he is himself a historical character of flesh and blood; his great letters are genuine beyond doubt, and can even be accurately dated'.[45] Thus, Farrer can argue that 'It is through St Paul, then, that our faith is rooted in history ... And so it is not necessary, even if it were honourable, to press the evidence about the authorships, date or sources of the Gospels further than it will go'. This is because, for Farrer, the evangelists are 'built like St Paul and like ourselves upon the common faith, the apostolic witness, writing anyhow early in the history of our religion, where there were memories of Christ still to be gathered, and when the Spirit of the same Christ was still most active in the special work of revelation'.[46]

Paul as historical person

Farrer focusses not only on Paul's writings, his historical context, and his influence on the Gospels, but also on Paul as a historical person. Paul is first and foremost 'the preacher of the resurrection' who, contextually, 'is converted to a Church already proclaiming it within some three years of the event'.[47] However, Farrer writes that 'it is often said that it would have amazed these writers to learn that their books would be viewed as "Scripture"', even though they 'were writing books of the *nature* of sacred scripture ... they had no idea of doing anything else'.[48]

Nevertheless, Paul, for Farrer, is not a flawless saint. As a preacher and teacher, Paul 'wears his heart on his sleeve' and it is because of this that Farrer can discern that 'pride was his besetting temptation'.[49] This pride, however, isn't the kind that seeks status and dignity for 'that sort of pride would not have led him to stitch tents in Aquila's shop, rather than draw an apostle's salary.' Rather, Paul's pride 'was of an altogether subtler sort; he would rather give than receive' and only over time did he 'learn to take'.[50]

Paul is also one who confirms Farrer's view that 'the world's a boasting-match, a confidence trick'. He writes that 'All men are insecure', even St Paul. So that even though Paul knows security is only obtained 'by accepting divine love', he still struggles.[51] Paul, however, takes a risk that many in Farrer's church are unwilling to take and thus serves as an example. For Farrer, Paul is an example who 'pitted himself against impossibilities, and never let himself off. And when he was weak, then, by the grace of Christ, he found himself strong. The strength was not his, and the fact gave him a deeper assurance. For every position of strength we build in this world is sure to crumble.'[52]

Farrer also brings the person of Paul to life in a number of his writings. For example, Paul serves as a critic against those with whom Farrer disagrees. When arguing against those who withhold themselves from communion on Sundays, Farrer asks 'What do you think St Peter or St Paul would have said if you had told them that you feared always to communicate, lest it should go stale on you?' To which Farrer replies: 'They would not have known what on earth you were talking about. It would have been all you could do to bring them to conceive the possibility of such emotional frivolity, such reckless individualism in a Christian'.[53] He then uses the language of Paul to continue his critique 'What,' he asks, 'is the body of Christ to lack a member because you are not feeling soulful?' Through the adapted words of Paul, Farrer's point is clear.

Elsewhere, Paul serves as an example of conversion and Farrer explicitly compares the stories of Jeremiah and of Paul. Farrer draws on Paul's words from Galatians 1 about God 'who from my mother's womb set me apart … that I might preach him among the nations' and compares them with Jeremiah 1 about the God who 'before thou camest forth from the womb … sanctified thee; I have appointed thee a prophet unto the nations'.[54] Farrer concludes that 'the Apostle has been taught to see himself in Jeremiah'.[55] As Farrer encourages his listeners in their own calling, he continues that 'Jeremiah's calling and St Paul's were both quite sudden; and other people were intrigued or perplexed by the violence of the change' and yet they are not surprised.[56] Certainly, their 'task might be as heavy as the cross, but the issue is as clear as daylight to those blessed saints of the two Testaments, to Jeremiah and to St Paul'.[57] By bringing their stories to life, Farrer is able to connect with the calling of his community.

Farrer also brings Paul to life in his own twentieth-century world. As he introduces an example of conversion in an essay on philosophical theology, he tells us much about what he thinks of Paul when he writes that 'the story I shall tell will be a true story. But I shall corrupt it in two ways. I shall make the convert more explicitly intelligent than he was and I shall make him a little more typical than he was – straighten out the kinks of idiosyncrasy.'[58] In the story that follows about someone 'whom it will be convenient to call Paul', this Paul was sent 'to a day school' where the headmaster is called Stephen and, later, his college chaplain at the University of Damascus is called Ananias. In a clever retelling of Paul's conversion to faith in Christ, Farrer focusses on the balance of divine and human communication[59] and the importance of experience. For this 'young Paul', 'learning to pray and to co-operate with grace is not easy'[60] and 'the revelation of the true Christ in the heart' cannot be achieved 'without a certain crucifixion, an agony of discovering the purity and supernaturality of the spiritual good'.[61] In an example laced with language from Paul's epistles, Farrer argues that experiences of the divine are not just any experience and 'cannot be understood profanely' as so many philosophers attempt to do.[62]

In one of his sermons, Paul the person is once again transformed first into a college chaplain who 'is sometimes here, sometimes away touring the Mediterranean, but not for reasons of health' and who sends letters occasionally back to the College 'taking you severely to task' for certain behaviours.[63] And then, in another sermon, Paul becomes a 'worker-priest'.[64] In the latter creative story of Paul's difficulties in Corinth, Paul is one who does business in tents and 'never took a penny from the Corinthian Christians'.[65] But when Paul goes away on a mission trip, a VIP shows up from Palestine, who stays at the 'Roma Hotel' in Corinth and is clearly 'in a different class entirely from Paul, the worker-missionary'. The Corinthians like someone of a higher class and assume that this VIP is 'a real apostle'.[66] As Farrer writes, the 'visit of the VIP weakened St Paul's authority, and that was a great pity' and it was this along with a few specific episodes concerning his charity for the poor 'which made St Paul explode ... and he certainly let them have it'.[67] At this point, Farrer has Paul speak directly to his students who, like the Corinthians, sometimes focus more on their own strength and class than on God which, according to Farrer's Paul, is 'idiotic'. By bringing Paul the person to life for his community, Farrer encourages them not only to enter into the story but also to be challenged and transformed by Paul's words, just as the Corinthians were.

Key issues connected to Paul's writings

As stated in the introduction to this chapter, Farrer does not shy away from some of the difficult debates raised by different interpretations of Paul's letters. These include questions of justification and faith, atonement, the incarnation and the Trinity.

When it comes to justification, Farrer writes that it 'would never have been heard of as a doctrine, but for St Paul's controversy with the Judaizers'.[68] Farrer uses this particular doctrine to counter all those who have 'in more recent times' tried to make justification the primary means to 'nourish the Christian soul'.[69] Farrer is keen to argue against those who say that justification is by faith and not by works, and pulls from 1 Corinthians 4, Romans 2 and Galatians 4 to show that salvation is through 'God's eternal decree, we were saved in Christ's work, we were saved when we were baptized into Christ; we are being saved daily through the Spirit; we shall be saved on the last day'.[70] Thus, anyone who says 'that St Paul rejected "justification by works" is false, unless "works" be given the special sense of "wage-service", "paid labour"'. Farrer continues, 'St Paul did not teach that man is saved by an inward act (believing) rather than an outward act (doing). He taught that man is saved, not by earning salvation, but by adhering to him who is salvation'.[71] But this adherence for Farrer, reading Paul, 'is actualized by deeds rather than by states of mind'[72] and thus while Paul speaks about justification in his letters, it cannot be disconnected from believing and doing in Christ.

The writings of Paul also come to the fore when Farrer turns to the figure of Mary. Farrer begins with the statement that 'The earliest and most copious of apostolic writers, St Paul, tells us not a word about her history',[73] except that Galatians 3.23—4.7 does contain 'all the essential themes of the doctrine of the virginal birth'.[74] Farrer sees Paul claiming that Christians are both 'Sons of God' and 'born of a woman, born under the law' just as Christ, 'the Son of God is born of a human mother'.[75] There are, for Farrer, a few issues with this reading of Paul, which he then clarifies, with a now familiar focus on context. For, he writes, this supposition that Paul clearly supports the 'virginal birth' has 'obvious difficulties', including the reality that 'St Paul does many times roundly declare that Christ died on the cross, and rose again. He nowhere states that he was born of a virgin'.[76] After a number of complex approaches to Galatians and Romans, Farrer concludes by stepping away from the argument and writing that whatever the argument about virginal birth, Paul's argument is always 'with the central object of faith': Christ.[77]

Paul and his writings are also a central focus when Farrer discusses the doctrine of the Trinity in his Bampton Lectures. One cannot, Farrer is clear, assume that 'St Paul or St John is, after all, a systematic theologian' as each is 'a very unsystematic systematic theologian, no doubt, too impulsive and enthusiastic to put his material in proper order or to standardize his terminology'.[78] The focus, for Farrer, must thus be on the images the Apostle Paul uses, rather than trying to find trinitarian concepts in his writings because looking only for concepts is like using 'a bulldozer for the cultivation of a miniature landscape-garden'.[79] Thus, 'without the statistics or the lexicography' it is obvious 'that St Paul's several imagery statements speak of personal divine action in the Father, the Son, and the Holy Ghost, and further, that St Paul was not a polytheist'. Problems arise with these images of Father, Son, and Spirit when 'we syllogize from them in the direction of our own questions which are not his' as then 'our process is completely invalid'.[80] Thus, while Farrer explores the idea of the Trinity, he also teaches his readers how to read Scripture through the words and images of Paul and his writings. As he concludes, Paul's images offer 'a tri-form experience of God, not the experience of a triune deity'[81] seen in Paul's prayers and 'the pattern of God, Lord, and Spirit on his homiletical paragraphs'.[82] But the limits of interpretation are clear since whether this 'is a triad of Divine Persons or a triad of saving mysteries, we still do not know'.[83]

One final issue on which Farrer draws on the writings of Paul is that of atonement, on which Farrer engages a debate that continues to this day concerning the language of propitiation and expiation. For Farrer, 'on atonement, new life, redemption, sanctification ... Paul piles figure upon figure in the attempt to describe what cannot be described, and especially the sacrificial cost'.[84] But even though Paul 'uses technical terms of sacrifice ... there is one thing that he does not say' when speaking about atonement. Paul 'never says that Christ propitiated the wrath of God, or propitiated God at all'.[85] Farrer can hear the counter that Paul does say 'Christ is a propitiation' but he clarifies 'The English versions say so; but you can take it from me that the English versions are wrong'.[86] Farrer argues that the word here is expiation, not propitiation, for a person is propitiated but a crime is expiated and Paul, according to Farrer, means the latter: God 'loved us enough to set forth Christ as an expiation of our sins through his blood'.[87] Paul's words, therefore, permeate the doctrine drawn out in Farrer's writings.

Paul's letters as example

While sometimes Farrer engages in deep exegesis of Paul's person or writings to expound doctrine, illuminate the Gospels and offer an example for living, the writings of Paul also permeate Farrer's thought in more subtle ways. Frequently, Paul's words serve as an example to support an argument, offered in passing but nevertheless serving a crucial role.

For example, when Farrer writes about messianic prophecy, part of his argument revolves around a question from Romans 3: 'What advantage has the Jew?' Farrer responds, 'and we may reply, still out of the Apostle's mouth: Much advantage on every side; and to begin with they were entrusted with the miracles of God'.[88] For Farrer, such an example points to the essential place of prophecy in the Old Testament and the importance of prophetic fulfilment, which he finds confirmed in Paul's Roman epistle.

Examples from Paul's writings also form the foundation for much of Farrer's Christology. In a section on the mystery of how Christ is both human and divine, Farrer turns to a question Paul poses in 1 Corinthians 2: 'Who has known the mind of the Lord?' in order to conclude that the 'natural mind could not understand Jesus in his historical existence ... Only God can understand God, even when God is incarnate'.[89]

Farrer also connects the messages of Paul and Jesus. When he speaks of salvation and death, he writes that 'The apostle talks of fire, and so did Christ. Many, says St Paul, will be saved, though they bring a world of rubbish with them, but none of them will be let off the ordeal of fire'. Farrer then quotes directly from 1 Corinthians 3 to make his point, before moving back to Christ's words from the Gospels.[90]

The words of Paul serve as examples to support Farrer's arguments in many other ways, some in passing and some more fully developed. For example, he uses Paul's letters to speak about the connection between resurrection and sacrament,[91] the defeat of 'the hostile powers' by Christ 'in his own flesh',[92] purgatory,[93] and God's providence.[94] Paul is a reference point when Farrer writes about the shining face of Moses,[95] the connection between death and salvation of the flesh,[96] and as a way into a sermon on Acts and Pentecost.[97] When writing about sanctification,[98] predestination[99] and sacramental life,[100] Farrer looks to examples from Paul's letters. And when speaking about the Day of Judgement, he both turns to Paul[101] and invites sympathy for Paul and his apparent contradictions about the eschaton. Don't be 'too hard on the Apostle' he tells his students, for 'How was he to know the very form and timing of the events yet to come?'[102] From his description of God's work in the world, in history, the mystery of the incarnation, and the Holy Spirit, the language of Paul is always close to hand.[103] The writings of Paul, in other words, permeate Farrer's writings.

The humorous side of Farrer's engagement with the Apostle

As a brief conclusion, Farrer's wonderful sense of humour is also encountered through his reliance on Paul. While certainly the adaptation of Paul to modern life, school and university is creative, Paul's writings also lead him to make some wonderful statements. Some are humorous asides, such as his conclusion that, 'St Paul does not say "Fais ta toilette et fais ton âme" because he doesn't happen to be writing French.'[104] Others are part of a wider point, such as a sermon on speaking in tongues in Corinth where Farrer concludes that 'Speaking with angel-tongues is a fine thing, but prophesying is finer; that is, inspired preaching is better than inspired yodelling'.[105]

Another rather playful conclusion can be found in a sermon on Paul as an example which begins: 'they used to tell schoolboys … that St Paul was a fine example of a Christian gentleman, because just look at what perfect manners his letters display.' As Farrer continues, 'since then I have looked at St Paul's letters a great deal, and I am not so sure about perfect manners'.[106] They are, for Farrer, 'the manners of a Jewish exile doing his best … but it is a bit too obvious'.[107] Nevertheless, he is able to use his sense of humour to make a serious point. He concludes the section: 'as I am not a primitive Roman elder but only a decadent English theologian, I am rather fortunate than otherwise to have the Apostle writing as he does … He may not be such a good model of manners … but he is a more useful example of the working of God's grace'.[108]

Conclusion

Paul was clearly a saint – one who points to Christ – for Austin Farrer. His writings infuse the writings of Farrer, his person serves as example time and again. While Farrer doesn't expect all whom he engages to agree with Paul, he pleads with them to give the Apostle a chance. While Paul remains enigmatic at times, inspiring at others, and downright pedestrian in some places, he is found across the writings of Austin Farrer. And thus it seems fitting to conclude in the words of Farrer himself: 'I told you that I would do my best to state exactly what St Paul says and means; and that I have now done, as best I could, in the time and in the words available.'[109]

Notes

1 Austin Farrer, *The Glass of Vision (Bampton Lectures for 1948)*, Westminster, Dacre Press, 1948, p. 38. Ironically, this statement falls within a series of lectures whose title is taken from 1 Corinthians 13.12, 'now we see through a glass darkly'.

2 Austin Farrer, *The End of Man*, London, SPCK, 1973, p. 44.

3 Austin Farrer, *Interpretation and Belief*, London, SPCK, 1976, p. 13.

4 James Leslie Houlden (ed.), *Austin Farrer: The Essential Sermons*, London, SPCK, 1991, p. 66.

5 Farrer, *Interpretation*, pp. 25–6.

6 Farrer, *Glass*, p. 37.

7 Ibid.

8 Austin Farrer, *Words for Life*, Charles C. Conti and James Leslie Houlden (eds), London, SPCK, 1993, p. 84.

9 Houlden, *Essential Sermons*, p. 13.

10 Ibid., p. 14.

11 Farrer, *Glass*, p. 38.

12 Farrer, *Interpretation*, p.12.

13 Farrer, *Glass*, p. 57.

14 Farrer, *Interpretation*, p. 9.

15 Ibid.

16 Ibid., p. 10.

17 Ibid.

18 Ibid., p. 11.

19 Ibid., p. 12.

20 Ibid., p. 41.

21 Ibid., p. 42.

22 Ibid., p. 43.

23 Houlden, *Essential Sermons*, p. 15.

24 Ibid., p. 46.

25 Austin Farrer, 'Infallibility and Historical Revelation' in *Infallibility in the Church: An Anglican-Catholic Dialogue*, London, Darton, Longman & Todd, 1968, pp. 9–23; p. 17.

26 Farrer, *Glass*, p. 52.

27 Ibid., p. 53.

28 Austin Farrer, *The Brink of Mystery*, Charles C. Conti (ed.), London, SPCK, 1976, p. 138.

29 Ibid.

30 Austin Farrer, *Said or Sung: An Arrangement of Homily and Verse*, London, Faith Press, 1960, p. 175.

31 Farrer, *Interpretation*, p. 61.

32 Ibid., p. 63.

33 Ibid.

34 Ibid., p. 64.

35 Farrer, *Glass*, p. 54.

36 Ibid., pp. 54–5.

37 Ibid., p. 55.

38 Farrer, *Interpretation*, p. 16.

39 Austin Farrer, *St Matthew and St Mark*, Westminster, Dacre Press, 1966 (2nd edn), pp. 153–4.

40 Farrer, *Interpretation*, p. 16.

41 Ibid., p. 106.

42 Ibid., p. 108.

43 Ibid., p. 111.

44 Houlden, *Essential Sermons*, p. 65.

45 Ibid.

46 Ibid., p. 66.

47 Ibid., p. 113.

48 Farrer, *Glass*, p. 54.

49 Farrer, *End*, p. 44.

50 Ibid., pp. 44–5.

51 Farrer, *Mystery*, p. 5.

52 Ibid., p. 26.

53 Farrer, *Said or Sung*, p. 75.

54 Austin Farrer, *Words for Life*, Charles C. Conti and James Leslie Houlden (eds), London, SPCK, 1993, p. 53.

55 Farrer, *Words*, p. 53.

56 Ibid., p. 54.

57 Ibid.

58 Austin Farrer, *Reflective Faith: Essays in Philosophical Theology*, Charles C. Conti (ed.), London, SPCK, 1972, p. 142.

59 Farrer, *Reflective Faith*, p. 144.

60 Ibid., p. 46.

61 Ibid., p. 147.

62 Ibid.

63 Houlden, *Essential Sermons*, pp. 65–6.

64 Farrer, *Mystery*, p. 22.

65 Ibid., pp. 22–3.

66 Ibid., p. 23.

67 Ibid., pp. 23–4.

68 Farrer, *Interpretation*, p. 95.

69 Ibid.

70 Ibid., p. 96.

71 Ibid., pp. 96–7.

72 Ibid., p. 97.

73 Ibid., p. 101.

74 Ibid.

75 Ibid., pp. 101–2.

76 Ibid., p. 103.

77 Ibid., p. 104.

78 Farrer, *Glass*, p. 45.

79 Ibid.

80 Ibid., pp. 45–6.

81 Ibid., p. 46.

82 Ibid., p. 47.

83 Ibid.

84 Houlden, *Essential Sermons*, p. 47.

85 Ibid., p. 48.

86 Ibid.

87 Ibid.

88 Farrer, *Interpretation*, p. 8.

89 Austin Farrer, *A Celebration of Faith*, London, Hodder and Stoughton, 1970, pp. 44–5.

90 Houlden, *Essential Sermons*, p. 12.

91 Austin Farrer, *The Crown of the Year: Weekly Paragraphs for the Holy Sacrament*, Westminster, Dacre Press, 1952, p. 29.

92 Farrer, *Interpretation*, pp. 30–1.

93 Farrer, *Saving Belief*, p. 155.

94 Austin Farrer, *Lord, I Believe: Suggestions for Turning the Creed into Prayer*, London, Faith Press, 1958, p. 28.

95 Farrer, *Lord, I Believe*, pp. 21–2.

96 Houlden, *Essential Sermons*, p. 1.

97 Farrer, *Words*, p. 18.

98 Farrer, *Mystery*, p. 37.

99 Ibid., p. 96.

100 Farrer, *Mystery*, pp. 134–6.

101 Ibid., p. 54.

102 Houlden, *Essential Sermons*, p. 57.

103 See Farrer, *Interpretation*, p. 4; *I Believe*, pp. 73–4; Houlden, *Essential Sermons*, pp.117–20.

104 Houlden, *Essential Sermons*, p. 155.

105 Farrer, *Mystery*, p. 27.

106 Houlden, *Essential Sermons*, p. 13.

107 Ibid.

108 Ibid.

109 Farrer, *Mystery*, p. 137.

Philosophy

4

Farrer's Relevance for Contemporary
Philosophical Theology

MARGARET YEE

Austin Farrer held firmly to the view that, without making unfounded theological presumptions, it was possible to present a critical and independent
philosophical pathway which could substantially underpin the very essence
of belief in God. As he wrote:

> Anyone who wishes to introduce the name of God into a philosophical
> treatise is confronted with the awkward choice between speculation
> and ecclesiasticism ... The dilemma is an awkward one. But we hope to
> avoid the worst faults on either side if we take up the traditional theology
> without having decided either what area of its extent is capable of direct
> philosophical support, or what degree of strength and demonstration
> that support can attain.[1]

The prime purpose of this chapter is to track the development of Farrer's
philosophical approach and its relevance for contemporary philosophical
theology. Through analysis of five of his most important philosophical
and theological writings, published over his lifetime, it will be seen that
vital principles for philosophical theology, and even more significantly for
twenty-first-century theology, were being developed and presented in his
metaphysical approach.

The main texts to be examined are his three earliest philosophical reflections on theology, namely *Finite and Infinite* (1943; second revised edition
in 1958), *The Glass of Vision* (1948) and *The Freedom of the Will* (1957),
and his last two published books, *A Science of God?* (1966, published in
US under the title *God is not Dead*) and *Faith and Speculation* (1967).

There are sound reasons for drawing attention to these five texts in particular. The most relevant kernels of Farrer's thought for contemporary
philosophical theology are articulated clearly in the first four of these texts.
In the fifth, he states explicitly that his philosophical enquiry has led him
ultimately to affirm a philosophy of action for traditional theology distinct
from the limited outlook of process theology prevalent at the time.[2]

The full import of Farrer's ingenuity and relevance for contemporary
philosophical theology will be best understood once key concepts in his

new metaphysics are properly identified and examined. In particular, two major advances in his philosophical argument as to how human minds apprehend knowledge of God both rationally and empirically, will be carefully analysed. These two phases of development, involving radical changes to his metaphysics, will help designate explicitly the steps taken by Farrer to arrive at his revisionary and dynamic philosophy of action for contemporary philosophical theology.

Where Farrer's methodological search began

The development of Farrer's methodological approach began in 1943 when he published his first major tome, *Finite and Infinite*. His initial philosophical endeavour was to investigate traditional theology, presented by Thomas Aquinas (1225–74) in *Summa Theologica*[3] and *Summa Contra Gentiles*.[4] Similar to Aquinas' medieval theological works, Farrer, in the twentieth century, sought to establish the credibility and substance of talk of God by pursuing a metaphysical approach comprehensible within his own time.

At heart, while Farrer's manner of approach was philosophical, his ultimate purpose was theological. Metaphysics was the methodology he sought to employ for demonstrating rationally that traditional theology was a discipline of high intellectual standing. For this reason, he has been deemed an early Anglo-Catholic neo-Thomist by John Macquarrie.[5]

In a manner similar to Aquinas, Farrer was not concerned with seeking a proof for the existence of God. More importantly, if talk of God could be shown to be philosophically logical and intelligible, the subject matter of theology would, without question, be accounted as a rational and serious area of study and enquiry, especially to philosophers. It would demonstrate that theology was about something, not nothing.[6]

Farrer stressed that in exploring and apprehending reality the mind thinks both *analytically* and *analogically*. When we think analytically, we proceed by using step-by-step reasoning and analysis. In this way we are able to make deductions and inductions. When we think analogically, the mind has the capacity to perceive things symbolically, connecting thoughts and concepts in a manner which can prove significant and illuminating. The form of reasoning used here is extrapolation, what Farrer called 'backward extrapolation'. Through critical analysis (*analytical thinking*) we perceive that we are finite and our minds also are finite. In this way we have the capacity to surmise that the finite is limited and bounded. However, when we reflect on the finite metaphorically or symbolically (*analogical thinking*) we are able to apprehend concepts of the infinite, and distinguish that the infinite is unlimited and boundless. These procedures are rational functions of the human mind; an integral aspect of its cognitive capacities.[7]

On the one hand there is exploration of the *particular* through analytical thinking applying critical and logical procedures, where the outcome is the identification of the finite. On the other, reflecting on the finite through analogical thinking, and exploring the *universal*, symbolic concepts of an apprehension of the infinite may be identified.[8] Working within this holistic frame of reference (universal and particular) and comparing perceived similarities and differences between concepts of the finite and those of the infinite, Farrer was able to distinguish the finite from the infinite and the infinite from the finite.

It is important to note that the prime focus and foundation of Farrer's metaphysics was the activity of human apprehension. 'Apprehension' is the key to rational thought, not least in philosophical theology. The mind's apprehension of the infinite proceeds rationally and sequentially by analogical reflection on the finite. As a consequence, the finite and the infinite (what may be described as the *mental objects* of cognitive thought)[9] are perceived reflectively via the capacity of the human imagination rationally. Each consideration is accounted for methodologically by philosophical reasoning. Each step is possible to check and cross check, namely 'theory with practice' and vice versa, systematically, preventing any mistaken mental connections, contradictions or conflicts.

Further, the thinking mind is that of a rational being, a human agent. By exercising the human mind, both universally and particularly, it is possible to apprehend the nature and form of being, substance, essence and existence philosophically. As one contemplates these aspects of reality, mental objects and the mind's response to its mental objects (reflective cognitive action and activities on its symbolic subject matter) are delineated rationally.[10]

Although the infinite is unlimited and unbounded, our understanding of the infinite is not vague and undefined. It is true that we cannot define the limits and boundaries of the infinite, since these are unlimited and unbounded. We can, nevertheless, specify the characteristics of the infinite by saying what it is not. Aquinas had referred to this aspect of theology as the *via negativa*.[11] Farrer, similarly, acknowledged that though we cannot say what the nature of God is absolutely, we know what it is not. The infinite is not finite, nor the finite infinite.

Within this broad, holistic, metaphysical framework of thought, involving the finite and infinite, Farrer argued that talk of the possibility of God's existence and the relation of creator and creation could in fact be pursued philosophically and rationally. Finite and infinite being and agency are apprehended through cognitive capacities of the human mind. Procedurally, it can be shown how the human agent comes to understand the self and the world rationally in this way.[12]

Throughout his life Farrer was never to divert from rationality as fundamental in acquiring knowledge of God. Nor did he depart from his holistic framework of thought in which he delineated reality in terms of the finite and the infinite, the particular and the universal. These most thoughtful and comprehensive analyses of human apprehension of God, presented determinedly in his first edition of *Finite and Infinite* in 1943, remained paramount and unchanged throughout his life. Apprehension is a rational activity of the human mind, involving multiple functions, exercised by the human agent in order to acquire knowledge of God.

At the close of his meticulous and carefully presented metaphysics, however, which could *rationally* underpin claims for the existence of God, Farrer acknowledged that he had not provided philosophical grounding for deeper theological concepts such as grace and providence. At the time, he simply noted that this was merely a matter still to be addressed rather than any lack or possible oversight in his metaphysics.[13] However, this was all to change radically.

Over the next 14-year period of Farrer's life (1943–57) it is possible, from documentary sources, to pinpoint the first of two major developments in his thought. Similarly, and also from documentary sources, a second major development occurred, though this was much later, in 1966.

As we examine these two changes in greater detail, it will be seen that the changes made were not only *rational* (involving logical, non-contradictory, critical thought, as is required of the humanities) but also *empirical* (involving findings from observation, experimentation, measurement and testing as fulfilled in the sciences).[14]

Quite amazingly, the full import of these *two phases* of development were presented chapter by chapter in his last book, *Faith and Speculation* (1967). As a consequence, the text presents in summary form, his final, overall defence for his 'new metaphysics' for philosophical theology, empirically grounded in a new revisionary and dynamic philosophy of action.

The following analysis of Farrer's first and second phases of change will set out explicitly not only a revolutionary and enlivening transformation of both his philosophical and theological thought, but also, in retrospect, his ingenious designation of the first principles for all knowing.

Farrer's new metaphysics: First phase

The first phase of Farrer's extraordinary changes of momentous effect to his metaphysics are fully documented in *The Glass of Vision* (1948) and *The Freedom of the Will* (1957), comprising his understanding of (i) the human imagination and (ii) human consciousness.

The human imagination and images

Farrer's *The Glass of Vision* has rarely been given much attention, let alone prominence, by philosophers of religion compared with the attention expended on his more specifically philosophical books *The Freedom of the Will* (1957) and *Faith and Speculation* (1976). This is not surprising. A quick glance at the contents of *The Glass of Vision* suggests that the text is concerned with addressing questions asked more by biblical theologians than philosophers of religion. However, the contrary is actually the case. Closer reading of the material and the issues raised by Farrer demonstrate that, even though the discussion would appear to be focussed primarily upon Christian doctrine and biblical revelation, underlying Farrer's whole presentation is a corresponding exposition of the rational role of the human imagination and images in the acquisition of knowledge of God.

In Chapter 1 of *The Glass of Vision*, statements such as the following, made at the start of his Bampton Lectures, stipulate that Christian theology needs to be rationally grounded rather than based on experiential or existential foundations:

... this is why, when Germans set their eyeballs and pronounce the terrific words 'He speaks to thee' (Er redet dich an) I am sure, indeed, that they are saying something, but I am still more sure that they are not speaking to my condition.[15]

Later, Farrer emphasized his rational stance even more strongly by describing apprehensions of God as 'movements of thought'.[16] These, he argued, were attributable to cognitive, rational functions of the human mind. In particular, these apprehensions of God could be distinguished from psychical understandings of life and the world which belonged to the bottom of the soul. By contrast, he held that spiritual understandings of God's activity in the life of Jesus belonged to activity at the top of the mind, typical symbolically of what one would expect to find at the peak of a cone.[17]

As early as 1948, in *The Glass of Vision*, the ingenuity of Farrer's philosophical thought was emerging in his insistence that knowledge of God is acquired rationally through the activity of the human imagination and its images. Chapter headings such as 'Images and Inspiration' and 'Archetypes and Incarnation', at face value, appealed primarily to those concerned with the interpretation of Christian doctrine and biblical revelation. Needless to say, engagement with the text itself inevitably involves one instead with Farrer's carefully expounded thought on the particular role and function of the human imagination and images in the search to know, especially in theological enquiry. His delineation of such activity, discussed in fuller detail in his chapters on 'The Metaphysician's Image' and 'The Rational Theologian's Analogy', unquestionably holds the significance of Farrer's overall intention. His stance was that rational thought in metaphysics in contemporary times was entirely amenable for underpinning traditional theology rationally as well. Toward the close of the book, in his chapter 'Prophecy and Poetry', he drew together the main threads of his illuminatingly presented approach. The cognitive capacity of the human imagination and images enables us to apprehend diverse spheres of understanding, and express our understanding through symbolic language, whether these apprehensions are philosophical, historical, theological or creatively poetical.[18]

It was the very dynamic of these forms of interactive function and exchange of distinctively theological concepts that he referred to as 'revealed images'.[19] A study of the lively interaction and interrelation of images could be critically tracked in unfolding events and action. As the images took on greater advancement in form and function so did the enrichment of their signification. The vibrancy of the images, relating to one another as is possible in the human imagination, ultimately gave rise to what Farrer called the 'dominant' and 'great images'[20] of Christian doctrine and revelation as thought and action were lived out in historical events. These actively perceived thoughts of human actions and behaviour, forming major concepts in the human mind, were conveyed through symbolic language, lived and thought in community. At this stage the very actions of 'lived belief' were being unpacked, step by step.

Emphasis on the function of language as symbolic, rather than merely pictorial and rigid in form, enabled him to show the means by which words in language and linguistics (and by implication numbers in the sciences, though not stated explicitly by Farrer) were capable of signifying the depths of the dynamic interrelation of divine/human activity and action in reality. The engagement of the finite with the infinite and the infinite with the finite were integral to the activity. In this way human understanding of the lived life of Jesus and incarnation, involving the interrelation of the finite and the infinite, the divine and the human, could be accounted for rationally.[21] The 'crisis of images' in which the paradoxical nexus of the finite and the infinite, the divine and the human were symbolically exemplified, reached the apex of rational expression in the life of Jesus. Here was the very essence of scriptural revelation, marks of the *immanent* and the *transcendent* in full union, lived out actively in history.

These dynamic revelatory images formed the building blocks of theology, which are basic to highly developed teachings of Christian doctrine. Time and again, in his discussion particularly of grace and providence, this foundational understanding remained undiminished in Farrer's thought as knowledge of God, apprehended rationally by the human mind.

Concurrent also with his analysis of the role and function of the human imagination and images was Farrer's recognition of the overlap of theological thought with the thought of other disciplines. Thus, in *The Glass of Vision* he acknowledged the need to adopt a multi-disciplinary approach to theology. For instance, symbolic images of the events, life, teaching and action of Jesus and the early church, signifying particular spiritual and theological significance, overlapped contextually with historical, physical, psychological and communal factors.[22]

Fully aware of the enormous breadth of perceived functions of the human mind articulated within the context of a multi-disciplinary view of the world, in the next decade Farrer's interests turned to pursuing a formal investigation of the complex relations in human consciousness itself. His determination to wrestle with these issues metaphysically, with due consideration of the human will and freedom, resulted in his major philosophical work *The Freedom of the Will* (1957).

Human consciousness and voluntarism

In coming to terms with the breadth of issues involved in human consciousness Farrer was concerned to begin with a broad canvas.[23] Methodologically, he considered that a holistic viewpoint would prevent discussion being hampered by overly restrictive contexts. Broad brushstrokes could set things in process, in which major questions relating to body and mind, the seat of consciousness, or issues such as motive, choice and freedom could be properly examined.

Most basic to his concerns was whether freewill and determinism were in any way reconcilable. Could it be said that there is choice and freedom in human living and, if so, could a rational defence of such conditions be established?

Far from accepting robotic concepts of consciousness, bordering on the mechanistic, Farrer decided to adopt a method of debate by which questions relevant to human agency could be properly explored step by step. Could it be argued rationally that human agency, while natural and physiological, was possessed also of mental capacities in which motivation, choice, responsibility and freedom were intrinsic characteristics? Could the co-ordination of nature and the lively activity of motive and choice, grounded in the human self, be attributed to human will, responsibility and freedom?[24]

Despite having already demonstrated a lively, non-reductionist, theological and rational view of mental activity in the human imagination in *The Glass of Vision*, in *The Freedom of the Will* Farrer insisted upon providing a purely philosophical and rational argument for human consciousness overall. Similar to his attempt to delineate a sound metaphysics in *Finite and Infinite*, in *The Freedom of the Will* he sought to wrestle with in-depth concerns related to freedom and necessity, by which metaphysics itself could be further justified as an acceptable branch of philosophy. In addition, he was now well aware that a more fully developed metaphysics than the one expounded in *Finite and Infinite* was required to underpin the theological concepts of grace and providence.

In 1957, therefore, in *The Freedom of the Will*, Farrer began with discussion on the relation of body and mind. Physiological and psychological functions, he argued, were not concurrent activities.[25] However, since perceptions of bodily action formed a unity of 'thoughtful bodily action',[26] physiological and psychological functions were clearly interrelated, even though the precise nature of the relation could not be fully stipulated.

Tests for human consciousness might well be undertaken psychologically, assessing thinking and reported sensory experiences of human agents. However, as Farrer pointed out, the function of the imagination, reflection and thought, needed accounting for more fully, since they could not be strictly classed as physical activities of the brain.[27] The activities were in fact mental capacities of the human brain involved with mental objects. What needed to be recognized was that mechanistic viewpoints of consciousness arose from neurological measurements in brain research. However, such mechanistic accounts failed to address distinct characteristics of human consciousness wholly.[28]

At the physiological level there were electrical, neurological, chemical and biochemical activities, sensory and reflective responses. A complexity of conditions enabled the unity of the functions of brain and mind in human consciousness. In the light of intricate and interrelated mental functions, including memory, recall, intention and choice, Farrer argued that mechanistic or hard deterministic accounts of human consciousness were, as a consequence, overruled. There are free actions of the human will which cannot be refuted, though not all actions are necessarily intentional, motivated or directly chosen. In human consciousness there are both voluntary and involuntary actions.

It is important to note that earlier in *The Glass of Vision* Farrer had probed an understanding of involuntary actions, which did not involve the human will. For instance, avoiding an accident, a car driver, without conscious thought, could swerve the car to safety. 'Once bitten, twice shy,' such involuntary action could later become conscious and voluntary, involving the human agent's choice to avoid driving on narrow roads in the future. It is this capability in human consciousness involving voluntary action which enabled the human agent the freedom to make rational decisions theologically in apprehending knowledge of God. The lively activity of the human imagination encapsulates what is revealed in history and event, not least through Jesus' action.

Integral to human consciousness is the function of the human will, *voluntarism*, expressed pragmatically in *volition*. Chapters in *The Freedom of the Will* are given to discussion of the lively, human activity of will, volition and invention. Farrer argued that acts of human volition needed to be seen for what they were in themselves, none other than human actions. However, he was only too well aware that human volition, a human action, could, with its freedom to choose, act contrary to divine will. Farrer therefore pointed out the need to distinguish between actions of the creator and that of the created. Without grace and providence through saving belief the alignment of human volition, the will of created human beings, with divine will, would not be possible.[29]

Farrer admitted that at this stage, even as a Gifford Lecturer addressing implicit notions of human volition such as motivation, intention, valuation and invention, he could only alert readers to the possibility of divine mystery. Deeper investigations of voluntarism in order to bridge the relation of human volition and divine will, demonstrative of grace and providence, would require his writing another robust book. Such theological concerns, therefore, had to be presently left as 'unfinished business'. Later, in 1964, he dealt with this theological issue of grace and providence and the relation of *human volition* and divine will in his *Saving Belief*.[30]

What Farrer held had been established by him philosophically, however, and could not be denied, was the voluntary capacity of the human agent to exercise volition and choice, decide or determine. In *The Glass of Vision* he had already demonstrated an explicit, rational account of knowledge of God of divine revelation through the life of Jesus, his actions, suffering, death, resurrection and ascension. Now in *The Freedom of the Will* he had been able to show that the lively activity of these great and dominant images of the human imagination, signifying the life and action of Jesus, could be suitably grounded philosophically through voluntarism.

Typical of Farrer's approach, dealing with first things first, in 1958, a year after establishing his philosophical grounding for a multiplicity of cognitive actions and activities in *The Freedom of the Will*, he corrected the error in his earlier metaphysics expounded in *Finite and Infinite* (1943). His defence of voluntarism, which supported the multiplicity of rational activities of human apprehension, could now replace the static, formalism of Aristotelian thought.[31] By correcting the error in his metaphysics in *Finite and Infinite* (1943) he provided a new multiple and active metaphysic, capable of grounding deep theological concepts such as grace and providence rationally.

Rather than rewrite *Finite and Infinite*, he thought it sufficient to acknowledge his metaphysical error in his new preface to its republication in 1958 and refer readers directly to chapters 7, 9 and 11 of *The Freedom of the Will* where the freedom of action of the human will, voluntary and involuntary, were fully discussed.[32]

This irreversible change, the first phase of his understanding of the multiple and dynamic activity of human apprehension, involving the human imagination and human consciousness, was ultimately to form the core of his legacy to Anglican theology. However, prior to this fulfilment, there was a further development still to come in Farrer's thought. This last change (his second phase of development) virtually served as his 'seal of completion' on a new metaphysics for philosophical theology.

Farrer's new metaphysics: Second phase

In 1966 Farrer published *A Science of God?* naming the first chapter 'Theology and Science.' Being a Lent Book, the text was gauged as suitable more for ecclesiastical purposes rather than being of philosophical importance. Contrary to all expectation, however, Farrer decided to introduce the second phase of development of his new metaphysics in this Lenten text, stating his intention as follows:

> I do not propose to report the views of enthusiastic theologians with foreign names; for that sort of thing, though no doubt stimulating, is of little use for the settling of our convictions. I propose to approach the being of God, and to approach it calmly, treating it as a matter of knowledge.[33]

Religious convictions and religious experience required rational grounding. One of Farrer's prime concerns in establishing rational knowledge of God was the necessity of distinguishing between psychical beliefs and scriptural inspiration. This requirement lay at the very heart of his second phase of development. The action necessary for achieving such distinctions, Farrer argued, was scientific and practical: 'We must approach the question in a scientific spirit, and examine all available evidence for, but equally the evidence against.'[34] For instance, criteria of judgement which could distinguish psychical or psychopathological mental images from psychologically healthy religious images were required for trustworthy assessment. This second phase of change was formidable. Theological claims, as in any other discipline, needed not only to be justified rationally, but the level of credibility needed also to be demonstrated empirically.

By insisting on these two requirements, the rational and the empirical, as methodologically inseparable in serious enquiry, Farrer considered that he had 'rounded off' and completed his method of approach. This change not only ensured that theology met metaphysical concerns (as required in philosophy), but also fulfilled scientific epistemological demands (as required in the physical and life sciences).

Extraordinarily, Farrer had now come to realize fully that what he had presented in *The Glass of Vision* as rational knowledge of God could also be submitted to empirical testing by applying a scientific approach. The viability of theological claims epistemologically (that is, as justifiable knowledge of God) needed also to be established as empirically credible via cross checking with relevant cross-disciplinary contextual evidences both for and against such claims. His approach was innovative. He adopted a pragmatic method, effective for testing the theological rational claims empirically and vice versa. For example, apprehensions of Jesus' life and actions as both human and divine had been signified as rational through the logical, symbolic and voluntary functions of the human imagination and human consciousness. Such rational knowledge of divine/human revelation could then be tested empirically through investigating evidences for and against. Historical, contextual, psychological criteria of judgement could show a level of credibility attributable to interpretations of scriptural revelation concerning Jesus. Rational (logical, non-contradictory) issues required cross checking with empirical (practical, evidential) aspects repeatedly. The epistemological viability of such theological claims (in other words the 'evidential force' of such claims) could be tested on both frontiers, back and forth, iteratively (similar to 'testing both sides of a coin', leaving no stone unturned).

These requirements, clearly stipulated in 1966 as his second phase of development, enabled Farrer to provide full philosophical grounding of the relation of human volition and divine will. Scriptural inspiration through the dominant and great images from the life and actions of Jesus provided the source of such knowledge. Where the Gospel narrative affirmed the words of Jesus: 'not my will but thine be done'[35] we find the efficacious union of divine/human action fulfilled. The salvific function of Jesus is not only signified in his life and action, but was apprehended by the human mind rationally and empirically. What human *volition* of created being, given its freedom, failed to fulfil, Jesus' life and action achieved, uniting divine and human will. The inexplicable offer of unconditional grace and providence was a redemptive act for all creation (as discussed in *Saving Belief*, 1964) which earlier, in *Freedom of the Will*, Farrer had attributed to Divine Mystery. Through such action, human beings were enabled by divine action to adopt life-in-grace through faith, uniting human volition of created being with divine will.

By applying a scientific spirit, it was possible to ascertain the epistemological credibility of apprehensions of knowledge of God in a world in which voluntarism and volition operated freely. Through his second phase of development in which empirical procedures were now also required, Farrer sought systematically to unravel the age-long epistemological conflicts since the rise of modern science (Copernicus, Galileo and Newton) between theology and the sciences, step by step.[36]

Theology, a discipline concerned with knowledge of God, had its own subject matter, requiring an appropriate method of approach. Its subject matter was very different from the subject matter of the sciences, such as physics, chemistry or astronomy. Thus, writing on 'God and the Stars' in Chapter 2 of *A Science of God*, Farrer made clear that studies in scientific areas such as astronomy would not bring us to knowledge of God. Studies of science are science. Theology is theology. A very different method of approach was required for theological enquiry; one that was critical, rational and practical rather than technological and experimental approaches of science. Methods of approach needed to be appropriate to the subject matter under investigation.[37]

Despite such differences between theology and the sciences, however, the first principles of critical enquiry in any search to know, whether in theology in its exploration of reality or in science where the concern was with the physical world, needed to be applied. The combination of rational and empirical demands were inescapable canons to be met for legitimate enquiry, whatever the study. It is possible also to surmise that his realization earlier of the multi-disciplinary approach in academic enquiry had begun to bear fruit also, as he continued his discussion, maintaining how the findings in scientific thought, as in other disciplines in the humanities, contributed to theological reflection:

> If the religious approach is concerned with the whole picture, it is concerned with everything that can contribute either detail or order to the picture. The map of the countryside is not the countryside, but if you are trying to get the countryside into your head, the map will help you.[38]

If theologians were unprepared to consider the findings of scientific explorations in the physical or life sciences when reflecting on the universe, and their possible relation to theological and practical aspects of the world, knowledge of God's relation to creation would be very limited. Knowledge acquired in all relevant areas of enquiry, whether in the humanities or the sciences, could not be ignored, since theology was concerned with the whole picture of reality.

This distinction between the subject matters of theology and the sciences and their relevant methodologies having been made explicit, Farrer moved onto his next central task which was to deal directly with the seriously prevailing issues at that time arising from conflicts over the theory of evolution and the doctrine of creation. The requirement of applying the scientific spirit in theological enquiry was dealt with substantially in Chapters 3 and 4 and even more significantly in Chapter 5 'The Nature of God'. Theologians must take into account dilemmas arising from scientific claims to evolutionary theory as also the ethical and moral claims concerning theodicy and human suffering.

In the light of Darwin's evolutionary theory, he enticed his readers in an intriguing manner to consider issues arising from both scientific and theological perspectives. The task was to assess the acceptability and logic of alternative explanations. The following discussion of poignant statements of Farrer's indicates his rational and empirical (what is currently described as 'empirico-cognitive'[39]) methodological stance for theology:

> That the forms of life must have come in gradually is a conclusion one can scarcely resist. The only alternative to an evolutionary account would be the supposition that new species were pushed in ready made when the time was ripe for them.[40]

The incredulity of such an alternative in attempting to bypass the outcome of empirical, scientific enquiry was clearly senseless. By employing the rational and empirical ('empirico-cognitive') capacity of the human mind, a deeper and more credible theological understanding would be acquired. Thus he argued: 'To sum up: the evolution of biological species is part of a total picture of the natural world, and it is not worth kicking at it unless we can have back the whole pre-nineteenth-century world-view.'[41]

Given the impact on enunciations of the creation of life, following an overall acceptance of scientific advances such as evolutionary theory, a further primary theological question arising was that of the God of Nature. In which ways is belief in God, exercised in the practice of religion, to be reconciled to such advances in scientific learning? Determined to deal without default when confronted with such dilemmas, Farrer expended inordinate care in probing deeply the issue of 'causality'. In his Lenten book, in seeking to assist believers to recognize the need to apply *empirical* procedures in order to access the full depths of knowledge of God as Creator, he argued: 'If we think about the God of salvation only, and take the Cause of nature for granted, we shall be forever misunderstanding the natural workings of God.'[42] Instead, he sought to encourage his readers to think about the world in its *universal* perspective, its marvellous wonder, grandeur and beauty, while taking into account also its *particular* factors, gained from careful study of the very intricacies of nature, its complex activities, the energy, liveliness, interaction of forces, multiple and multi-levelled, yet diverse in form and function.

The finite and immense activities of nature are infinite in number, whether of plants, species or physical elements, each functioning according to their own nature yet also integral to one overall reality. The findings of scientific enquiry will provide detailed knowledge and information of the world and of nature, but profound questions relating to causality still required explanation. In applying both rational and empirical canons to theological enquiry, knowledge of God as Creator of a highly complex, intricate and active world, finite and infinite, could be grounded epistemologically. This would be assured, as first principles, required of all disciplines, would have been properly met. Thus he argued: 'The way to study God's mind in nature is to let things show us how they go.'[43]

In his discussion of the God of Nature, we find him drawing together his initial open, unlimited, holistic framework of *Finite and Infinite* in which infinite aspects of the finite are apprehended through the power of the human imagination through the lively activities of voluntarism. The apprehended images of revelation may be critically assessed applying the stringent cross-checks of both rational and empirical procedures, one or the other, by which the lively interaction of the finite and the infinite at the highest of all levels in the life and actions of Christ crucified are understood and grounded. Similarly, wider implications in human volition and operative in our world may also be tracked. Through such an approach, conflicts between God and Nature, and theology and science, would be better understood as not 'God or Nature' but rather as 'the God of Nature' in which *anima mundi*, the lively nexus of the finite and infinite, continues in active holistic relation. On these grounds he ends the chapter on the God of Nature with these words:

... it is because God makes the world make itself; or rather, since the world is a single being, he makes the multitude of created forces make the world, in the process of making or being themselves. It is this principle of divine action that gives the world such endless vitality, such vital variety in every part. The price of it is, that the agents God employs in the basic levels of structure will do what they will do, whether human convenience is served by it or not. Yet the creative persuasion has brought it about that there is a world, not a chaos, and that in this world there are men.[44]

In this second phase of development, Farrer's methodological approach had been shifted philosophically from metaphysics to epistemology. Theology was to be thought and lived out in practice. A rational and empirical route in which the lively action and activity of the finite and the infinite, the divine and the human, creator and creation were involved had shown that theology was certainly about something, not nothing!

Farrer's Relevance for Contemporary Philosophical Theology: A Revisionary and Dynamic Philosophy of Action

As we come to Farrer's last publication, *Faith and Speculation* (1967), we find the harnessing of all the kernels of thought, which had fulfilled such significance in the development of his philosophical thought, under a single concept, 'the conceivability of a divine action in the world'.[45] The whole outcome constituted his epistemological method for a grounded traditional theology. This text, which included his Deems Lectures on 'Grace and Freewill', 'Nature and Creation' and 'Revelation and History', was directly focussed on the lively action and activity of the relation of the divine and the human, considered from both universal and particular perspectives.

Beginning with the thinking human agent in his first chapter on 'The Believer's Reasons', Farrer indicated, with wit and humour, the philosophically invalid religious responses often offered. From this stance he quickly moved his reader onto a discussion of his second chapter on the importance of meeting 'The Empirical Demand' in any search to know. The marks of his new metaphysics were effectively applied throughout his discussions. These first principles for acquiring knowledge of God, operative contextually within the vital action and activity of the voluntarism of mind and imagination, mapped a route forward for his philosophy of action. His revisionary and dynamic philosophy of action had avoided the hazardous pitfalls of the empiricism of David Hume and ridded itself of the dross of Aristotelian formalism on the one hand, while ensuring not to succumb to inadequately founded Christian apologetics of neo-orthodoxy or liberal theology on the other.[46] In the end of the day, the very relation of finite and infinite, divine and human, affirmed by human apprehension or 'movements of thoughts' (i.e. rational and evidential functions of the human imagination and human consciousness) was designated. They are shown as rationally operative in the lively, vital, lived out nature and communication of being with being, the limited with the unlimited, forged by the human mind, and conveyable to others.

Farrer's phrase 'multiplicity in the world'[47] described well the complexity of interactive functions involved in the universe, similar to the multiple activity of the human mind he had raised much earlier. Such unity of action and activity of human apprehension was best encapsulated within an expanding revisionary and dynamic view of reality. Critical questioning and pragmatic testing of all thought, religious or otherwise, was essential. We cannot begin with a *tabula rasa*. Even our assumptions require investigating, as in empirical enquiry.

The endpoint of Farrer's explorative search was a philosophy of action, capable of underpinning the breadth and depth of the lively relation of the finite and the infinite, the divine and the human, the transcendent and the immanent, all perceived as intrinsic to traditional theology. His new metaphysics with its empirical grounding had placed theology in its rightful place, an authentic discipline, critical and open to academic investigation, as any other serious area of enquiry.[48]

In an increasingly secular world, in which an ever-widening gap between the sciences and humanities has continued unabated, at times even challenging theology's standing as an academic discipline, the want of an even more explicit delineation of first principles for all academic enquiry has been long awaited. Farrer's epistemological stance, incorporating clear systematic principles of theory and practice for theological enquiry, would seem to be a methodological approach which has answered that very search.[49]

Notes

1 Farrer, *Finite and Infinite*, Westminster, Dacre Press, 1943, p. v.

2 Farrer, *Faith and Speculation*, London, Adam & Charles Black, 1976, p. 170.

3 London, Eyre & Spottiswoode, 1964.

4 Brian Davies, *Thomas Aquinas's Summa Contra Gentiles – A Guide and Commentary*, New York, Oxford University Press, 2016.

5 John Macquarrie, *Twentieth Century Religious Thought* (revised edn), London, SCM Press, 1981, pp. 283–90.

6 *Finite and Infinite*, 1943 and 1958, p. 1.

7 Even at this early stage Farrer's thought on the functions of the human mind foreshadowed later research in cognitive psychology by major thinkers such as Philip Johnson-Laird, *Mental Models: Towards a Cognitive Science of Language, Inference, and Consciousness*, Cambridge University Press, 1983.

8 *Finite and Infinite*, pp.19–25.

9 Ibid., pp. x–xi and ch. 9. See also Philip Johnson-Laird, *How we Reason*, Oxford, Oxford University Press, 2006, pp. 230, 428.

10 Ibid., chs 5–9, 15–16.

11 Ibid., p.43. Traditional theology does not consider that *via negativa* excludes *via positiva.*

12 Ibid., chs 20–1.

13 *Finite and Infinite*, p. 300.

14 *Finite and Infinite* 2nd edn., 1958, p. ix. Also *Faith and Speculation*, p. v. in which he expressed his wish to affirm clearly to all the irreversible change to voluntarism that he had made in his metaphysics.

15 Farrer, *The Glass of Vision*, Westminster, Dacre Press, 1948, p. 8.

16 *Faith and Speculation*, p. 122.

17 *The Glass of Vision*, p. 22.

18 Ibid., chs 4–7.

19 Ibid., pp. 76, 90, 93–5.

20 Ibid., pp. 42–4, 47–51, 136.

21 Ibid., pp. 36–44, 90–2.

22 Ibid., p. 78.

23 Farrer, *The Freedom of the Will*, London, Adam & Charles Black, 1957, p. vii.

24 Ibid., pp. 1–2.

25 Ibid., pp. 6–7.

26 Ibid., pp. 6–13, 316.

27 Ibid., chs 1–2.

28 Ibid., pp. 98–100.

29 Ibid., ch. 14 'Valuation and Invention' and ch. 15 'Liberty and Theology'.

30 Austin Farrer, *Saving Belief: A Discussion of Essentials*, London, Hodder & Stoughton, 1964.

31 Charles C. Conti, *Metaphysical Personalism*, Oxford, Clarendon Press, 1995, provides an important analysis of Austin Farrer's theistic metaphysics. Consider also Anthony Kenny on brain and mind in *What I Believe*, London, Continuum, 2016, ch. 6. See also *The Glass of Vision*, pp. 87–9, for Farrer's thought on involuntary and voluntary thinking.

32 *Finite and Infinite* (2nd edn, 1958), pp. ix–x.

33 Farrer, *A Science of God?*, London, 1966, p. 9.

34 Ibid., p. 10.

35 Luke 22.42b, New Revised Standard Version.

36 Ibid., pp. 12–13, 23–5.

37 Ibid., pp. 25, 26–38.

38 Ibid., p. 23. See also Charles Pasternak (ed.), *What Makes Us Human?*, Oxford, Oneworld, 2007.

39 Margaret Yee, 'Austin Farrer's Science of God' in *Philosophie, Théologie, Littérature: Hommage* à Xavier Tilliette, SJ, Louvain, Paris, Miklos Veto, 2011; and Yee, 'Theological Studies' in Rom Harré & Fathali M. Moghaddam (eds) *Questioning Causality*, Praeger, 2016, ch. 21, for a full discussion of Farrer's thought on science and theology, to which the terminology 'empirico-cognitive' (Yee's neologism) has been applied.

40 *A Science of God?*, p. 42.

41 Ibid., p. 43.

42 Ibid., p. 71.

43 Ibid., p. 87.

44 Ibid., pp. 90–1.

45 *Faith and Speculation*, p. v.

46 '… a theologian attempting to steer between the Scylla of irrationalism and the Charybdis of apriorism' – a most fitting description of Farrer's thought on revelation by Ninian Smart, 'Revelation and Reasons' in *Scottish Journal of Theology*, 11/4, Dec. 1958, p. 352. See also *Faith and Speculation*, pp. 70ff.

47 *Faith and Speculation*, ch. 10; p. 175.

48 For instance, Janet Soskice, *Metaphor and Religious Language*, Oxford, Clarendon Press, 1985; Caroline Franks Davis, *The Evidential Force of Religious Experience*, Oxford,

Clarendon Press, 1989; and Olivera Petrovich, *Natural-Theological Understanding from Childhood to Adulthood*, London, Routledge, 2019; all of whom were either doctoral students of or advised by Prof. Basil Mitchell, himself a close friend and member of The Metaphysicals with Austin Farrer.

49 Harré, Rom & Fathali Moghaddam (eds), *Questioning Causality*, Santa Barbara, CA, Praeger, 2016, Editors' Commentary, p. 381: 'This would tend to make a rapprochement between the divine and the human more acceptable, by the criticisms of the purely empirical analysis provided by David Hume.'

5

Providence and the Problem of Evil in Farrer's *Love Almighty and Ills Unlimited*

LEIGH VICENS

In his short book *Love Almighty and Ills Unlimited* (1962; hereafter *LAIU*), Austin Farrer sets himself the large task of tackling the 'theoretical' or philosophical problem of evil,[1] i.e. the problem of making sense of why an omnipotent and wholly good God would allow evil in the world. Farrer takes evil to call into question not God's *existence* (in fact, he thinks the 'mixture of good and evil' in our world gives us positive reason to believe in God)[2] – but rather God's *providence*,[3] the idea that God is in control of events and processes in the natural world and human history, guiding them according to divine purposes. Farrer's response to the problem of evil is sometimes commonsensical, sometimes radical, sometimes simply suggestive and open to interpretation. In the course of summarizing what I take to be some central points in Farrer's thinking about evil and providence, I will offer some interpretations at variance with other commentators, note some similarities between his ideas and those of contemporary philosophers, and suggest some developments of his reasoning not explicit in *LAIU*, which seem to me independently plausible.

After laying out his starting assumptions and approach to the problem in chapters 1 and 2, Farrer begins, in chapters 3 and 4, to 'break [the problem] up into parts' – for, 'since we cannot take all particular evils one by one, we want a rational principle, to divide them into kinds'.[4] Responses to the problem of evil often take such a 'divide and conquer' strategy, usually considering two categories of evil: moral and natural.[5] The former are evils for which (created) people are responsible, whereas the latter are *not* brought about by responsible agents. Thus one might expect Farrer to begin by reasoning about the cause of one or another of these categories of evil. Instead, he considers 'the thousand million years when there was a universe, and nothing lived' and asks how we should think about destructive events like the death of a star.[6] This seems an odd entry point to the problem of evil, since no one worries about the prehistoric death of a star; unlike natural evils such as hurricanes or cancer, destructive events which occurred long before anyone lived do not have a negative effect on anybody, and so are not usually considered evils at all.

However, Farrer begins where he does for a reason: his consideration of the problem of evil follows the direction of God's own creative process. Farrer writes, in a later chapter: 'I think that God's creation begins from below with a chaos of non-rational forces ... and I view the degree of order and the complication of structure which Providence has drawn from these beginnings as a miracle of patient overruling.'[7] Thus, if we are to understand Farrer's reasoning about evil at a higher level of organization than in a 'cohesive mass of molten rocks'[8] – such as in the pain suffered by an animal, or the malicious action of a human being – we would be wise to start with him, 'from below'.

So then, let us ask: is the death of a star, in a universe with no sentient life, a *bad* thing? Farrer suggests we might be tempted to think so, given how it seems to us that 'nothing worthwhile can exist ... without a high degree of stable organization, whether it is the organization of stellar systems ... or the atomic structure of physical substances, not to speak of the great elaboration of cellular arrangement which is necessary for plant or animal life'.[9] On such grounds, it is natural to 'identify the will of the Creator with the development or preservation of system or structure' and so to take the explosion of such a structure as a setback for the Cosmic Designer.[10] But physical destruction cannot be eliminated from the universe, given the nature of the physical world – 'an interaction of systems innumerable'.[11] Farrer's understanding of the nature of the physical world was informed by the science of his – and our – time. He writes: 'The first and most elementary energies of the world, by their mutual action upon each other, constitute a diversified field of force which is both the space and matter of the universe. But for them, the higher systems with which alone we are directly acquainted would have nowhere to be, and nothing of which to consist.'[12]

Farrer understands the fundamental 'energies', as well as the more complex systems they constitute, to 'act of themselves, and from the principle of their own being; which is, to build and perfect and maintain their own organization, seizing on the matter which suits them, and resisting interferences'. From this, he reasons that 'strife' between these systems is unavoidable,[13] and so concludes:

> If God was pleased to create a physical universe, he was sure to set going an infinity of forces and a plurality of systems ... acting upon one another in accordance with the limited principle incorporated in each. Such a universe must inflict much accidental damage on the systems it contains; a damage which is the essential form of natural evil.[14]

Thus, the nature of the physical universe has implications not only for explosions of stars, but for events we generally take to be natural evils. For where one physical system waxes, another wanes: bacteria grow in number and strength, making a creature weak and ill; a tornado gains power and speed, wreaking havoc on the structures and living things that stand in its way – and so on.

In chapter 5, on animal pain, Farrer writes: 'It is superfluous to repeat for living creatures in particular what we have explained with reference to physical systems in general. For animals, whatever else they may be, are physical systems, and suffer as such the reign of accident.'[15] Rather than repeat the superfluous, he considers whether, subject to natural destruction, animals would be better off without the experience of pain. In response, Farrer notes that the evolutionary function of pain is to help animals protect themselves from harm, and so is essential to animal survival.[16] Thus the suffering of animals is justified given the nature of the physical world and the purpose of pain.

Having dealt with animal suffering, Farrer moves on, in chapters 6 and 7, to discuss human sin, beginning with its origins. He considers and rejects the hypothesis that Satan tempted humanity to commit moral evil, for this hypothesis merely pushes the question back, from why *human beings* first sinned to why some *angelic creature* did. While Farrer finds the Satan story non-explanatory, he has no better alternative to offer in its place. The origin of sin, he says, is a total mystery – 'the one irreducible surd in the arithmetic of existence'.[17] Yet he finds it unmysterious how, once occurring, sin could propagate, to become such a pervasive, inescapable feature of human existence. Here Farrer proposes a modified version of the doctrine of original sin; and just as he gleans insights from contemporary physics and evolutionary biology to explain the necessity of natural evil in a physical world, so he demonstrates an appreciation of modern developmental psychology in his account of human nature and the heritability of sin:

> Our humanity itself is a cultural heritage; the talking animal is talked into talk by those who talk at him; and how if they talk crooked? His mind is not at first his own, but the echo of his elders. The echo turns into a voice ... and each of us becomes himself. Yet by the time we are aware of our independence, we are what others have made us. We can never unweave the web to the very bottom, and weave it up again. And if the inculcated attitudes were warped, or the suggested ideas corrupt, we shall never be rid of the influence, and we may be incurably vitiated by it. Nor is it only parental impresses of which we are the helpless victims. How many persons, how many conditions have made us what we are; and, in making us so, may have undone us.[18]

In sum, Farrer suggests that, just as natural evil is an unavoidable consequence of the nature of the physical world, so moral evil, once introduced into society, is unavoidable given the nature of humanity. For just as it is the nature of the physical world to be an interaction of innumerable systems, so it is the nature of humans to be social creatures, whose cognitive and behavioural dispositions are formed by others. And since those who form us themselves have corrupted minds, they pass this corruption on to us, and we to our children.

While Farrer eschews explaining the origin of sin – how, that is, some first human(s) came to have warped attitudes and corrupt ideas ... I believe he has the resources to offer an explanation. For humans, he notes, are animals too, sharing both 'the good and evil of animal nature'.[19] He notes this in the context of discussing human susceptibility to *natural* evil, but our animal nature would also seem to contain the seeds of sin, conceived as prioritizing the self above all else. Of course, we do not fault non-human animals for this kind of self-centredness, because they do not know, and cannot do, any differently. But Farrer understands our humanity to be animal nature wedded to rationality[20] ... and the rational person does know better.[21] Thus the origin of sin could be located in our natural self-centredness winning out over our moral conscience.

Perhaps Farrer does not account for the origin of sin along the lines I have proposed because such an account might be said to make God – the author of our nature, both animal and rational – the 'author of sin'. It is a common move for those who, like Farrer, affirm God's 'universal causality'[22] to throw up their hands and call sin a 'surd'.[23] But to affirm God's universal causality just is to affirm the divine authorship of all things; and so to then backpedal and call sin a 'surd' seems obfuscatory. Instead, Farrer should stand by what he has said – that 'if the God who saves us is the author of nature, then *the evil from which he saves us is part and parcel of the nature he has made*';[24] this is no less true of human sin than animal suffering.

It may soften the blow to consider, as suggested above, that human sin is somehow a necessary concomitant of creating human persons – something God could not avoid if he wanted to create rational animals. Brian Hebblethwaite has proposed, along these lines, that a theodicy of moral evil is 'implicit in [Farrer's] picture of the necessary conditions of the fashioning of rational – creaturely persons in a physical world'.[25] Noting that Farrer endorsed a libertarian (i.e. indeterministic) view of human freedom in *The Freedom of the Will*, Hebblethwaite proposes an Irenaean theodicy dependent on a libertarian view, according to which such freedom 'is necessary in the first stages of the creation of persons, namely, ... the building up of creatures from below in a morally ambiguous environment'.[26]

While Hebblethwaite may be right, that a free will defence is implicit in *LAIU*, another way to explain why such a response to the problem of evil is not explicitly stated there – which Hebblethwaite calls 'one of the most puzzling features of the Farrer corpus'[27] – is simply that Farrer changed his mind, and in *LAIU* backed off from his early libertarian commitments. After all, in explicating his understanding of original sin, Farrer repeatedly emphasizes his belief that individual persons are not fully responsible for the moral evil they commit. As already noted, Farrer describes human beings as 'helpless victims' of the conditions which have formed us, and which we cannot resist or undo. He later notes a 'common though not always acknowledged observation', that 'the gospel is preached to multitudes with whom its acceptance is not a live option, or a psychological possibility' – and he attributes the difference between those who accept God's saving grace, and those who do not, to 'a hundred circumstances outside the control of either parties'.[28] When Farrer does talk of human freedom in the context of moral evil, he says:

> The world is our natural habitat, not of our bodies only, but of our thoughts. Our lungs can breathe no other air, our minds can move in no other universe ... *Within this world, so constituted as it is, the scope of our freedom is found* ... We cannot ask that when we sin, we should sin for ourselves alone ... What is true of us is true of all; as others will be our victims, so we are the victims of our progenitors. To understand sin is to understand original sin; the sin behind our birth, which casts its shadow over our life.[29]

The scope of our freedom thus seems severely limited, on Farrer's more mature view.[30] Hebblethwaite acknowledges the seemingly 'deterministic picture' in *LAIU*, which he admits is 'surely incompatible with ... *The Freedom of the Will*,' but then notes two qualifications of this picture:

> First, regarding our condition in this life, [Farrer] points out that while we may not be responsible for the false orientation in which our will is set, we are responsible for its continued hold on us, and for our failure to correct it (p. 150). And, secondly, regarding the future of man, he supposes that, beyond the grave, all men and women will be confronted unambiguously by Christ and the redeemed and none will be found unable to respond but by their own fault (p. 130). So free will is maintained, as we should expect.[31]

I do not know what Hebblethwaite is referring to in his first point. Nowhere on the cited page does Farrer say anything close to what Hebblethwaite suggests. Farrer does describe the doctrine of original sin as teaching that 'the race is fallen, so that every individual person born into the world starts in a position somehow analogous to that of a man fallen from grace *by his own fault*'.[32] But he immediately goes on to say he believes in original sin (only) 'with reservations' – and modifies the view in the ways described above. With regard to his second point, Hebblethwaite is correct – Farrer does seem to think that at the eschaton, every created person's freedom of choice will be restored, so those bound for hell will be fully responsible for their own damnation. However, to affirm that human freedom will be ensured on the Day of Judgement is certainly consistent with the denial of much significant freedom in this life; and the free will defence Hebblethwaite attributes to Farrer is about building human persons *here and now*.

I've suggested so far that it's consistent with Farrer's own thinking in *LAIU* that human sin is the inevitable consequence of God's project of person-making. This is not because such a project requires created people to have freedom over which God cannot exercise control, but because human persons are, on Farrer's view, fundamentally rational animals, and animals have a tendency toward self-preserving behaviour that, when coupled with a moral conscience, makes them liable to moral evil. So, on this Farrer-inspired approach, moral evil is a consequence of our human nature just as natural evil is a consequence of the nature of the physical world.[33]

Having proposed a kind of amendment to Farrer's theodicy, I proceed to raise some questions about his view as whole, and to consider how Farrer might respond, beginning with his theodicy for natural evil. We've been told that it is the nature of the physical world to be a collection of systems interacting with each other and inflicting damage on each other, and that pain is essential to help sentient beings who are part of the physical world to protect themselves from harm. Yet, we might wonder, couldn't there be *less* damage, or *less* pain than there is in the actual world, while still maintaining the 'goods' that the physical world makes possible? Similarly we might ask, regarding Farrer's account of moral evil: couldn't there be *fewer* warped attitudes or corrupt ideas, or evil behaviours that result?

Or, does Farrer think that *every single* instance of evil in the world is necessary for some greater good intended by God, so that God could not remove any without contravening his purposes? The answer to this last question is a definite 'No.' Farrer clearly finds a 'Yes' answer both obviously false – for starters, 'there are many useless and excessive pains in animals'[34] – and morally problematic: 'it is intolerable to assert that the agony of God's creatures, not to say their sin, serves him as a means perfectly calculated to produce ulterior ends'.[35] What Farrer seems to be condemning here is an instrumental justification of *individual* evils; for, as we have seen, he offers his own instrumental justification of evils *in general*. We might wonder what the moral difference is. I think the answer lies in his use of the word 'ulterior'. Farrer insists that God makes creatures *for their own sakes*,[36] with features, such as pain, that are generally good for the organisms that have them. But in some cases, those features do not serve the organisms – for instance, in 'the pain [an] animal feels in being mauled, when it is destined to be devoured'.[37] If we suppose that when it is not beneficial to the creature, pain is 'a divine visitation, inflicted in each case for the special good it will do',[38] we would be led to the (intolerable) conclusion that God does not care about the wellbeing of the individual creature who He makes to suffer as a means to some divine end.

This does not mean, as Simon Oliver has proposed, that Farrer is resisting an 'anthropomorphism characteristic of philosophical theodicy, namely the attempt to "justify the ways of God to man" from a supposed "Archimedean point" of moral judgement'. Oliver argues that Farrer rejects the assumption that there is some moral standard that applies to God in his treatment of creatures, such that God must have a 'moral reason for allowing the pain and suffering we experience'.[39] Admittedly, Farrer does say, in criticizing Job's friends, 'In justifying Providence they come near to justifying evil; and evil can never be justified'.[40] Yet even here, Farrer seems to have in mind a justification of the *particular* evils that befell Job, and his friends' failure to see that Job's suffering neither did him good, nor was a penalty for his faults.[41] But Farrer repeatedly describes what he takes to be the *general* reasons why God creates certain things as a 'justification' of them – as in, 'We place the justification of animal life in a good intrinsic to life itself'[42] – and he even says that while 'Job's comforters mismanage their task ... it is a proper enough task in itself.'[43]

So Farrer does seem intent on justifying the *general* ways of God, while he resists the urge to offer a justification for any *particular* evil that does not seem to serve the general purpose of its kind. Yet, none of this answers the question of why there is so much apparently gratuitous evil – why, for instance, God does not create a world where dying creatures do not experience intense agony. Granted, God primarily 'works through natural forces and natural characteristics' so that 'no natural regularities are violated'.[44] But why does God not make the natural regularities a bit different? Surely in the infinity of possible worlds God could have created, there were physical worlds with sentient beings and rational persons, with less natural (not to say moral) evil. Isn't it the project of theodicy, after all, to explain why God created *this* world, rather than some other?

Farrer doesn't think so, and abstains from the possible-worlds language so common in contemporary analytic philosophy. In discussing the attempt 'to vindicate God for making the world as he has made it, rather than otherwise,' Farrer writes, 'this would involve the serious pretence to conceive the predicament of Almighty Wisdom, in choosing what sort of world to make. And is not such a pretence fantastic? If it is even right to speak of creation as the choice of a world, it cannot be supposed that such a choice is anything like the choices with which we are familiar.'[45] After considering and rejecting various human analogies to divine choice, Farrer says:

> God's mind ... does not labour, like ours, through a multitude of suggestions; he goes straight to the goal of his choice. He does not start with shadowy might-have-beens, and fill one of them out with the substance of being. He simply decrees what is; the might-have-beens are accompanying shadows of the actual, the other ways in which God knows he could have created, and did not.[46]

Hebblethwaite takes such passages to suggest a rejection of Molina's doctrine of middle knowledge, or the idea that God knows all truths about how possible creatures with libertarian freedom would behave in all possible circumstances, and on the basis of such knowledge, chooses to 'actualize' one set of possibilities. Hebblethwaite rejects the possibility of middle knowledge on the grounds that 'it requires a deterministic ... account of finite freedom after all. Only so could one make sense of the idea of the actualization of specific determinate futures.'[47] This is a common criticism of the doctrine of middle knowledge,[48] but I doubt Farrer would make it, for three reasons. First, as I have already noted, Farrer seems to back off his endorsement of libertarian human freedom in *LAIU*. Second, I think he would take his doctrine of double agency, developed more fully in his 1967 *Faith and Speculation*, to entail not only that God is the universal cause of all free creaturely actions, but also that, being the cause, God *can* foreknow such actions. And third, in the above quoted passage, Farrer is saying not simply that God does not foreknow *free choices* or even *indeterministic events*, but that God does not consider *any* alternative possibilities before he creates; so his reason for thinking this must be more general than some consideration about the nature of libertarian freedom or indeterminist events.

My take on Farrer's eschewing of possible-worlds language is different, and focusses on his claim that God 'goes straight to the goal of his choice' and 'simply decrees what is'. Despite his qualification immediately following – 'We may say such things; we cannot think them'[49] – and his insistence that 'All human analogy fails us',[50] I wonder if a *different* human analogy might shed more light on Farrer's understanding of God's choice. The analogy I have in mind is offered by David Bradshaw in a discussion of Greek patristic conceptions of divine freedom:

> When I choose to paint a landscape, I may or may not think of doing so as one among a discrete set of possibilities; I might instead, for example, be so moved with eagerness to create a landscape that the many other possibilities simply do not occur to me. This does not mean that my action does not involve a choice, but only that it does not involve a choice *among discrete possibilities*, for I did not consciously formulate and deliberate upon these possibilities beforehand; I simply acted spontaneously, in the fullness of my freedom. Likewise, when I choose to begin *this* brushstroke *here* and end it in just *this way*, I almost certainly do not think of this act as one specific possibility among others. Instead I freely express my overall intent and design through the brushstroke, directing the act as I perform it in a way that answers to that intent. This is of course only an analogy, but it nonetheless illustrates that 'choice' even in human action need not be conceived as a selection of one possibility among others, but is often simply the free expression of a creative intent.[51]

Perhaps God's creative freedom is analogous to such human freedom, at least in the negative respect that it does not necessarily involve a choice between possibilities. This is not to say, as Hebblethwaite insists, that the actualization of our particular world, among infinitely many known possibilities, is a metaphysical impossibility for God. It is rather to say that choosing from among such possible worlds is not God's *style*. What is more God's style than comparing and contrasting various possibilities, and actualizing the one with the best balance of good over evil? Perhaps simply creating a world with much goodness, because God judges it good and loves it. Farrer suggests that such a (human) choice would be a free one when he says in *The Freedom of the Will*, 'What can be more voluntary than a project with nothing against it, immediately seized by the whole energy of our will; when, for example, on a day of leisure, we embrace an invitation to visit the person whom we love?'[52] One might argue that this is not only a fine example of free choice, but a fine example of a *good* choice – despite the lack of prior deliberation about the various alternative ways one might spend one's day, and the costs and benefits of each.[53]

A critic might object to this line of reasoning as follows: whereas how one spends 'a day of leisure' is relatively inconsequential, and so perhaps need not require deliberation over alternative possibilities, the choice of what world to create is momentous; and considering the tremendous amount and severity of apparently gratuitous evil in the world, it seems that a God who cared about individual creatures would not disdain to choose from among alternative possibilities a world that contained less evil, while still realizing God's good purposes. But we might pause and press the critic here: given all the evil that we are aware of in the world, would it be at all reassuring to think that God chose to create this world because it had the least amount of evil God could get for the good He purposed? Marilyn McCord Adams raises this question in the face of what she calls 'horrendous evil', or evil that makes an individual question whether her life is worth living.[54] Considering what she calls 'generic and global approaches' to the problem of evil, which attempt to establish the possibility that this is the best possible world God could create (or something similar), Adams writes, 'Could the truck driver who accidentally runs over his beloved child find consolation in the idea that this middle-known but unintended side-effect was part of the price *God* accepted for a world with the best balance of moral good over moral evil he could get?' Adams thinks the answer is 'No' – it may be no comfort to the individual who experiences such a horror to know that, somehow, the world benefits. Indeed, it might even paint for the individual 'a picture of divine indifference' to his plight.[55]

My guess is that Farrer would agree with Adams. God would not appear any more loving or caring of individual creatures who suffer tremendously in this life on the supposition that there is no possible world God could have created with a better balance of good over evil. But what *would* be of comfort to the individual sufferer? Adams argues that comfort lies not in 'the overbalance/defeat of evil by good on the global scale' but in 'the overbalance/defeat of evil by good within the context of *an individual person's life'*[56] ... and that while horrendous evil is 'incommensurate' with any earthly goods, 'the good of beatific intimacy with God would *engulf* ... even the horrendous evils humans experience.'[57] Farrer concurs, saying of 'the promise of an invisible and eternal good' – that is, seeing the face of God – 'There is no other consolation but this which carries any force.'[58]

Adams goes further, reasoning that since 'it is the nature of persons to look for meaning, both in their lives and in the world,' God must 'make all those sufferings which threaten to destroy the positive meaning of a person's life meaningful through positive defeat'; and she proposes that God might do so by 'integrating participation in horrendous evils into a person's relationship with God'[59] – for instance, through identification with Christ, or as a vision of the inner life of God.[60] While Farrer does not give such concrete proposals, he also does not think God simply tacks an eternal happy ending on to an earthly life filled with horrors. So while he rejects the view, mentioned already, that suffering and sin serve God as 'a means perfectly calculated to ulterior ends', he does say, 'God would never have allowed evils to subsist in his creation, were it not that he might find in them the occasion to produce good things unique in kind, and dependent for their unique character on the character of the evils in question'.[61] Farrer further suggests that the sufferer may find comfort in this:

> A patriot, wearing away his life in a reactionary prison, is not merely to be told that his sufferings will be compensated by some good in the end. He can be told that the divine will has a unique purpose to achieve through them; that he can himself adhere to this purpose, and co-operate with it, if only by his faithful endurance. Even the sinner fallen from grace by his own fault can be assured that the inexhaustible inventiveness of divine mercy has prepared a unique good to be achieved through his repentance; and this in spite of the fact that he would have had a straighter path to higher good by not sinning at all.[62]

While Adams insists that there must be a particular reason why God permits each individual horrendous evil,[63] and Farrer, as we have already seen, thinks such an assumption is problematic, they agree not only that God will bring good out of each evil He permits, but that, as Adams says, 'it is not necessary to find ... reasons *why* God might permit [horrendous suffering]. It is enough to show *how* God can be good enough to created persons despite their participation in horrors.'[64]

I find in these points a resolution to difficulties I have with Farrer's theodicy. For his claims about the general reasons why God allows natural evil in the world seem to me unsatisfying. It is hard for me to believe, for instance, that omnipotence could find no better way to help living creatures protect themselves from harm than by the experience of pain, and I'm not totally convinced that it is a necessary feature of any physical world that much damage be inflicted on the constituents of it. But if it is true that no matter how much evil we (and, I should hope, all sentient creatures) experience, *our lives will be worth living* – and if it is also true that God will bring good out of each instance of horrendous evil, even those not particularly intended for any good – then I don't think it matters whether the evil was necessary to begin with. Maybe God could have created a world without pain; but this world is still good, and good for us – so let us rejoice and be glad in it.

Returning to her distinction between (not) knowing God's reasons for allowing evil, and knowing God's goodness toward us, Adams offers two illustrations:

> The two-year-old heart patient is convinced of its mother's love, not by her cognitively inaccessible reasons, but by her intimate care and presence through its painful experience. The story of Job suggests something similar is true with human participation in horrendous suffering: God does not give Job His reasons-why ... rather Job ... sees God's goodness face to face![65]

While most of us will not know God through a face-to-face encounter in this life, Farrer says that by faith we may apprehend a truth which 'speculation alone is powerless to reach'.[66] Farrer's response to the problem of evil seems unique among philosophical treatments in emphasizing the 'practical aspect of faith' – that is, what the individual facing evil may do in response to it. He writes: 'The Christian sufferer need not know why the blow was struck. He wants to discover what God is doing in face of it, *so that he may do it too*.'[67] While it may be impossible to tell, in some cases, what God is doing, Farrer suggests that those who take evil as 'God's invitation to succour his world', and so who 'give themselves to the work of relief', may very well find God there:

> Those who take the practical alternative become more closely and more widely acquainted with misery than the onlookers; but they feel the grain of existence, and the movement of the purposes of God. They do not argue, they love; and what is loved is always known as good. The more we love, the more we feel the evils besetting or corrupting the object of our love. But the more we feel the force of the besetting harms, the more certain we are of the value residing in what they attack; and in resisting them are identified with the action of God, whose mercy is over all flesh.[68]

While in response to the 'speculative' question of why God created a world with evil, speculative answers may be given – for instance, regarding the nature of the physical world, the purpose of pain, and so on[69] – the 'apprehension of truth' of the matter can be had only through practice. In other words, *finding* God (and good) in the midst of evil requires 'leaning in' (as it were) to suffering, and engaging the will of God that we can only perceive by so doing.

Notes

1 Austin Farrer, *Love Almighty and Ills Unlimited*, London, Collins, 1962, p. 7.

2 Ibid., pp. 8–9.

3 Ibid., p. 10.

4 Ibid., p. 30.

5 Cf. Richard Swinburne, *The Existence of God* (2nd edn), Oxford, Oxford University Press, 2004, p. 236.

6 Farrer, *Love Almighty*, p. 32.

7 Ibid., p. 146.

8 Ibid., p. 33.

9 Ibid., p. 36.

10 Ibid.

11 Ibid., p. 51.

12 Ibid., p. 56. Some interpreters read Farrer's formula 'to be is to act' as an expression of his early commitment to the Aristotelian view of God as 'pure being', from which Farrer distanced himself in later works (cf. Simon Oliver, 'The Theodicy of Austin Farrer', *Heythrop Journal* 39:3 (1998)). But another way to understand this formula, which shows up in *LAIU* in his description of physical creatures – 'They are action-systems, for to act is to be; they are what they do, or what they are apt to do' – is as an expression of dispositionalism, the view that the most fundamental properties of physical objects are how they are disposed to act under various conditions. For instance, the electrical charge of an electron or proton is simply its disposition to attract or repel particles of like or opposite sort – and it is the charge of the particle (along with other dispositional properties) that *makes* it an electron or proton. Hebblethwaite identifies Farrer as an essentialist – one who believes 'that certain properties are essential to objects ... being what they are' – in the tradition of Saul Kripke (Brian Hebblethwaite, *The Philosophical Theology of Austin Farrer*, Leuven, Peeters, 2007, pp. 80–1); I take dispositionalism to be a kind of essentialism.

13 Ibid.

14 Farrer, *Love Almighty*, p. 59.

15 Ibid., p. 82.

16 Ibid., pp .87–8.

17 Ibid., p. 140.

18 Ibid., p. 114.

19 Ibid., p. 106.

20 Ibid., pp. 106–7.

21 This point, I think, serves to answer Farrer's concern that 'it is quite unrealistic to describe the damaging part of our inheritance as the brute or the savage clinging to us, and not yet shaken off' for 'There are vices of which the primitive, not to say the animal, is incapable' (p. 151). After all, animals are incapable of vices because they lack the intelligence with which humans are endowed. So it is only because we have *both* animal *and* rational nature that we are capable of sin.

22 Ibid., p. 44.

23 Cf. Kathryn Tanner, 'Human Freedom, Human Sin, and God the Creator,' in Thomas Tracy (ed.), *The God Who Acts: Philosophical and Theological Explorations*, University Park, PA, Pennsylvania State University Press, 1994, p. 112. Tanner is herself echoing Karl Barth and Bernard Lonergan.

24 Farrer, *Love Almighty*, p. 14, emphasis added.

25 Brian Hebblethwaite, 'Freedom, Evil and Farrer' in *New Blackfriars*, 66:778 (1985) p. 185.

26 Ibid.

27 Ibid., p. 179.

28 Farrer, *Love Almighty*, pp. 114–15.

29 Ibid., pp. 158–9, emphasis added.

30 Of course, the idea that our freedom is *limited* might simply mean that free actions are rare – but that when we do freely act, our actions are still necessarily undetermined. (Thanks to David McNaughton, personal communication, for reminding me of this.) I do not think there is anything in *LAIU* that speaks decisively against such a picture; so Farrer may very well have remained a libertarian. But his emphasis on the conditioned nature of our choices – especially the important choices that shape our characters and determine whether we come to a saving knowledge of God in this life – suggests that Farrer was not relying on a libertarian Irenaean theodicy as Hebblethwaite proposes. For on such a theodicy, free will is valuable in this life precisely because it allows people to 'build' their own characters and 'fashion their own lives' for good or ill (Hebblethwaite, op. cit., p. 180); and Farrer seems to deny such significant person-building in *LAIU*. Instead, libertarian freedom seems important, if at all, at the Day of Judgement, when individuals who have been found 'unresponsive in this life' – 'by force of circumstances' (Farrer, *Love Almighty*, p. 123) – are raised from the dead and confronted with 'the completion of Christ's Incarnation,' which is the Church (ibid., p. 130). Then (and, I take it, only then) 'none will be found unable [to respond] but by their own fault' (ibid.).

31 Hebblethwaite, 'Freedom, Evil and Farrer', p. 183.

32 Farrer, *Love Almighty*, p. 150, emphasis added.

33 While Peter van Inwagen offers an Augustinian free will defence according to which the origin of sin 'must be mysterious to us', he similarly appeals to the combination of our animal and rational nature in explaining the propagation of sin (Peter Van Inwagen, "The Argument from Evil," in Kevin Timpe (ed.) *Arguing About Religion*, New York, Routledge, 2009, pp. 218–19.

34 Farrer, *Love Almighty*, p. 89.

35 Ibid., p. 162.

36 Ibid., p. 101.

37 Ibid., p. 90.

38 Ibid., p. 89.

39 Oliver, 'The Theodicy of Austin Farrer', p. 286.

40 Farrer, *Love Almighty*, p. 15.

41 Ibid.

42 Ibid., p. 84.

43 Ibid., p. 16. William Wilson and Julian Hartt, like Oliver, maintain that Farrer rejected 'the very project of modern theodicy'. But in his sermon that they quote to support this interpretation, Farrer says, 'Shall we put together the cosmic puzzle, and so justify the ways of God? No; God will justify himself, by his deeds' (quoted in 'Farrer's Theodicy,' in David Hein and Edward Hugh Henderson's *Captured by the Crucified: The Practical Theology of Austin Farrer*, New York, T & T Clark International, 2004, pp.104–5). This seems consistent with my interpretation of Farrer in *LAIU*, for there, after describing Job's comforters' task as 'proper enough', he goes on to write: 'The sufferer accuses God; and is not the believer to defend him? Not, of course, in the spirit of an advocate defending a client. For the client is supposed incapable of his own defence … But God is a living, self-justifying truth, and to plead for him can only be to say what he says, to capture an echo of his meaning in the idioms of our stammering speech' (Farrer, *Love Almighty*, p. 16). So again, Farrer seems not opposed to the project of justifying God's ways as such; instead, he is highlighting the failure to see that in doing so, we are simply expressing what God has already revealed through nature and human history.

44 Farrer, *Love Almighty*, p. 99.

45 Ibid., pp. 61–2.

46 Ibid., p. 64.

47 Hebblethwaite, 'Freedom, Evil and Farrer', p. 73.

48 William Hasker, *God, Time and Knowledge*, Ithaca, NY, Cornell University, 1989.

49 Farrer, *Love Almighty*, p. 64.

50 Ibid., p. 63.

51 David Bradshaw, 'Divine Freedom in the Greek Patristic Tradition' *Quaestiones Disputatae*, 2:1/2 (2011), p. 68.

52 Austin Farrer, *The Freedom of the Will*, London, Adam & Charles Black, 1957, p. 111.

53 After writing this I rediscovered an article in which Robert Merrihew Adams argues that it is not part of the Judeo-Christian worldview that God must create the best possible world (supposing there is one), and that, in fact, 'God's choice of a less excellent world could be accounted for in terms of His grace, which is considered a virtue ... of character in Judeo-Christian ethics' ('Must God Create the Best?' *The Philosophical Review* 81:3 (1972), pp. 318–19). Adams thinks the first claim, that God is justified in creating a less-than-best possible world, is fair at least if we assume that in the world God creates, 'None of the creatures ... has a life which is so miserable on the whole that it would be better for that creature if it had never existed' – a point discussed below, which Marilyn McCord Adams emphasized.

54 Marilyn McCord Adams, 'God and Evil: Polarities of a Problem' (1993), *Philosophical Studies* 69 2/3, pp. 167–86. Adams was, like Farrer, an Anglican priest and philosopher; and it seems she was familiar with his work, since she at least once cited *LAIU* (1993, footnote 17). Perhaps some of Adams' ideas discussed below were inspired by Farrer's.

55 Marilyn McCord Adams, 'Horrendous Evils and the Goodness of God' (1989), reprinted in Michael Peterson et al. (eds), *Philosophy of Religion: Selected Readings*, 5th edn, Oxford, Oxford University Press, 2014, p. 377.

56 Ibid., emphasis added.

57 Ibid., p. 379.

58 Farrer, *Love Almighty*, pp. 168–9.

59 Adams, 'Must God Create the Best?', p. 379.

60 Ibid., pp. 379–80.

61 Farrer, *Love Almighty*, p. 163.

62 Ibid.

63 Adams, 'Must God Create the Best?', p. 378.

64 Ibid., p. 379.

65 Ibid., pp. 378–9.

66 Farrer, *Love Almighty*, p. 187.

67 Ibid., p. 171, emphasis added.

68 Ibid., p. 188.

69 Ibid., p. 187.

6

'The Evidence of Faith': Austin Farrer, Diogenes Allen and Reformed Epistemology

ROBERT MACSWAIN

One of the most important and controversial movements in twentieth-century Anglo-American philosophy of religion developed in the early 1980s with Alvin Plantinga, Nicholas Wolterstorff and their associates under the title 'Reformed epistemology'. While not all those gathered under this banner were Calvinists, they shared a common set of convictions on the rationality of religious belief. Reformed epistemologists rejected what they called 'classical foundationalism' and the concomitant need for religious belief to depend upon propositional *arguments* and *evidence* for the existence of God in order to be considered rational. Rather, they insisted, belief in God was 'properly basic' – that is, based upon non-inferential modes of perception or an inbuilt sense of the divine – or rightly held on the basis of communal testimony and formation. If so, then religious belief may be rational without depending upon the traditional arguments of natural theology. To be more precise, religious belief was 'innocent until proven guilty', in that it still needed to defend itself when called upon by answering objections such as the problem of evil or other standard criticisms. But religious belief did not need to justify its basic content in some foundationalist, rationalist or evidentialist manner.[1]

With that background information in place, this essay will proceed as follows. I first summarize a recent survey of contemporary Anglo-American epistemology, both general and religious, that links four important trends with those associated with Reformed epistemology, and in particular Alvin Plantinga and William P. Alston (d. 2009). I then show how Austin Farrer anticipated all four of these current trends in his philosophical work beginning with *Finite and Infinite* in 1943 and concluding with *Faith and Speculation* in 1967. The next section argues that Farrer's American student Diogenes Allen (d. 2013) developed proposals in the early 1960s that not only influenced Farrer's *Faith and Speculation* but that bore a striking resemblance to the project Reformed epistemologists developed independently two decades later. The implications of all this will then be considered in a brief conclusion.

Four trends in contemporary epistemology, general and religious

In a recent survey of general epistemology relevant to religious epistemology, John Greco identifies four trends dating from the 1980s which continue to shape contemporary discussions: (1) rejecting narrow foundationalism, (2) rejecting internalism, (3) knowledge versus understanding and (4) explanation versus vindication.[2] He begins by noting the broad rejection of narrow foundationalism, which he describes as 'a theory that tries to explain all knowledge in terms of a narrow range of sources'.[3] More specifically, narrow foundationalism is preoccupied with 'a narrow range of evidence, or kinds of evidence' – that is, with what counts as legitimate evidence for a rational belief and what does not. Rationalists and empiricists answer this question differently, with rationalists focussing on 'certainty' and empiricists focussing on 'experience', but narrow foundationalists go on to insist that only their preferred form of evidence is acceptable. Such narrow foundationalism is traditionally manifest in religious epistemology by insisting that knowledge of God requires 'proofs' or 'demonstrations'. By contrast, Greco says, 'contemporary religious epistemology takes seriously the idea that our knowledge of God is a kind of knowledge of persons. But in general our knowledge of persons is by means of our interpersonal interactions with them as well as by what they reveal about themselves with their own words and actions. Religious epistemology is nowadays interested in pursuing analogous models of our knowledge of a personal God.'[4]

The second trend of 'rejecting internalism' could also be described positively as 'accepting externalism'. Both of these theories come in various forms. The primary claim of internalism is that for a belief to be rational its basis must somehow 'be "immediately" accessible to one; that is, it must be immediately knowable, or knowable "by reflection alone"'.[5] That is, everyone is personally responsible to ensure that their beliefs are rational by the exercise of appropriate reasons or arguments. There is thus a close connection between such internalism and what the Reformed epistemologists call classical foundationalism, 'which restricts the sources of knowledge to such things as a priori reason, conscious introspection, and what is "given" in experience'.[6] But such internalist theories are now widely (although by no means universally) rejected in favour of externalism. By contrast with internalism, externalist theories insist that 'knowledge requires appropriate causal contact with the object of knowledge. It also requires ... healthy cognitive functioning and an enabling cognitive environment'.[7] That is, externalism says that what makes a belief rational is 'external' to the direct individual consciousness and more dependent on reliable mental functions in appropriate contexts. Like the first trend, when applied to religious epistemology externalism also discourages emphasis on theistic arguments: while they may play some role, 'there is a general consensus that they are not the basis for ordinary beliefs about God'.[8] Greco writes: 'there is now increased interest in how religious believers might come to know God through experience or revelation. Just as general epistemology has turned its attention to the actual grounds of "ordinary" knowledge, and away from the rational reconstructions of philosophers, religious epistemology is now concerned with ordinary persons in the pew (or in prayer, or in distress, or in joy, or in service to others).'[9]

The third trend of 'knowledge versus understanding' both distinguishes between these two concepts and prioritizes the former over the latter, at least in regard to ordinary beliefs. As Greco puts it, 'there is an important difference between *knowing that* such-and-such is the case and *understanding why* or *how* such-and-such is the case'.[10] For example, one might *know* that food is good for one's health without *understanding* the biology of nutrition, digestion, and so forth.[11] Understanding is thus important and valuable in its own right, but it is not necessary for knowledge. Therefore, Greco says, 'there is now logical space for ordinary knowledge of God without philosophical or theological understanding. For example, one might know that God loves His people and wants His creation to flourish, but not understand how suffering is compatible with this.'[12] This distinction also provides a legitimate role for natural theology after all: not to justify basic religious knowledge, but to enable deeper understanding.[13]

The fourth and final trend is 'explanation versus vindication'. If the epistemic project is vindication, then we must engage sceptics on their own ground and try to establish by *their* criteria that we know anything at all: a game impossible to win and thus pointless to play. But if the epistemic project is explanation, then 'the aim is not to establish (against the sceptic) that we have knowledge, but to explain (to ourselves) the difference between knowing and not knowing. It is also to consider how beings like us, in the circumstances we find ourselves, might achieve the sort of knowledge in question.'[14] Greco thus concludes:

What this means for religious epistemology and the epistemology of theology is a retreat from apologetics. In older days, the task was to develop arguments in favour of God's existence, to answer objections against these, and to critique arguments against God's existence. The entire process was framed as a debate, with each side trying to prove its case against the other, using only premises that all could accept. This makes perfect sense if the project is vindication, but no sense at all if the project is explanation. Accordingly, present-day religious epistemology deals more in explanations than in proofs; that is, theories are put forward regarding what knowledge of God would require for beings like us, and models are put forward regarding how we might fulfil those requirements.

Having presented these four recent trends, Greco goes on to associate them in both general and religious epistemology with the groundbreaking work of Plantinga and Alston, both of whom are still historically identified with 'Reformed' epistemology despite Alston's avowed Anglicanism and Plantinga's later preference for what he more ecumenically calls an 'Aquinas/Calvin model'.[15]

Greco then considers various objections to their views such as counterevidence, the lack of universal religious belief, and religious diversity.[16] In the final section of his essay, he offers an interesting take on what he calls the 'social turn' in contemporary epistemology – that is, 'how the knowledge of individuals depends in various ways on the knowledge, activities, and properties of groups' – and in particular on the epistemology of testimony.[17]

Austin Farrer: from rational theology to the evidence of faith

Greco's four trends are all associated with Reformed epistemology and thus contrasted sharply from previous views, and that may well be the case in regard to mainstream Anglo-American discussions of natural theology, apologetics and religious epistemology. However, I will now show that all four of these trends were anticipated by Farrer between 1943 and 1967, sometimes explicitly, sometimes incipiently.[18] As I have argued at greater length elsewhere, Farrer's mature thinking on faith and reason passed through various stages, so my presentation here will be chronological, but along the way I will note how Farrer's developing thought intersects with Greco's contemporary trends.[19]

In his first major work, *Finite and Infinite*, Farrer took his basic cosmological and analogical inspiration from Thomas Aquinas in the twin task of arguing against (i) logical positivism's rejection of metaphysics as well as (ii) Karl Barth's insistence on revelation alone as the source of human knowledge of God. And to that extent, Farrer seemed more sympathetic to the project of traditional natural theology. Yet in this book Farrer also rejected textbook Thomism's conviction that human knowledge of divine reality depended on valid deductive arguments. Farrer thus asserted that *Finite and Infinite* was an exercise in what he called 'rational theology' even though he was not committed to 'the perfect demonstration of even one basic theological proposition. We may find that we can only show its possibility or probability.'[20] Here we already see a rejection of narrow foundationalism and the emergence of what has been called soft rationalism.[21] Farrer goes on to clarify that by 'rational theology' as opposed to 'natural theology' he means a focus on *analysis* rather than *dialectic*, which precisely mirrors Greco's contrast between explanation and vindication.[22]

On the subject of the contested question of the existence of God, Farrer argues that while it cannot be formally *demonstrated*, it can still be rationally *apprehended*.[23] By 'apprehension' Farrer means a non-inferential, intuitive grasp of divine reality on the basis of what he calls the 'Cosmological Idea': that is, through directly experiencing our own existence, as well as through recognizing the existence of other finite realities, including other persons, we come to understand our source in the unique creative activity of an infinite Agent. In light of Greco's emphasis on explanation rather than vindication – that is, putting forward theories and models rather than demonstrations and proofs – note Farrer's interesting claim that 'the theist's first argument is a statement; he exhibits his account of God active in the world and the world existing in God, that others may recognise it to be the account of what they themselves apprehend – or, if you like, that others may find it to be an instrument through which they apprehend, for perhaps apprehension is here not separable from interpretation'.[24] The non-inferential, interpretative character of apprehending God is at least analogous to Reformed epistemology's emphasis on proper basicality, and I will return to the crucial connection between knowing persons and knowing God below.

In regard to Greco's trend of 'knowledge versus understanding', even in 1943 Farrer explicitly endorsed Greco's view that (religious) epistemology is more about ordinary (religious) belief and less about formal philosophical reconstructions of it, and this conviction became even more pronounced as Farrer's thought developed further, as we will see in the following section. Thus, in *Finite and Infinite* Farrer says that he is simply seeking to understand 'the Jacob's-ladder of living religion', and in his correspondence with Diogenes Allen in the 1960s he summarized Allen's thesis by saying: 'Justification ought not to construct bypasses to God, but to test the roads by which he comes to us.'[25]

So far we have seen Farrer's early articulation of ideas expressed in Greco's trends of 'rejecting narrow foundationalism', 'explanation versus vindication' and 'knowledge versus understanding'. Since there is an admittedly strong internalist element to Farrer's argument in *Finite and Infinite*, and since contemporary externalist theories of epistemology did not develop until the 1970s, to claim that in Farrer we also find Greco's 'rejecting internalism' may seem implausible. But in an intriguing passage, Farrer suggests that even revelation must be intelligible to the human mind before it can be accepted, and so we must be properly designed to receive it: 'unless I had some mental machinery for thinking the bare notion of God, could I recognise His revelatory action as that of God?'[26] The term 'mental machinery' has a strongly externalist ring. And in a later passage in *Finite and Infinite*, we find even more explicitly externalist ideas. To understand human cognition it is necessary to 'abandon the path of logical rectitude, and to consider evolutionary theory and biological probability'.[27] That is, we must recognize that we are not immaterial 'thinking substances' but evolved organic beings who can only understand things in similarly-embodied ways within environments conducive to such knowledge. This is how what Greco calls 'beings like us' come to know things.

Recall that in articulating the religious significance of the move away from narrow foundationalism, Greco says that 'contemporary religious epistemology takes seriously the idea that our knowledge of God is a kind of knowledge of persons. But in general our knowledge of persons is by means of our interpersonal interactions with them as well as by what they reveal about themselves with their own words and actions. Religious epistemology is nowadays interested in pursuing analogous models of our knowledge of a personal God'.[28] Recall also his statement that externalism requires 'appropriate causal contact with the object of knowledge.'[29] Given these comments, it is thus fascinating to see how Farrer's thought moved increasingly in both of these directions in the 1950s and 60s.

For example, his 1957 Gifford Lectures at the University of Edinburgh marked an epistemic shift from his earlier focus on 'contemplative apprehension' to 'causal interaction'. Even in *Finite and Infinite* Farrer had argued that 'we cannot think about anything about which we can do nothing but think',[30] and that 'we know things as they condition or effect our vital operation'.[31] This minor theme in *Finite and Infinite* assumed more prominence in Farrer's later philosophical work where it was eventually applied not just to our knowledge of the physical world but – perhaps surprisingly – to God as well. Thus, in *The Freedom of the Will* Farrer wrote that 'the physical is known to us by the way it conditions our physical motion; and the divine will, which is God himself, is known to us in limiting or evoking our dutiful action, through all the persons with whom we have to do'.[32] That is, it is precisely through recognizing our moral obligations to others *and acting accordingly* that we come to recognize and respond to the divine reality as well. Likewise, in *Faith and Speculation*, Farrer maintained that:

> to know real beings we must exercise our actual relation with them. No physical science without physical interference, no personal knowledge without personal intercourse; no thought about any reality about which we can do nothing but think. Is not this the highest possible generalisation of the empirical principle? Theology must be at least as empirical as this, if it is to mediate any knowledge whatsoever. We can know nothing of God, unless we can do something about him. So what, we must ask, can we do?[33]

Farrer's answer regarding what we can 'do' about God is that we can 'devote ourselves to [God's] will; that is, we can place ourselves in [God's] action as we suppose it to be disclosed'. And in such obedient devotion we find a confirming response of 'life' and 'blessing'.[34]

In these various statements we hear a significant development in Farrer's thought that arguably finds its clearest (although not final) expression in the opening chapter of *Saving Belief*, titled 'Faith and Evidence'. The crucial question is how what Farrer here calls 'the evidence of faith' is perceived and evaluated.[35] The question is crucial because Reformed epistemology self-consciously defines itself as a form of non-inferential 'anti-evidentialism', and yet Farrer insists that evidence for God is still necessary for rational belief. However, Farrer also insists that we must be properly positioned to perceive the evidence correctly, and what positions us is 'faith' understood as a form of openness and receptivity to God – or at least to reality. The attitude of faith is required to interpret the objectively-compelling evidence. Thus, he says that without

> the readiness of faith, the evidence of God will not be accepted, or will not convince. This is not to say that faith is put in place of evidence. What convinces us is not our faith, but the evidence; faith is a subjective condition favourable to the reception of the evidence ... [T]he evidence is intrinsically and of itself convincing, but only under conditions which allow it to be appreciated. Faith supplies the conditions.[36]

Diogenes Allen and Reformed epistemology

The previous section argued that Farrer exemplified in proleptic fashion all four of Greco's contemporary trends in both general and religious epistemology. Assuming that Greco's account is correct, Farrer anticipated these trends about 40 years before they became widely influential in Anglo-American philosophy. Precisely why Farrer was so far ahead of his time, on these and many other issues (such as his literary approach to biblical interpretation) is an interesting question that cannot detain us further here, other than to note that it might help explain his relative obscurity both then and now.

However, although Greco associates all four trends with Reformed epistemology, I have not argued that Farrer himself was a proto-Reformed epistemologist. Things are rather different with Diogenes Allen, who as an American Ph.D. student at Yale spent a year in Oxford working with Farrer on his doctoral thesis in 1963–64.[37] The son of Greek Orthodox immigrants from Turkey who became a Presbyterian as an undergraduate at the University of Kentucky, Allen was then a Rhodes Scholar at St John's College, Oxford, before returning to the USA for further theological and philosophical studies at Yale. Allen, Plantinga and Wolterstorff were all born in 1932, and Allen's undergraduate mentor was Jesse DeBoer (1912–90), who studied and taught at Calvin College, the Dutch Reformed *alma mater* of Plantinga and Wolterstorff. Although two decades older than them, DeBoer shared the experience of being taught by their mentor, William Harry Jellama (1893–1982).[38] Especially given Allen's early embrace of Presbyterianism (albeit moderated by his Orthodox upbringing and modified yet further by his later membership and ordination in the Episcopal Church), it is plausible to suggest that his studies with DeBoer provided some shared intellectual DNA with Plantinga and Wolterstorff.

Such biographical speculations notwithstanding, Allen's doctoral thesis and subsequent publications advanced a proposal remarkably similar to early Reformed epistemology, although 20 years beforehand. As Farrer engaged with Allen on these topics in 1963–64, Farrer was himself challenged and stimulated by Allen's argument, as his correspondence with Allen and published citations bear witness.[39] In a series of letters Farrer summarized and raised various objections to Allen's position. The penultimate letter, written on 29 June 1966 after Allen sent Farrer an *American Philosophical Quarterly* article containing the core of the thesis, reads as follows:

> Dear Diogenes,
> Thank you for the offprint of your very substantial paper, which I have read with high appreciation. By the time I received it I had completed the MS of a book containing the Deems Lectures of 1964 [*Faith and Speculation*], in which your ideas (not unacknowledged) furnish the substance of the first chapter ['The Believer's Reasons']. I do not altogether agree with you but I think what you say is very important. I think it comes to this: The believer, qua believer, rightly says 'I believe because the grace of God' (or the like) 'persuades me.' But the philosopher's business is not (mainly) to say: 'Quite right, my boy, that's how believing goes' but to examine the assumptions upon which the facts through which 'the grace of God persuades' come to be taken as instruments, effects or evidences as the Grace of God.[40]

Readers are directed toward the first chapter of *Faith and Speculation* to see Farrer's public engagement with and partial endorsement of Allen's ideas, but in the remainder of this section I turn directly to Allen's article. Allen first proposes a distinction between what he calls 'motives' and 'rationales'. A motive is the *actual reason* why someone holds a certain belief. It is specific to her as an individual, and Allen sometimes refers to it as 'biographical'. A rationale, by contrast, is a *possible reason* that one *could* provide, not to justify the belief itself as *actually* held by the person, but as a general reason why the belief *might* be true or even *ought* to be held. So whereas motives are actual and personal reasons, rationales are possible and impersonal.[41]

In regard to religious beliefs, Allen holds that most people's motive for belief is faith, aroused biographically. In some rare instances, the *actual reason* someone believes might indeed be the cosmological or some other theistic argument, but this is neither normal nor necessary. Crucial to Allen's position is the claim that not only is it *actually* the case that most people's religious beliefs are based on faith (which is fairly uncontroversial), but also that this situation is perfectly *rationally acceptable*. As he puts it, such faith-based 'biographical' reasons are 'a proper basis for the affirmation of Christian beliefs. The motives one has for one's adherence to religious beliefs are not grounds which warrant other kinds of assertions, but they are a basis for the assertion of religious beliefs. To believe on the basis of one's motives is not to act arbitrarily, blindly, or without any reason.'[42]

Furthermore, Allen makes the stronger claim that to insist that religious beliefs must be based on arguments is to distort their true character: 'To seek to give religious beliefs an evidential basis results in turning them into something else. In particular, it makes religious beliefs appear to be like other kinds of metaphysical assertions.'[43] Metaphysical beliefs are based on reasoning that makes inferences about realities beyond empirical investigation. Religious beliefs, on the other hand, while they may well imply or even entail certain metaphysical commitments, are not based on such reasoning. Rather, they arise in response to personal confrontation with a message about God – 'the gospel' – which one encounters either through growing up in a religious community, or through reading the Bible, or through hearing a street preacher for example.[44]

Although Allen maintains that to grow up within the Christian community is itself a valid motive to hold Christian beliefs (assuming, as we shall see in a moment, that one has not encountered insurmountable objections to them), in fact there is more to faith on his account than biographical considerations, namely appropriate *grounds*. According to Allen:

> The grounds are that a man has come to have faith in response to the witness of the Christian community and in the condition of faith he finds his soul nourished. By praying, by reading the Scriptures, by fellowship with other Christians, he finds his life is beginning to conform to what Paul described as the new life. This nourishment is his assurance and ground for the condition of faith in which he finds himself; and the very response of faith itself (which includes receiving nourishment) is a ground for faith.[45]

Thus, having faith is not merely assenting to a particular set of groundless beliefs just because one was taught them as a child, but rather to actively receive what Allen calls 'nourishment' from them – nourishment which itself provides the necessary grounds on which they are rationally held.

What then of 'rationales', or possible reasons? Do they play any role at all in this scheme? Yes, for religious believers often encounter *objections* to their belief, objections which arise either internally or externally, which cause them to doubt or perhaps even to abandon their faith. Although Allen holds that religious beliefs are 'innocent until proven guilty', he fully acknowledges that sometimes they do need to be defended. Rationales may thus be a necessary component of the life of faith, answering accusations and dealing with doubt. However, as with metaphysical beliefs, Allen insists that rationales still need not – and perhaps even should not – become the believer's *actual* motive or ground: she should still believe because of the *nourishment* she has actually received from the gospel, not because of an impersonal, objective argument.[46]

I do not have space to make a close comparison between Allen's position here and the original version of Reformed epistemology articulated by Plantinga, Wolterstorff, Alston and others in the 1980s, but the parallels are remarkable. In both cases we see an emphasis on the *prima facie* rationality of ordinary religious belief, a pervasive anti-evidentialism, the idea of 'grounds' rather than 'arguments' as the basis of belief, and the need for 'negative apologetics' to answer objections. It is also striking to recall Greco's claim that 'religious epistemology is now concerned with ordinary persons in the pew (or in prayer, or in distress, or in joy, or in service to others)'.[47] Such common and communal practices of faith are precisely what Allen presented in the mid-1960s as the primary justification for religious belief as well. And if Farrer did not follow Allen all the way in this regard, his final book *Faith and Speculation* still wrestled with this then-radical and still-controversial epistemic proposal, namely that 'it is the actual motives or grounds for religious believing which demand the philosopher's attention'.[48]

Conclusion

I thus conclude with a question and an observation. The question is, 'Why are Farrer and Allen not better recognized for their trailblazing accomplishments in religious epistemology?' More specifically, why is Farrer not included in contemporary epistemological discussions, and why has Allen's anticipation of Reformed epistemology been so neglected? My brief answer is that they were both so far ahead of their time that their work fell on the proverbial rocky soil. More empirical and formalist forms of philosophy were so deeply entrenched in the United Kingdom and the United States during the 1940s, 50s and 60s that it took several decades for an atmosphere more congenial to alternative approaches to develop. It may also be the case that Farrer and Allen simply were not as effective as others in getting a hearing for their ideas, either because of their style of presentation or because of their chosen publishers. So I am certainly not accusing Greco of negligence or Reformed epistemologists of conspiracy: the absence of Farrer and Allen here is pervasive and systemic rather than accidental or intentional. But that situation should be remedied and their work engaged with more deeply.

My observation is that both Farrer and Allen continued to develop as thinkers in commendable ways and they continue to be relevant to the current conversation. Consider, for example, the crucial question of 'the evidence of faith': that is, should religious belief be based on evidence or not, and if so then what kind and how much? Despite being challenged by his proposals, Farrer thought that Allen had gone too far in his youthful anti-evidentialism – and Allen later agreed. That is, Allen eventually came around to Farrer's position in 'Faith and Evidence' that the evidence 'is intrinsically and of itself convincing, but only under conditions which allow it to be appreciated'.[49] Accepting this claim then opens important connections between epistemology and both moral and spiritual development (that is to say, matters of the *heart*), for what does it take for those necessary faith-conditions to obtain? Thus, against Reformed epistemology William J. Wainwright defends the thesis that 'mature religious belief can, and perhaps should, be based on evidence but that the evidence can be accurately assessed only by men and women who possess the proper moral and spiritual qualifications'. He adds, 'This view was once a Christian commonplace; reason is capable of knowing God on the basis of evidence – but only when one's cognitive faculties are rightly disposed'.[50] Likewise, Sarah Coakley argues for the essential but neglected role of spiritual practices and increased attention to both body and gender in the *transformation* of our epistemic capacities to become more astute in recognizing the reality of God.[51] And while Harriet Harris is less convinced than Wainwright and Coakley about the need for evidence in establishing the rationality of religious belief, she claims that a major problem with Reformed epistemology is precisely that it 'wastes the opportunity' to turn its commendable epistemology into a more robust spirituality.[52] Whether fair in this specific instance or not, her general challenge for philosophers to better integrate their intellect and affect, head and heart, mind and spirit is worth heeding. And in this respect, both Farrer and Allen offer valuable models to emulate.[53]

Notes

1 Although other publications followed as their arguments became more sophisticated, the *locus classicus* is Alvin Plantinga and Nicholas Wolterstorff (eds), *Faith and Rationality: Reason and Belief in God*, Notre Dame, IN, University of Notre Dame Press, 1983. In his introduction to the volume (1–15), Wolterstorff already noted that the term 'Reformed epistemology' was not entirely felicitous (7), and Plantinga later expressed regret that some readers interpreted it in a triumphalist manner: see his 'A Christian Life Partly Lived', in *Philosophers Who Believe: The Spiritual Journeys of 11 Leading Thinkers*, ed. Kelly James Clark, Downers Grove, IL, InterVarsity, 1993, pp. 45–82, citing p. 67.

2 John Greco, 'Knowledge of God', in *The Oxford Handbook of the Epistemology of Theology*, William J. Abraham and Frederick D. Aquino (eds), Oxford, Oxford University Press, 2017, pp. 9–29. For my purposes here, I will take Greco's survey at face value and not engage critically with either his choice of trends or his interpretation of them. However, in comments on an earlier version of this essay, David Brown observed that, despite being presented as a general account, Greco's survey is in fact more focussed on the American than the British context, a thought to which I return in note 17 below.

3 Ibid., p. 10. 'Foundationalism' refers to a family of epistemic theories that all conceive of belief along the architectural analogy of a building with a foundation on which higher levels are then built. 'Narrow' and 'classical' foundationalism, while not identical, are both restrictive about what belongs in the foundational level, whereas other versions are more generous: Reformed epistemology is a form of generous or broad foundationalism (see note 6 below). Foundationalism is often contrasted with 'coherentism', a family of theories that construes belief along the organic analogy of a web.

4 Ibid., pp. 10–11.

5 Ibid., p. 11.

6 Ibid. For Plantinga, classical foundationalism restricts the foundational or 'basic' beliefs to what is self-evident, evident to the senses, or incorrigible (cannot be doubted), but it also allows for additional rational beliefs validly derived by argument from these foundations. By contrast, Reformed epistemology allows for belief in God to be included among the foundations, even if it is not self-evident, evident to the senses, or incorrigible: see 'Reason and Belief in God', in *Faith and Rationality*, Alvin Plantinga and Nicholas Wolterstorff (eds), pp. 16–93.

7 Ibid., p. 12.

8 Ibid.

9 Ibid.

10 Ibid.

11 I take this example from C. S. Lewis, *Mere Christianity*, London, Macmillan, 1953, pp. 43–4.

12 Greco, 'Knowledge of God', p. 13.

13 Ibid. For this claim, Greco cites Nicholas Wolterstorff, 'The Migration of the Theistic Arguments: From Natural Theology to Evidentialist Apologetics', in *Rationality, Religious Belief, and Moral Commitment: New Essays in the Philosophy of Religion*, ed. Robert Audi and William J. Wainwright, Ithaca, NY, Cornell University Press, 1986, pp. 38–81.

14 Ibid.

15 Ibid.

16 Ibid., pp. 14–23, 25–6. In this section Greco focusses on Plantinga's 'Reason and Belief in God'; Alvin Plantinga, *Warranted Christian Belief*, New York, Oxford University Press, 2000; and William P. Alston, *Perceiving God: The Epistemology of Religious Experience*, Ithaca, NY, Cornell University Press, 1991. For previous engagements with these figures and texts, see Robert MacSwain, 'An Analytic Anglican: The Philosophical Theology of William P. Alston', *Anglican Theological Review* 88 (2006), pp. 421–32 and 'Sensus Divinitatis or Divine Hiddenness? Alvin Plantinga and J. L. Schellenberg on Knowledge of God', *Anglican Theological Review* 99 (2017), pp. 353–62.

17 See ibid., pp.23–7, and here citing p. 23. As noted above, David Brown points out that Greco's survey is arguably more focussed on the contemporary American context than the British one. Without denying the influence of Plantinga, Wolterstorff and Alston in British philosophy of religion, Brown observes that Richard Swinburne's inductive and probabilistic approach remains the standard point of reference on the rationality of theism (in either agreement or disagreement), and also that the so-called 'New Atheists' still accept the foundational and evidentialist frameworks rejected by Reformed epistemology. For Swinburne's position see *The Existence of God*, Oxford, Clarendon Press, 1979, republished in a substantially revised second edition in 2004. A more accessible version may be found in Richard Swinburne, *Is There a God?*, Oxford, Oxford University Press, 1996, revised edition 2010. Exploring the comparison between Farrer and Swinburne would thus be a worthwhile project for another essay. For an interesting comparison between Swinburne and Wolterstorff in conversation with Farrer, see Basil Mitchell, 'Two Approaches to the Philosophy of Religion', in *For God and Clarity: New Essays in Honor of Austin Farrer*, ed. Jeffrey C. Eaton and Ann Loades, Allison Park, PA, Pickwick Publications, 1983, pp. 117–90.

18 Although I will not cite them below, for helpful and relevant analyses see two essays by Edward Henderson, 'Knowing Persons and Knowing God,' *The Thomist* 46 (1982), pp. 394–422 and 'Valuing in Knowing God: An Interpretation of Austin Farrer's Religious Epistemology', *Modern Theology* 1 (1985), pp. 165–82.

19 For more detail on the material covered in this section, see Robert MacSwain, *Solved by Sacrifice: Austin Farrer, Fideism, and the Evidence of Faith*, Leuven, Peeters, 2013, chs 3 and 4. For a brief introduction to Farrer's thought, including his work in biblical studies and theology as well as philosophy, see Robert MacSwain, 'Austin Farrer', in *Twentieth-Century Anglican Theologians*, ed. Stephen Burns, Bryan Cones and James Tengatenga, 2020 (forthcoming).

20 Austin Farrer, *Finite and Infinite: A Philosophical Essay*, Westminster, Dacre Press, 1943 (2nd edn, 1959).

21 The term seems to have been coined by Rod Sykes in 'Soft Rationalism', *International Journal for Philosophy of Religion* VIII (1977), pp. 51–66.

22 See Farrer, *Finite and Infinite*, pp. 5–6. Farrer thus also anticipates the later focus of analytic philosophical theology in engaging directly with Christian doctrines such as Trinity and incarnation without initially seeking to demonstrate their truth.

23 Ibid., p. 8.

24 Ibid., pp. 9–10.

25 Ibid., p. 4 and Farrer's 1963 letter to Allen on pp. 241-2 of MacSwain, *Solved by Sacrifice*.

26 Farrer, *Finite and Infinite*, p. 2.

27 Ibid., p. 232.

28 Greco, 'Knowledge of God', pp. 10–11.

29 Ibid., p. 12.

30 Farrer, *Finite and Infinite*, p. 294.

31 Ibid., p. 231.

32 Austin Farrer, *The Freedom of the Will: The Gifford Lectures delivered in the University of Edinburgh, 1957*, London, Adam and Charles Black, 1958; 2nd edn, 1963, p. 309.

33 Austin Farrer, *Faith and Speculation: An Essay in Philosophical Theology*, London, Adam and Charles Black, 1967, p. 22. Note the self-quotation from *Finite and Infinite*, p. 294.

34 Ibid., p. 57. In making these claims Farrer was influenced by Diogenes Allen: what Farrer calls 'blessings' Allen calls 'nourishment'. In context it is clear that both Farrer and Allen are speaking of spiritual rather than material benefits and so such talk should not be confused with what is sometimes called the 'prosperity gospel'. I am grateful to Ben Cowgill for pointing out the need for clarification here.

35 Austin Farrer, *Saving Belief: A Discussion of Essentials*, London, Hodder and Stoughton, 1964, pp. 11–34. 'Faith and Evidence' has been reprinted in *The Truth-Seeking Heart: Austin Farrer and His Writings*, ed. Ann Loades and Robert MacSwain, Norwich, Canterbury Press, 2006, pp. 168–84; the phrase 'evidence of faith' is found on p. 26 of the original and p. 179 of the reprint.

36 Farrer, 'Faith and Evidence', p. 22 (176 in the reprint). For more detail, see MacSwain, *Solved by Sacrifice*, pp. 160–72. In my view, this development amounts to a shift from soft rationalism to a subtle form of moderate fideism, although this claim has been contested: see, for example, Brian Hebblethwaite's review of *Solved by Sacrifice*, *Faith and Philosophy* 31 (2014), pp. 490–2. For a more sympathetic response to this aspect of my argument, see Sergio Sorrentino's review, *European Journal for Philosophy of Religion* 9 (2017) pp. 209–12.

37 For the basic details of Allen's life and career, see MacSwain, *Solved by Sacrifice*, pp. 40–1, 174-5. He eventually succeeded John Hick as the Stuart Professor of Philosophy at Princeton Theological Seminary.

38 For DeBoer, see https://archives.calvin.edu/index.php?p=collections/findingaid&id=42& q=#bioghist; for Jellama, see https://calvin.edu/academics/departments-programs/philosophy/ lecture-series/ (both accessed 21 September 2019).

39 The version of Allen's doctoral thesis read by Farrer was *Motives, Evidence, and Religious Commitment* (1964), the revision accepted by Yale for the PhD was *Faith as a Ground for Religious Beliefs* (1965), and the final version was published as *The Reasonableness of Faith: A Philosophical Essay on the Grounds for Religious Belief*, Washington, DC, Corpus Books, 1968. Allen presented the central argument in 'Motives, Rationales, and Religious Beliefs', *American Philosophical Quarterly* 3 (1966): 111–27. For Farrer's letters to Allen, see *Solved by Sacrifice*, Appendix (B), pp. 240-9. Farrer acknowledged Allen's influence in the preface to *Faith and Speculation*, vi, and cited Allen's 'Motives, Rationales, and Religious Beliefs' in the first chapter on 10.

40 MacSwain, *Solved by Sacrifice*, Appendix (B), Letter 6, p. 248.

41 Allen, 'Motives, Rationales, and Religious Beliefs', pp. 111–12.

42 Ibid., p. 111.

43 Ibid.

44 Ibid., pp. 112–13. The first two examples are Allen's, but he clearly does not limit himself to them.

45 Ibid., p. 113.

46 The preceding five paragraphs were adapted from MacSwain, *Solved by Sacrifice*, pp. 177–82.

47 Greco, 'Knowledge of God', p. 12.

48 Farrer, *Faith and Speculation*, p. 1: note how he explicitly used Allen's terms of 'motives' and 'grounds'.

49 See Diogenes Allen, 'Faith and the Recognition of God's Activity', in *Divine Action: Studies Inspired by the Philosophical Theology of Austin Farrer*, ed. Brian Hebblethwaite and Edward Henderson, Edinburgh, T & T Clark, 1990, pp. 197–210 and *Christian Belief in a Postmodern World: The Full Wealth of Conviction*, Louisville, KY, Westminster/John Knox Press, 1992.

50 William J. Wainwright, *Reason and the Heart: A Prolegomenon to a Critique of Passional Reason*, Ithaca, NY, Cornell University Press, 1995, p. 3. See also his *Reason, Revelation, and Devotion: Inference and Argument in Religion*, New York, Cambridge University Press, 2015.

51 See, for example, Sarah Coakley, 'Response' to William P. Alston, 'Biblical Criticism and the Resurrection', in *The Resurrection: An Interdisciplinary Symposium on the Resurrection of Christ*, ed. Stephen Davis, Daniel Kendall SJ and Gerald O'Collins SJ, Oxford, Oxford University Press, 1997, pp. 184–90; 'The Resurrection and the "Spiritual Senses": On Wittgenstein, Epistemology and the Risen Christ', in Sarah Coakley, *Powers and Submissions: Spirituality, Philosophy and Gender*, Oxford, Blackwell Publishers, 2002, pp. 130–52; and 'Dark Contemplation and Epistemic Transformation: The Analytic Theologian Re-Meets Teresa of Ávila', in *Analytic Theology: New Essays in the Philosophy of Theology*, ed. Oliver D. Crisp and Michael C. Rea, Oxford, Oxford University Press, 2009, pp. 280–312.

52 See Harriet A. Harris, 'Does Analytical Philosophy Clip our Wings?', in *Faith and Philosophical Analysis: The Impact of Analytical Philosophy on the Philosophy of Religion*, ed. Harriet A. Harris and Christopher J. Insole, Aldershot, Ashgate Publications, 2005, pp. 100–218.

53 I am grateful to David Brown, Ben Cowgill, Stanley Hauerwas, Ann Loades and the editors for helpful comments on earlier versions of this essay.

7

Farrer's Theism: *Finite and Infinite*

PAUL DEHART

Finite and Infinite, Austin Farrer's first book (1943), is one of the most penetrating and ambitious essays in philosophical theism to appear in the twentieth century.[1] Its initial impact, however, was muted; its subsequent influence has likewise been difficult to discern. Why should this be? Some difficulties are internal to the work itself. The scope and complexity of the argument is exacerbated by Farrer's style of writing; his pursuit of a richly varied and allusive language tends to sacrifice transparency and immediacy. Nor were external conditions promising for a ready reception. Its appearance during the middle of World War Two did not help, and its commendation of classical theism had to swim against the rapidly swelling tide of logical positivism and linguistic analysis within English philosophy (Ayer's *Language, Truth and Logic* had appeared in 1936).

Beyond these obvious hindrances lies a more subtle consideration; Farrer's book presented from the outset difficulties of classification, and continues to do so. He insisted that it was a work of philosophy, not of doctrinal or systematic theology. But the age of the grand philosophical theisms (Alexander, Tennant, Whitehead etc.), a genre to which the book belongs even if as a polemical response, was ending; philosophy of religion was coming to designate a quite different style of thinking, as it still does today. There remained circles in which a more lasting echo might have been expected, namely those committed, like Farrer, to the retrieval of that classical monotheistic scheme (transcendent deity, creation *ex nihilo*) perfected, for many, by Thomas Aquinas and his commentators, medieval and modern. Yet here is in some ways the most curious circumstance of all. The ground for a resurgence of this venerable approach had been laid in the Anglophone world at least since A. E. Taylor's influential article on 'Theism' (1922) for Hastings' *Encyclopaedia*.[2] Creative Neo-Thomist thinking had been percolating for more than a decade in Catholic circles, especially in France (Gilson, Maritain). And yet Farrer's brilliant elaboration of this tradition seems scarcely to have been noticed within Catholic theology, while his potential role as its flag-carrier within Anglicanism was immediately usurped by E. L. Mascall, whose book *He Who Is* (much easier to digest but decidedly superficial by comparison) arrived the same year as Farrer's.[3]

In fact, though Farrer claimed Thomist inspiration for his book, to conventional eyes it looked nothing like what such a volume should look like. The result has been that, to this day, even amid the lively conversations among Catholic and other philosophical theologians developing the thought of Thomas Aquinas, Farrer is all too rarely mentioned. Though the book's profound intelligence has always been acknowledged, a relatively brief flurry of discussion, most influentially at Yale under Julian Hartt, soon gave way to neglect.[4] This is true even within discussions centring on Farrer's thought. During his lifetime the latter's work as a New Testament exegete generated much discussion; his sophisticated meditation on revelation in the Bampton Lectures (*The Glass of Vision*) was another touchstone for commentary. As for philosophical theology, his influence within several more specialized conversations has largely been mediated by his later, more compact texts: *Love Almighty and Ills Unlimited* (theodicy), *A Science of God?* (religion and empirical knowledge), *Faith and Speculation* (divine action within the world).[5]

So what was Farrer up to, after all, in *Finite and Infinite*? He understood himself to be constructing a rational argument for a more or less traditional or classical theistic understanding of God as absolute or transcendent creator. In his day this involved him, as he put it, in a debate between 'Thomists' and 'Moderns', and it is the highly original position he staked out within this conflict that is the key to understanding the nature of the book, its spotty reception and its potential contributions in the present.[6] For Farrer took both sides of this debate with unusual seriousness; as will soon be seen, he grasped those aspects of traditional theistic argument that must appear doubtful under contemporary philosophical conditions, and allowed these critical insights to alter in decisive ways his appropriation of tradition. In order to see how this is so, the intent and logical articulation of his book as a whole must first be summarized. Only then will it be possible to highlight three areas in which Farrer has departed from the main lines of Aquinas's own approach to the creator God. In light of these findings, the chapter will end by briefly addressing two questions. First, does his 'modernity' call into question Farrer's own sense that his essay was essentially Thomist? Second, what promising insights does this book bequeath to later philosophical theologians, especially those endeavouring to think through the classical theistic model?

The preface (in both its original version and in its revision for the second edition of 1959) is highly illuminating as to Farrer's intentions. His goal is to take up the traditional theology of the creator God developed and refined over the centuries prior to modernity, and to see how much of this edifice of thought can be supported by purely rational argument, apart from any appeal to divine revelation.[7] Such an argument will work through a philosophical analysis of limited or finite being or worldly process that discloses its incapability, precisely as finite, of maintaining itself in existence.[8] That is, the very structure of finite worldly units and relations in their operation contains an implicit, and necessary, reference to a unit and an operation that is not finite, and upon which they depend. This systematic relation of dependence between the multiple finite and the one infinite is what Farrer calls the 'Cosmological Idea'.[9]

Such, in broad outline, has been the perennial rational theology that Farrer seeks to retrieve in updated form. He further introduces certain stipulations that will determine the strategy and components of his particular version. Very early he makes a distinction between analysis and dialectic. The former examines the logical elements of the Cosmological Idea, laying bare relations of evidence, inference and analogy; it seeks to show how it 'works' in rational terms, without seeking persuasion or assertion of its truth. Dialectical reasoning, on the other hand, begins by drawing the attention of persons to aspects of the world and its ordering within experience as commonly interpreted that implicitly demand God's activity. The dialectic proper then proceeds to 'start from their scraps of crypto-theism and show how these can only be upheld in a fully theistic position, and how the denial of such a position removes them wholly.'[10] In other words, dialectic (which has provided the basic form of the various historically propounded arguments for divinity) works to 'enlarge the vision' of people such that they are led to see how the world they encounter is actually an ingredient within that larger structure of being unveiled by analysis: 'God as effecting the world and the world as the effect of God,' i.e. the Cosmological Idea.[11]

Farrer's other main stipulation springs from the fact that the Cosmological Idea works via analogies based on agency; finite agents are the key to grasping the infinite agent they deficiently reflect. But that requires an understanding of finite activity-in-general (being) in its varied modes as distributed into *things*: structured and relatively continuous centres of activity, more or less well-defined packets of agency. That activity persists in such abiding and organizing patterns and leads to the identification of substrates of manifold operation, or what has traditionally been called substances. Now, everyday human experience of the world spontaneously organizes itself into just such a picture of things-in-relation. But in philosophy, the combination of empiricist scepticism and scientific reductionism has for centuries relegated substance to the status of a redundant fiction. If, then, the Cosmological Idea, the central analogy upon which depends the rational construal of the creator God, employs substances or things as its evident starting point, then before one can even begin conceiving God rationally one must get clarity on the reality and status of substances or 'things' as authentic metaphysical elements. Clearly this leaves Farrer considerable work to do.

These stipulations account for the two most striking features of Farrer's tripartite undertaking. Farrer is convinced that any attempt to manoeuvre observers into a rational assent to, or even sympathetic entertainment of, the Cosmological Idea is logically secondary to a delineation of the conceptual structure of that Idea. As a result, the book's first part is given over to such an analysis, while the third part is left to lay out the different possible modes of arguing for the factuality of the God–world relation. The relative cogency of the different sorts of argument (more bluntly, their respective degrees of speciousness) is determined from the basic structure of the Idea itself. Thus, in a nod to Kant, *Finite and Infinite*'s discussion of God comprises an Analytic and a Dialectic. But these opening and conclud- ing parts are dwarfed by the mammoth second part sandwiched between them (200 of the book's 300 pages). God, the infinite agent or substance, is not the topic here at all, but rather finitude as such. In light of modern epistemic assumptions, Farrer held that the standard conceptual anat- omy of substance developed in ancient and medieval thought could not be sustained. But substance (defined units of agency) there must be if the Cosmological Idea is to be vindicated. Hence the necessity, and the length of this middle part; as he put it, Farrer had to 'reconstruct' the doctrine of substance.

A hasty overview of each part will give some sense of the scope, intricacy and ambition of Farrer's project. The first part clarifies the goal: not to discover new, hitherto unknown grounds for theistic belief, but rather to clarify what has always been confusedly known[12] in monotheistic religious consciousness, by revealing the 'mental machinery' of the Cosmological Idea.[13] According to this notion each and every creature bears an identical relation of dependence upon the creator, a relation that is utterly unique in kind. Descartes provides the initial orientation as to how this implicit idea of the creator can be brought to light; not as the conclusion of a line of inferential reasoning, but rather as an idea already apprehended in and through the apprehension of the creative effects.[14] Since the relation of the creator to effected finite things is not an instance of a class of relations, it can only be 'quasi-described' by analogies with the metaphysical relations obtaining within and between finite things.[15] Such relations are specified through the metaphysical discernment of a real order within the world that is neither 'accidental concomitance' nor 'logical implication'.[16] The basic elements of this order are the finite substances themselves.[17]

If these substances are discrete instances of agency, that is units of activity characterized and differentiated (and hence limited) by particular modes, then the infinite analogue will precisely be sheer or pure activity, without limiting mode. But how can 'absolute existence' possibly be characterized rationally?[18] Through extrapolation from finite agency. Traditionally, a 'scale of nature' was constructed, a hierarchy of types of substances ris- ing toward the perfection of divinity, but this problematically presumed acquaintance with substances in their essential ordering. Yet there is one finite unit of activity that is accessible to us, for it is our self: '[O]ur own voluntary conscious acts form a continuous scale of ascent and descent.' Through direct insight into our own personal acts we can note their increas- ing or decreasing realization of 'the forms of apprehension (objective grasp of realities), rationality (appropriate response to them), and will (freedom)'.[19] By postulating to their perfect extent our own fragmentary acts of freedom and noesis, we intellectually realize ourselves as *imago dei*.[20] After we mentally *ascend* the ladder of our own perfection (though awareness of non-human finite substances prevents the mere apotheosis of the human), we must then *extend* these features of spirit in the forms proper to perfect being by denying their inherent limitations. The result is a (negative) characterization of absolute act: absolute unity, complete independence, universal relevance.

We can prescind from much of the detail of the long second part; though an extraordinary achievement in philosophical analysis of human selfhood and agency, its actual contribution to the Cosmological Idea is only indirect, forming the requisite finite presupposition of the infinite analogy. Though the execution is a delicate matter, his plan is simple: to liberate our notion of substance from its traditional Aristotelian conception by portraying our cognitive apprehension of 'things' as such in and through our internal perspective on our own agency. This involves four steps. The first step is to show how meaningful propositions about substance and being are possible at all,[21] in face of two sorts of critique. On the one hand, Farrer concedes that the structure of language as such does not reflect the real order of things but is conditioned by human mental processes;[22] the Aristotelian metaphysic naively projects the logical ordering of propositions (subject–predicate) onto reality (substance–accident). He responds that Aristotle was indeed wrong in assuming a necessary symmetry between world and thought, but his true insight was to show how our ordinary language expresses the setting of our actual traffic with substance:[23] namely, as relatively stable selves interacting with a world of things possessing a persistent unity and independence sufficient to function as counterparts to our action.[24] On the other hand, Farrer agrees with the empiricist principle that meaningful utterance about entities is premised upon their presenting discernible and practically-relevant differences within the field of our experience.[25] But he has a retort to the anti-metaphysical corollary that substance and being are universal and hence meaningless in this regard. Propositions about substance can signify because being (activity) is not an indifferent universal but a diversifying principle; it is distributed into different bundles, and the patterns or modes of bundling are in turn of different types.[26]

With these logical preliminaries out of the way, Farrer turns in his second step to that locus within our experience where the shape of our own agency is most sharply evident to us, namely in the struggle of moral decision-making. Will is defined here as the power that organizes and focusses the mental and bodily elements of a human person toward the processual enactment of a chosen pattern of action,[27] an intervention in the world based on an intelligent apprehension of it. The pattern passes (at least in intent, unless defeated by circumstances) from envisionment to actualization; it is exclusively due to will's marshalling of subordinate bodily and mental units into a real pattern that subordinates and integrates them, in effect realizing the agent *qua* that act. It is in the struggle of explicit choice that will is most self-aware and free, though Farrer notes this is only the most transparent instance of willed action, since most of our enactments lie on a spectrum of decreasing consciousness and increasing automatism. But in its highest degree of evidence will becomes the template for grasping all substantial relation: 'how real connection creates real units relevant for it'. As he puts it, the act of will 'posits its own final phase as a complex,' holding together its elements which 'would not ever exist unless the whole pattern were there to be the form of an act of will'.[28]

If the single act of will is 'a complex unit with a unity that is metaphysically real,' its relation to the larger complex called the self, of which it is itself a component, must be explored in a third step. Here Farrer builds up his model of the agent-self by expanding the point-unity of the single act of will into multiple, more encompassing and temporally extended modes of unity: starting from the basic pattern of maintaining organic bodily functioning, elaborating along the margin of this pattern a 'super-pattern' of evolving projects of the self, and temporally concentrating in each specific act prior phases of the self as integral components of its present actuality. The unity of the self as such is indescribable but these different abstractions from it help to characterize its unity as a focussing of many acts in one and a continuity of activity from one act to the next.[29] With this difficult ground laid the fourth and final step is relatively easy. Though one's knowledge of things in general is never directly presented ('empty'), Farrer shows how they are apprehended through a schematic extension of the only substance that can be immediately known, one's own self.[30]

The prime theological relevance of the knowledge of finite substance that he has taken such pains to secure is made clear by Farrer in an important summary:

> For (a) one type of analogical and causal knowledge prepares us for another yet further removed: (b) the existence of several sorts and degrees of substance prepares us for the possibility of a quite other degree, the absolute: (c) we use of necessity the analogy of distinct sorts of substance and of their external relation in thinking of God and the world related: (d) the plurality, variety and mutual externality of finite substances reveal by contrast the unity and necessity of God's being, and so constitute a springboard for theological dialectic, additional to that provided by the mere metaphysical finitude of the individual self: (e) the demonstration that all that is, is substance ... enables us to understand everything, and not our own conscious being only, as dependent upon the creativity of God.[31]

With all the essential analogical elements of the Cosmological Idea now laid out and rationally articulated Farrer is ready in the relatively short third part of the book to classify and evaluate the different proofs of God's existence by showing how each takes up one or another of the now schematised aspects and relations of finite agency. Instead of an historical inventory of these proofs, Farrer uses the scheme he has already developed to provide an abstract classification of possible modes of theistic argument. Two different kinds of differentiation are combined to present a grid of possibilities; the concrete arguments actually recognised from history are then assigned their places within this scheme. This has the advantage of clarifying the logical relationships between the different kinds of argument, as well as indicating their relative strengths and weaknesses. Because dialectic of its nature must combine logical consistency with persuasive appeal, in any given kind there is a trade-off between conceptual rigour on one side, immediacy and impact on the other; hence for Farrer there is a utility in their aggregation that belies their individual weaknesses.

All theistic arguments for a creator begin from the experienced fact of constitutive but contingent combinations of elements that go to make up finite things and relations. One axis of Farrer's classifying grid is provided by different modes of appeal from these evident finite distinctions to an infinite agency grounding their combination.[32] Thus 'immanental' arguments accept one element as given, positing divine action as the provision of the other; 'transcendental' arguments rather begin from the combination as such, grasping its very 'composition' as evidence of derivation from a reality displaying the relevant content as pure identity or simplicity; finally, 'experiential' arguments adduce actual instances of finite combination as intuitive apprehensions of divine activity. The other axis concerns not the mode of appeal, but the scope of experienced finitude on the basis of which the appeal is made.[33] Here Farrer distinguishes (1) arguments from the limitations inherent within beings in general, i.e. the way the total possibility of existence or activity is contingently pared down to distinctly circumscribed modes; (2) arguments from substantial relations, i.e. the way finite agency in general must combine the intelligible character of its activity with its gradual actualization or serial repetition or its 'chaotic' determination by external agency etc.; and (3) anthropological arguments, i.e. appeals to the need to account for the inherently meaningless limitation and division to which specifically human agency is subject (the functional 'impurity' of intellection and of willing in themselves, their juxtaposition as related yet distinct expressions of intelligent act, etc.).

With the achievement of this scheme of arguments for transcendent theism, accompanied by Farrer's different evaluative judgements, 'the true conclusion of this book' is attained.[34] He means that in securing the logical coherence and meaningfulness of infinite act and finite freedom, purely rational theology has done all it can do. It cannot go on to deduce properly theological positions such as providence, grace or human immortality, but it presents a metaphysical scheme in which their possibility cannot be fore-closed. The preceding quick sketch cannot do justice to the care and detail of Farrer's argumentation, nor to his concessions and frank assessments of the limits and difficulties of the various lines of reasoning involved. But it has now given sufficient orientation to the nature of Farrer's project to allow us to discern those ways in which it departs from that style of think-ing in which transcendental theism historically received its most elaborated and influential form: Thomism. I will suggest three areas in which Farrer's decisions noticeably part ways with the venerable Thomist tradition.

The first difference concerns mode of argumentation. Aquinas shared with his entire intellectual generation an exhilarating confidence in the ability of syllogistic reasoning as codified by Aristotle to achieve conclu-sive results within every sphere of intellectual inquiry. It was entirely in line with his age's scientific ideal for Aquinas to cast his great theological syntheses in the form of demonstrations, and this replicated the formal pedagogy of the university as well. Testimony to his faith in formal proof was his assumption that no false conclusion was susceptible of properly premised and logically correct demonstration. The far more nuanced, even ambiguous role assigned by Farrer to the proofs of God's existence immedi-ately marks the different intellectual universe of *Finite and Infinite*. Deeply concerned as he is with the rationality of theistic assertions, he has aban-doned any notion that they can be derived in a logically compelling way from a universally available starting point. Instead, his model argumenta-tive strategy is to elicit the vision of deity latent within the very structure of our everyday experience of ourselves interacting with the world. The combination of analysis and dialectic is intended to draw out the implicit, unrecognized apprehension of infinite divine agency already involved in our encounter with finitude.

A second difference between Aquinas's theism and Farrer's lies in the primary metaphysical function assigned to deity. For Aquinas, reason's entry point into the thought of God is the question of universal causality; the meaning and cogency of the concept 'God' is the meaning and cogency of the concept of the source of all actuality, order and change. He derives from this basic notion the two master concepts upon which he hangs much of his rational elucidation of God's being: that of the absolutely unmoved mover of all things, and that of the absolute perfection combining the removal of all limitation with the concentration of all worldly excellence. Farrer's master metaphysical concept, by contrast, is the ideal of action as such. The initial perspective assumed is that of the self's own exercise of rational and voluntary agency. The idea of being as actuality, of substance as the persistent patterning or formal organization and unification in act of relatively disaggregate elements ('matter') and of intelligent grasping and freely chosen shaping of reality: all these emerge from within our direct acquaintance of being agents. The entry point into the concept of God is the unlimited extrapolation of this: the sheer exercise of activity as activity, completely unfettered by limits of modality or material resistance, under-stood as the ultimate extension or purification of the spiritual operations of intellect and will.

The crucial analogical role assigned here to human intelligence and free-dom within the concept of God is of course present in Aquinas; precisely as universal cause or creator God displays the supreme excellence of mind. But this points to a third and final way in which Farrer has differently con-structed his theistic arguments, namely through his privileging a different analogy of eminence. Both Aquinas and Farrer employ the model of human spiritual activity to account for the way in which the totality of positive metaphysical qualities present in the finite order find their ideal and original unity in the divine being, freed from the dispersal, mutual interference and inherent constraints of their creaturely agency. Thus both recognize the essential part played in theistic conceptions of eminent containment, the prior and perfect possession of every creaturely actuality within the divine act.

But each chooses to develop a different aspect of human mental operation as the primary analogy for understanding this eminence. For Aquinas, it is the cognitive operation, understanding, that provides the model for scaling up finite qualities into infinity. The removal of multiplicity, randomness and limitation within the divine plenitude is conceived along the lines of a per-fect act of intelligence, where the profuse data delivered through sensuous contact with the world are grasped as so many fragments of a higher con-ceptual unity, logical elements of a rich universal pattern. Farrer, however, appropriates the volitional side of the human act to picture the eminence of the finite in the infinite. His approach runs from being as activity, to its distribution into substances as centres of coherent patterns of activity, to willed, conscious exercises of choice as the paradigm case of directly accessible substantial agency. Thus the conception of God as pure being (activity) is oriented toward the willed act in its perfect form: maximal focal integration (*contra* functional dispersal), independence (*contra* exter-nal conditioning), scope (*contra* locality) and creativity (*contra* constrained options).

These three departures mark Farrer's independence of textbook Thomism; they might well appear major aberrations from Thomistic teaching. Even more disorienting is the undeniable paucity of reference to Aquinas; *Finite and Infinite* refers to him only six times, mostly in passing. The word 'Thomist' adds another five to the tally (nor are all these references positive). Consider that Leibniz and Bergson each claim a similar number of appear-ances, while Descartes receives 22 mentions, and Kant 25.[35] Readers might have justifiably asked whether this is really a work of Thomism at all; is it the 'Moderns' who actually triumph in Farrer's book? Against this impres-sion there are three things to be said.

First, we have Farrer's own vigorous assurances as to the true nature of his convictions. 'The Thomists possess the true principles for the solution of the problems of rational theology and above all the problems of analogical argument and analogical predication.'[36] In writing the book Farrer was 'possessed by the Thomist vision'.[37] Second, there are any number of specific positions assumed or developed throughout the book that are clearly Thomist in inspiration, even though Aquinas is not mentioned. Consider the following examples (they could be multiplied): the identity of essence and existence in God;[38] the agnostic element in all theistic analogy;[39] the classic divine attributes;[40] the cognitive achievement of intellect[41] and the role of omniformality;[42] the entire analysis of freedom within the human act;[43] will as universal appetite;[44] and the key role of disposition or habit in human agency.[45] But above all, third, the entire scheme of transcendent deity and its relation to finite creation, the way limited being is understood as the fragmentation or diminution of an absolutely prior act (i.e. the divine being itself), and the framework of analogical predication that conceptualizes our epistemic access to this unique metaphysical relationship: all this is manifestly Farrer's faithful restatement of an essentially Thomist scheme. As he says, the Cosmological Idea is simply his name for the 'Analogy of Being'.[46] And his insistence on the absoluteness of the creative relation in such a scheme[47] is the intended rejection of Thomism's modern rivals: correlative or 'dipolar' accounts of the God–world relation, whether of Hegelian or Whiteheadian stamp.

What then of Farrer's departures from Aquinas? These are indeed moments in his discussion where his modern philosophical sensitivities lead him to move aspects of the overall argument onto firmer ground, avoiding medieval presuppositions that now inevitably appear scientifically obsolete, linguistically naïve or epistemically overconfident. And yet even in the three select cases it must be said we are dealing not with oppositions or fundamental incompatibilities but with shifts in emphasis within a shared overarching vision. It is just these decisions of Farrer which point to the potential fertility of his first book for the conceptual elaboration of Christian theism even today. Already in 1896 Maurice Blondel said this about Thomism: 'Once a man has entered this system, he is himself assured; and from the centre of the fortress he can defend himself against all assaults and rebut all objections on points of detail. *But first he must effect his own entrance.*'[48] Getting inside Thomism's conceptual frame of reference: that is where the obstacles lie for moderns, according to Blondel. And that is where the continued fruitfulness of Farrer's essay is to be found.

Each of his three departures from standard appropriations of Aquinas serves to remove impediments to contemporary intellectual entrée into Thomism's theistic construal of reality. Releasing Aquinas's scheme from the pressure of demonstrative form not only heightens initial plausibility. It disentangles the logic of Aquinas's account of creation from a whole host of ancient cosmological and metaphysical presuppositions whose prior acceptance allowed the 'proofs' to get off the ground. Rather than delivering deity as the conclusion of a syllogism, Farrer uses Aquinas's ideas to evoke the vision of God tacitly projected by our active schematization of the worldly horizon. Similarly, the move from universal cause to ideal agent relieves the theologian of the burden, rendered much more difficult by vastly increased scientific knowledge, of drawing all classes of creatures onto a single trajectory of ascending proximity to the divine fullness of being. This strategy also enables a more direct conceptual path to the personal aspects of that fullness. Finally, locating the primary personal analogate within the volitional rather than the cognitive side of our subjectivity has several advantages. For one thing, it rebalances a problematically one-sided 'intellectualist' emphasis within the Thomist tradition (but thereby also points to some of those suppressed aspects of Aquinas's own understanding of cognition that Pierre Rousselot had emphasized).[49] Second, it sidesteps for purposes of theistic argument the modern difficulty of conceptualizing the act of intelligence in its true scope (a problem later tackled by Bernard Lonergan, though he began exploring it in Farrer's day).[50] Third, it links the rational idea of God more closely to the aspect of subjective agency that is both more intuitively available to us and more intimate to our sense of individual identity.

In fact, here in sum is to be found the power of Farrer's approach, what he absorbs from the 'Moderns'. His retrieval of Aquinas partakes of the fundamental philosophical revolution of modernity, already recognized as unavoidable by Blondel: the need to begin the exposition of being from within an account or estimate of the structure of human subjectivity, its achievements and demands. Not only does Farrer's focus on our own agency highlight the most epistemically available access point for analogizing. It also, as he is quite aware,[51] closely connects the rational conception of God with spirituality; the deity argued for, though literally and properly unimaginable,[52] is palpably identical in sublimity and function with the object of Christian prayer throughout the centuries. I do not wish to suggest that Thomists will have no difficulties with some of Farrer's decisions. They will perhaps want to address the need to reintegrate will and intellection more thoroughly. They might demand further elaboration of the metaphysical principle of formality that is presupposed by Farrer,[53] but the neglect of which arguably allowed him later to lapse into a questionable dualism of formalism and voluntarism. In spite of these or other queries, Farrer's brilliant accomplishment, his assimilation and extension of Aquinas's theism, remains undiminished. Indeed, this chapter cannot communicate the extraordinary richness of *Finite and Infinite*; a keen insight or startlingly suggestive formulation is to be found on virtually every page. Farrer is most definitely a Thomist, but he has employed the reasoning of Aquinas not as a dialectic battering ram but in a manner far more delicate and persuasive. As if responding to Blondel's challenge, he deftly restates the analogy of being to usher us *into* the Thomist theory by way of its most natural yet surprising conclusion: that we are all already 'inside' the experience of God.

Notes

1 Unless otherwise indicated, citations will be to the second edition: Austin Farrer, *Finite and Infinite: A Philosophical Essay*, Westminster, Dacre Press, 1959. The first edition from 1943 has identical pagination except for the preface, which partially differs between the two editions. Citations to the preface of the first edition will be noted as such.

2 Alfred E. Taylor, 'Theism', in the *Encyclopaedia of Religion and Ethics*, ed. James Hastings, vol. 12, Edinburgh, T & T Clark, 1921.

3 Eric Lionel Mascall, *He Who Is: A Study in Traditional Theism*, London, Longmans Green, 1943.

4 Julian Hartt, 'Austin Farrer as Philosophical Theologian' in *For God and Clarity: New Essays in Honor of Austin Farrer*, ed. Jeffrey C. Eaton and Ann Loades, Allison Park, PA, Pickwick Publications, 1983, pp. 1–11.

5 This neglect of *Finite and Infinite* among Farrer students has also, I suspect, sometimes been driven by, and perhaps contributed to, a vague sense among many readers that he eventually moved on from that extravagant early work, that it did not represent the 'mature' Farrer. This is incorrect, though space prevents treating the problem in detail. To be sure, he had decided criticisms of certain aspects of the argument. See especially the preface to the second edition (ix–x) and Austin Farrer, *Faith and Speculation: An Essay in Philosophical Theology*, London, Adam & Charles Black, 1967, pp. 112–18. But a careful perusal of these discussions will show the quite specific character of his later demurrals from *Finite and Infinite*, alongside a general reaffirmation of its approach and arguments as a whole. The significance of his decision 16 years after its first appearance to reissue the book unaltered needs no comment.

6 For 'Thomists' and 'Moderns' see Farrer, *Finite and Infinite*, p. vi (1st edn).

7 Ibid., p. vii.

8 Ibid., pp. viii–ix.

9 Ibid., p. vi.

10 Ibid., p. 10.

11 Ibid., p. 12.

12 Ibid., p. 4.

13 Ibid., p. 2.

14 Ibid., p. 8.

15 Ibid., p. 24.

16 Ibid., p. 19.

17 Ibid., p. 20.

18 Ibid., pp. 35–6.

19 Ibid., p. 45.

20 Ibid., pp. 49–50.

21 Ibid., p. 63.

22 Ibid., p. 64.

23 Ibid., p. 65.

24 Ibid., p. 68.

25 Ibid., p. 71.

26 Ibid., p. 79.

27 Ibid., p. 115.

28 Ibid., p. 170.

29 Ibid., pp. 228–9.

30 Ibid., p. 230.

31 Ibid., p. 246.

32 Ibid., p. 263.

33 Ibid., pp. 264–5.

34 Ibid., p. 299.

35 For these numbers I use the index helpfully compiled in Brian Hebblethwaite and

Edward Henderson (eds), *Divine Action: Studies Inspired by the Philosophical Theology of Austin Farrer*, Edinburgh, T & T Clark, 1990, pp. 230–9.

36 Farrer, *Finite and Infinite*, vi (1st edn).

37 Ibid., p. ix.

38 Ibid., pp. 33–4.

39 Ibid., pp. 50–1.

40 Ibid., pp.59–60.

41 Ibid., p. 75.

42 Ibid., pp. 19, 151.

43 Ibid., pp.113, 128 et al.

44 Ibid., p. 148.

45 Ibid., p. 194.

46 Ibid., p.vi (1st edn).

47 Ibid., pp.37–8, p. 61.

48 Maurice Blondel, *The Letter on Apologetics* and *History and Dogma*, ed. and trans. Alexander Dru and Illtyd Trethowan, New York, Holt, Rinehart & Winston, 1964, p. 146 (italics added).

49 Pierre Rousselot, *Intelligence: Sense of Being, Faculty of God* [1908], trans. Andrew Tallon, Milwaukee, Marquette Univ. Press, 1999.

50 Bernard Lonergan, *Insight: A Study of Human Understanding*, London, Longmans, Green, 1957. The year *Finite and Infinite* was published, Lonergan was initiating the research into the shape and possibilities of Aquinas's account of intellection that bore fruit in the famous series (1946–9) of *Verbum* essays. See Bernard Lonergan, *Verbum: Word and Idea in Aquinas*, vol. 2 of *Collected Works of Bernard Lonergan*, Toronto, University of Toronto Press, 1997.

51 Farrer, *Finite and Infinite*, p. 3.

52 Ibid., p. 56.

53 Ibid., p. 42.

Language and Symbolism

8

Through a Glass? Farrer, Coleridge and Revelation

STEPHEN PLATTEN

In the process of arranging a seminar on Austin Farrer's works, the fiftieth anniversary of his death, four unpublished lectures were discovered, delivered in 1966, in the USA, just two years before he died. The third lecture was titled: 'How Far is Christian Doctrine Reformable?' Early on in the lecture Farrer touches on the theme of revelation and epistemology. He notes:

> Much has been talked in recent times, by way of setting up a contrast between a revelation of God in action, or event and a revelation of God in propositions or statements; of course to the disfavour of the second alternative. We are told that our predecessors conceived of divine revelation as a set of divinely dictated propositions from which learned theologians were to draw syllogistic inferences. True enough; only it is really quite a long time since people thought quite like that.[1]

Nonetheless, in spite of Farrer's final reflection there, one of his seminal contributions to twentieth-century theology was an original and pioneering theory of revelation which aimed to offer a proper and reasoned alternative both to a revelation of God in action or event, and the propositional theories of revelation to which he is referring above. Indeed, in the same essay he continues:

> In contrast to such propositionalism one is happy to say that the revelation of God in Christ, just as much as the works of nature, is what he does. But then what Christ does has the nature of meaningful human action, and a man's words are an essential part of his conduct; not to mention the fact that apart from a revealed instruction about the nature of Christ's person and action the mere things that happen to him do not signify what we mean by a unique revelation of God.[2]

Farrer is clear in what follows that there is a:

> divine concord ... between the words of Christ in Galilee or in Jerusalem, and the subsequent teaching of the Holy Ghost.[3]

Here, as throughout his metaphysic, Farrer is keen to allow no division to be drawn between human and divine action. This has essential implications for his entire theological corpus, alongside his specific writing on the nature of revelation. It is in his Bampton Lectures, published exactly as he delivered them,[4] *The Glass of Vision*, that he sets out his understanding of the nature of revelation most systematically. Elsewhere he reverts to the same theme and sometimes to expand on the themes encompassed in the Bampton Lectures in response to his critics.[5]

To revert to the main theme, however, Farrer states sharply in his third Bampton Lecture:

> It does not seem as though the theory of revelation by divine events alone is any more satisfactory than the theory of dictated propositions.[6]

It is not only in his philosophical works and biblical theology, however, where Farrer establishes the basis of his theory of revelation. It surfaces regularly in his sermons and in his devotional writings. There is a living *co-inherence* (a term to which we shall return), so, for example in his Lent Book for 1965, he writes:

> ... the Gospel narratives will often cast identification with Christ's act or attitude, and so (to use the traditional language of religion) he (the Christian) meditates what he reads.[7]

Farrer offers, then, a rich and integrated vision of the Christian life which both embraces and requires a clear understanding of the nature of revelation. God is the 'Creative Mind' and as such his thought wills us into existence and our actions become one with his. Humanity is co-creator with God, and so the finite and infinite co-inhere. The natural and the supernatural are to be seen as a continuum, and the ultimate exemplification of this is, of course, in Jesus: 'The God of religion is not different from the God of rational enquiry.'[8] Farrer was a thinker of great originality, and hardly used the modern scholarly apparatus of footnotes, endnotes and references, which makes it all the more difficult to speculate on precise sources. Nonetheless, we may seek influences or resonances with other writers and notably in this area of revelation (and indeed, in the key area of metaphysics) within which Farrer bound together the human and the divine.

One clear starting point in relation to Farrer's focus upon images and human imagination relates to the wider circle of scholars with whom he engaged in Oxford. In contrast to the Dionysian *via negativa*, Farrer's work is rooted in the *affirmation of images*. Farrer's closest confederate in this field and pursuit of truth was the novelist and theological writer, Charles Williams. Moreover, both Williams and Farrer either directly or by implication used the term *co-inherence*.[9] This term, used implicitly by the

Cappadocian Fathers, is echoed in the correlative concept of *perichoresis*. Williams writes:

> Coinherence had been the very pattern of Christendom; we were not to be merely inheritors of the name of salvation. Baptism signifies this: As it passes from the most material coinherence it is received into the supernatural.[10]

Williams is less precise than Farrer in his use of language but the two writers include very strong mutual resonances within their thinking. So Williams notes more precisely elsewhere:

> From Childbirth to the Divine Trinity Itself, the single nature thrives; there is here no difference between the *natural and that supernatural.*

Both writers also conceive of the nature of the Eucharist in these terms; so Williams:

> The great rite of this (as of much else) within the Christian Church is the Eucharist, where the coinherence is fully in action. 'He is in us and we in Him'.[11]

Farrer echoes this too, using very similar language to that which he uses in his Bampton Lectures:

> The natural and the supernatural joined, when Christ was conceived in Mary by the Holy Ghost. The mystery is continued and extended in this Holy Sacrament.[12]

Coinherence is a useful concept in emphasizing the inseparability of the divine and thus also talk of co-creation.

It is more than likely, then, that Farrer and Williams will together have explored this continuum of the human and divine imagination. Might there, however, be still earlier influences on Farrer in this essential element of his metaphysical theology? One of the possible influences that has been explored by scholars of literature and theology is that of Samuel Taylor Coleridge. The resonances between the thought of Coleridge and Farrer are remarkable in themselves. The key starting point here must be in the correlation or inseparability of the human and divine and the impact of this on the essence of divine revelation. In exploring the resonances here, we begin with an extract from Coleridge's *The Destiny of Nations*. He writes:

> For what is freedom, but the unfettered use
> Of all the powers which God for us had given?
> But chiefly this, him First, him Last to view.

Through meaner powers and secondary things
Effulgent, as through clouds that veil his blaze.
For all that meets the bodily sense I deem
Symbolical, one mighty alphabet
For infant minds; and we in this low world
Placed with our backs to bright Reality
That we may learn with one unwounded Ken
The substance from its shadow.[13]

These lines capture vividly Coleridge's understanding of both symbol and imagination. These lines underscore his belief that the universal is captured in the particular, the infinite in the finite (precisely reflected in Farrer), the objective in the subjective – 'one mighty alphabet for infant minds'. A similar coming together of the universal and the particular is there in his poem, 'The Eolian Harp':

And what if all of animated nature
Be but organic harps diversly fram'd,
That tremble into thought as o'er them sweeps
Plastic and vaste, one intellectual breeze,
At once the soul of each, and God of all.[14]

Again there is in Coleridge a clear integrated vision which encompasses his religious philosophy: Holy Scripture, for him, captures that 'one intellectual breeze', that 'alphabet', but it does not monopolize or exhaust it. Nor indeed does it suggest an understanding of Scripture requiring to be seen in a *propositional* manner wherein we may capture God's activity through an individual miracle or one piece of history. This suggests an almost exact parallel with the extract from Farrer with which we began, where he wrote:

> ... not to mention the fact that apart from a revealed instruction about the nature of Christ's person and action the more things that happen to him do not signify what we mean by a unique revelation of God.[15]

This leads one to a key point in understanding Coleridge's view of biblical inspiration:

> Does not the universally admitted canon – that each part of scripture must be interpreted by the spirit of the whole – lead to the same practised conclusion as that for which I am now contending; – namely that it is the *Spirit* of the Bible [my italics] and not the detached words and sentences, that is infallible or absolute?[16]

Coleridge's theory of biblical inspiration goes beyond this relatively limited assumption and builds upon what is described as his 'polar logic'[17], so that the inspiration of the biblical material is encountered in the poetic and symbolic. As the artist or author is inspired to write with the assistance of the divine Creator, so the Bible communicates its images in a similar manner. Elsewhere, again in the posthumously published *Confessions of an Inquiring Spirit*, Coleridge makes this point directly:

> Is the grace of God so confined, are the evidences of the present and activating Spirit, so dim and doubtful, that to be assured of the same, we must first take for granted that all the life and *cogency* [my italics] of our humanity is miraculously suspended?[18]

This reinforces the sense in which Coleridge's understanding of revelation issues from his basic philosophy of religion and 'polar logic'. Just as the poet is endowed with what Coleridge calls his 'shaping spirit of imagination', so is Scripture a product of the imagination. Here the imagination defines that intersection of the subjective and objective. In poetic imagery the books of Scripture communicate the infinite, the divine. So, in *Confessions* he notes:

> Whatever finds me, bears witness for itself that it has proceeded from a Holy Spirit.[19]

There are thus striking parallels between Coleridge's theory of biblical inspiration and that of Austin Farrer's Bampton Lectures. Thus, in what is perhaps one of the key paragraphs of his lectures, Farrer writes:

> Here, anyhow, is what I took from Spinoza. I would no longer attempt, with the psalmist, 'to set God before my face.' I would see him as the underlying cause of my thinking, especially of these thoughts in which I tried to think of him. I would dare to hope that sometimes my thought would become diaphanous, so that there should be some perception of the divine cause shining through the created effect, as a deep pool, setting into clear tranquillity, permits us to see the spring in the bottom of it from which its waters rise. I would dare to hope that through a second cause the First Cause might be felt, when the second cause in question was itself a spirit, made in the image of the divine Spirit, and perpetually welling up out of his creative act.[20]

Here, then, are clear resonances between Farrer's and Coleridge's understandings of biblical inspiration. In both writers the authority or inspiration of the Bible springs from a series of inspired poetical images. In each writer there is captured this same sense of what Coleridge calls *co-agency* and Farrer describes as co-creation. None of this argument has passed without criticism.[21] In relation to Farrer's argument, H. D. Lewis was unhappy with the notion that the key biblical images remain both plainly human constructs and yet also carry with them the marks of divinity. Was Farrer not wishing to have his cake and eat it? Oddly enough, Lewis is effectively falling into the same trap as some of the eighteenth-century rationalists against whom Coleridge was writing. There is an assumption that the two spheres cannot come together, and in making this assumption metaphysics itself is threatened. Far from assuming that the great controlling biblical images are beyond criticism, both Farrer and Coleridge are clear that the images will be subject to continued scrutiny and clarification. So, vividly, Farrer writes:

> ... images are *crucified* [my italics] by the reality, slowly and progressively, never completely and not always without pain: yet the reality is better than the images. Jesus Christ clothed himself in all the images of messianic promise, and in living them out, crucified them; but the crucified reality is better than the figures of prophecy.'[22]

Was Farrer influenced, then, by Coleridge, or did his own theory of scriptural inspiration spring up quite independently? The question is unanswerable. Throughout his writing, Farrer focussed upon the figural imagination in his biblical scholarship,[23] his philosophical theology,[24] his homiletical writings and, supremely, in his Bampton Lectures on scriptural inspiration. It is inconceivable that Farrer knew nothing of Coleridge, but whether he had encountered his prose writings on biblical inspiration is uncertain. Farrer noted that his great love outside his academic work was poetry. There is, however, another intriguing sentence from Coleridge's thought which is a further possible bridge between him and Farrer, and others in Farrer's intellectual circle. Coleridge writes:

> Revealed religion (and I know of no religion not revealed) is in its highest contemplation the unity, that is, the identity of co-inherence, of Subjective and Objective.[25]

Such language is resonant with Farrer's style, expression and content, the term coinherence offering a fascinating link. Both Farrer and Coleridge offer a constructive approach to Scripture – and indeed to the perennial and wearying arguments about *natural* and *revealed* theology. In both writers the natural and supernatural continuum is lost neither through inhabiting a private subjective religious world nor by adopting a rationalist and reductionist approach to the text. Farrer and Coleridge are keen to hold together the human and the divine, the finite and the infinite. To understand fully Farrer's use of the figural imagination as a key to biblical inspiration and thus to revelation returns us to the grounding of all this in Farrer's metaphysical/philosophical theology.

Recently, Rowan Williams has returned to this key area in Farrer's thought in his academic monograph which seeks to offer a clear understanding of Christology rooted in a theology of creation.[26] Williams' analysis of Farrer's work, which we shall discuss in more detail later, not only offers an essential starting point for his [Williams'] Christological reflections, but also offers clarifying insights on Farrer's broader philosophical theology. It also adds clarity to and strengthens Farrer's approach to revelation and his determination to hold together an integrated theology which includes the natural and the revelatory.

The beginnings of this crucial analysis are there in Farrer's first book, *Finite and Infinite*, which is a highly technical discussion of Thomist thought. Nonetheless, in his analysis here, Farrer lays the foundations for his notion of *double agency*, the coming together of natural and supernatural in divine activity. Farrer's notion of a double agency has been the source of continuing debate. There was a celebrated exchange focussing on this issue in the journal *Theology*, sparked off by a letter to the journal from David Galilee in 1975.

Galilee opines in a comment on Maurice Wiles' monograph *The Remaking of Christian Doctrine*:[27]

> Wiles' basic weakness is that he has apparently ignored the writings of Austin Farrer, the one English theologian who has recently tackled the thorny problem of how an action may be both God's and man's ... Farrer's treatment of the problem of the 'causal joint' in God's action in nature, history and man remains an outstanding and germane contribution to the very problem which Wiles so rightly tried to tackle.[28]

In 1981, Wiles returned to the fray acknowledging that both Galilee's critique and a similar critique by Brian Hebblethwaite[29] merited a response. So Wiles notes in responding to Farrer's language about the divine as an 'infinitely higher analogue':

> If divine agency is an infinitely higher analogue of human agency and cannot be conceived in action (which on the face of it seems a reasonable thing to try to do with the concept of agency) without degrading it to the creaturely level, how do we know whether or not we are talking sense? Can we be sure we are preserving the religious realities of the biblical witness, and not just keeping the language while substantially changing the sense?[30]

Later Wiles asks:

> Is complete agnosticism about how God acts compatible with belief that he does? Farrer insists that it is.[31]

Our understanding of how the biblical material communicates starts at the heart of this debate with Wiles signing off by arguing:

The struggle to come to terms with it (double agency), to which Galilee and Hebblethwaite have rightly directed me, has only served to strengthen my conviction that the process of trying to make sense of the biblical witness and of the experience of grace may well involve substantial modification of the concept of double agency or even its replacement by some other conceptuality altogether.[32]

The debate did not rest there and Galilee and Hebblethwaite replied responding to the issue of dissimilarity and noting:

We repeat that agnosticism over the modality of divine action is not to be confused with agnosticism over the meaning of the basic analogy of action with which Farrer operates or over the necessity of its use.[33]

Wiles came back with a final riposte in the same edition of the journal, taking up the image used by Galilee and Hebblethwaite of God as the 'author'. He asks whether a better model is of an improvised drama and concludes thus:

The resultant drama would be both his and theirs, a true case of double agency, even though one would be hesitant to speak of the author as the agent of any of the particular happenings within the drama.[34]

At this point the debate is left unresolved and there is a sense in which none of the dramatis personae in the debate has actually reached down to the basis of Farrer's understanding of the interrelationship of human and divine action.

If this is the case, the problem may be rooted in an inability of theologians to resort to what one might describe as Farrerian 'first principles'. Underlying this problem is the technical complexity of Farrer's first monograph in which he explores in detail and depth the relationship between the divine and the human in Thomistic categories. It is here that Rowan Williams' recent writing can move us on from the increasingly sterile debate noted above, a debate within which all engaged in the argument have not touched the roots of Farrer's analysis. Williams' reading of Farrer's Bampton Lectures is thus set within the context of his earlier analysis in *Finite and Infinite*. Williams argues that talk of *infinite causality* should not be used to close gaps within *finite causality*. Instead there is a personal relatedness between the divine and the human within both the divine life and the highest levels of the finite. So he notes:

... this relationship transformingly illuminates how human intelligence and love are rooted in infinite agency.[35]

We are at the very heart of understanding the basis of Farrer's theory of divine revelation within Scripture. Williams expands this by noting:

What it promises is an unlimited and conscious growth into an enhancement of human intelligence and love in communion with God's infinite action.[36]

So Farrer:

... [God] works through second causes effects which do not arise from the natural powers of those causes. It is by reference to the powers of second causes that events or states are called 'supernatural'. Nothing is supernatural to God, because his nature is infinity, and no action exceeds it. But many acts may be supernatural to man, because many conceivable achievements exceed his natural faculties to learn, for example, the mystery of Trinity in the Godhead.[37]

Here, then, Farrer extrapolates from the technical analysis of *Finite and Infinite* an understanding of the double agency of finite and infinite which both underpins his philosophical theology and his perception of how the divine is communicated from infinite agency or reality to the finite mind. In a telling image, Williams writes of the

... stuff of the world ... reorganised as if around a new magnetic point of focus.[38]

Returning then, for a moment to the vexed issue of agency, Farrer writes:

... in some true sense the creature and the Creator are both enacting the creatures' life, though in different ways at different depths.[39]

Here Farrer uses the unlikely example of the story of the 'Ass of Balaam' to illuminate his discussion of causality. In conclusion from this, he notes:

Upon this personal double agency in our one activity turns the verbally insoluble riddle of grace and freewill, or of Godhead and Manhood in Christ's One Person, or of the efficacy of human prayer.[40]

Relating this to Scripture again, Williams notes:

Farrer says, we embark on a search for clusters of metaphor in Scripture that point toward the presence of the unlimited within history,[41] ... the search for a hermeneutic of scriptural imagery that allows us to have our imaginations enlarged in the direction of that which cannot finally be 'imaged' with any adequacy – the reality of an unlimited actuality that can be thought of only in some sort of association with love and intelligence.[42]

Farrer's holding together the finite and the infinite, the human and the divine in his understanding of revelation offers a credible but also a critical appreciation of how the divine is communicated within the human being such that the often heralded divide between *natural* and *revealed theology* is itself seen too simplistically. That human consciousness engages with both the natural world of God's creation and of revelation of the divine action and will in Scripture is undeniable. Farrer's philosophical theology, however, indicates that both of these are part of one continuum whereby the finite and infinite are correlated.

Very early on, in *The Glass of Vision*, his Bampton Lectures, he argues:

Indeed, to distinguish between natural and revealed theology is positively misleading; it would be better to substitute other distractions: say the distinction between a theology based on God's action in particular historical facts – in the lives let us say, of prophets and saints. It would be more significant on this showing to call Christianity an historical religion than to call it a revealed religion.[43]

A critical edge is thus added to the key biblical hermeneutic. Biblical images must be set within the wider context both of individual books/genres in Scripture and within Scripture as a whole; selective use of scriptural quotation entirely ignores Farrer's understanding of revelation. Moreover, as Farrer himself notes, there is an abiding danger of reading into Scripture rather than allowing the text to speak for itself. He gives one illuminating example in relation to the doctrine of the Holy Trinity; nowhere in the New Testament is the doctrine of the Trinity argued or stated working from first principles. It is not discernible within the pages of Scripture either by philosophical analysis or by lexicography, but instead:

If we want to find the Divine Trinity in the New Testament, we must look for the image of the Divine Trinity. We must look for it as a particular image, here or there. Most of the time other images will be occupying the page: we must be content if we can find it anywhere. Our next endeavour, after we have found it must be to isolate it and distinguish it from other images, not to show that other images are really expressed in terms of it, for they are not. The Trinity is one of the images that appear, it is not a category of general application.[44]

Farrer's work, then, releases us from some of the captivity which different approaches to revelation can so easily entrap the human mind. As we have noted, embracing his broader philosophical theology not only offers a rational and imaginative (in every sense) understanding of the nature of revelation but also an integrated vision for theology, as Rowan Williams indicates, in using Farrer as the starting point for Christological reflection. At the same time, there is an opening out of how our religious epistemology and religious sensibility relates to human consciousness. There remains much debate about how unique the notion of consciousness is that key factor which defines humanity as a species. Undoubtedly, however, *religious consciousness* does mark off homo-sapiens from others within the animal kingdom. Here, Farrer's work on revelation speaks more widely within human sensibility. In relation to our possibility to conceive the supernatural, Farrer writes:

> I reply that the possibility derives from the very form of our active existence. We are primarily aware of ourselves as active beings, engaged in interaction with a whole environment of other active beings ... we have large scope for freedom, and the sense of freedom easily begets the dream of passing right beyond our nature into supernatural action.[45]

Further on he engages directly with the theme of consciousness itself. Reflecting on the more weird phenomena of clairvoyance and telepathy, he continues:

> We entirely agree that they belong to the top of the soul, for they are nothing but the specially striking manifestation of a power which accompanies rational consciousness throughout. The excellence of the mind consists of conscious intelligence, but of a conscious intelligence based upon acute senses and riding upon a vigorous imagination.[46]

This leads Farrer into a careful analysis of the relationship between religious sensibility and the imagination and distinguishing this from what he labels as the 'weird'. Being careful to retain a proper sense of human autonomy in this area, he notes:

> There is no question then of the finite excluding the infinite, as the finite excludes the finite. We can, no doubt state the limiting case: there is a point beyond which infinite God could not divinise his creature without removing its distinctive creaturely nature, and as it were merging it in himself: an act which would be exactly equivalent to its annihilation. But, short of this, we can set no limits to the supernatural enhancement God can bestow.[47]

Here, once again, is set out the possibility for our consciousness to engage with the supernatural, the infinite completely integrated with the human imagination. John Habgood captures this well and indeed refers to his connection to Farrer in his own Bampton Lectures:

> We get closer to the truth, I believe, if we describe the process of forming ideas about God and about humanity in terms of interaction. This seems to be what was happening in the story of Trinitarian theology. Ideas

about God and ideas about human personhood can be seen as developing together, each shaping and enriching the other. The late Austin Farrer in his book *The Glass of Vision* has a memorable paragraph describing a similar process in the growth of the idea of kingship.[48]

In this passage, Farrer indicates how he believes the two come together:

In fact the human King and the divine architect arrive at once, they are inseparable: each makes the other.[49]

In concluding an essay on Farrer's theory of imagination and revelation, Douglas Hedley notes:

It is the great virtue, I believe, of both Austin Farrer and Basil Mitchell to have defended a vision of theology in which the continuum of human creativity and divine action is so ably asserted.[50]

Hedley's comment here succinctly conjoins two essential contributions which proceed from Farrer's metaphysic, a metaphysic re-echoed in his late philosophical work[51] which revisited his arguments in *Finite and Infinite*, and which are also explored in his Gifford Lectures *The Freedom of the Will*.[52] Farrer's contribution is seminal in the manner in which the human and the divine, the objective and subjective, the finite and infinite are held together. Not only does this offer a creative approach to divine revelation, and indeed hold together an integrated theology rooted in Scripture and reflection upon nature, it also offers a dynamic model for the coinherence of human and divine action. Farrer's overall Thomist framework (pace Rowan Williams) gives a clear foundation for a metaphysical understanding of the universe. Supernatural terminology no longer defines a magical or crudely interventionist God, but an incarnational God coinhering with all creation in a proper pneumatology:

... the second cause in question ... [is] ... itself a spirit, made in the image of the divine Spirit, and perpetually welling up out of his creative act.[53]

Notes

1 *Austin Farrer, Oxford Warden, Scholar, Preacher*, ed. Stephen Platten, Markus Bock-muehl and Nevsky Everett, London, SCM Press, 2020.

2 Ibid.

3 Ibid.

4 Cf. Leonard Hodgson, Review in *The Guardian* (a weekly church magazine and not the national daily of that name), 28 January 1949: 'Unlike many others in the series, they are

printed exactly as they were delivered, even to the inclusion of the ascription with which each was closed in the pulpit.'

5 See, for example, in *Interpretation and Belief*, ed. Charles Conti, London, SPCK, 1976, 'Inspiration: Poetical and Divine.' Miss Helen Gardner demolished the literary side of my comparison in her Riddell Lectures, and Professor H. D. Lewis the theological in 'Our Experience of God.' There is some irony in Farrer's use of 'demolish' here, as he proceeds to expand positively on his earlier work in *The Glass of Vision*.

6 Austin Farrer, *The Glass of Vision*, London, Dacre Press, 1948, p. 38.

7 Austin Farrer, *The Triple Victory*, London, Faith Press, 1965, p. 12.

8 Austin Farrer, *A Science of God?*, London, Geoffrey Bles, 1966, p. 14.

9 Cf. Charles Williams, *The Image of the City*, London, Oxford University Press, 1958, pp. 154ff.

10 Charles Williams, *The Descent of the Dove*, London, Oxford University Press, 1939, pp. 162, 217.

11 Cf. Charles Hefling, *Jacob's Ladder*, Cambridge, MA, Cowley Publications, 1979, pp. 102f.

12 Austin Farrer, *The Crown of the Year*, London, Dacre Press, 1952, p. 47.

13 'The Destiny of Nations' in the *Complete Poetical Works of Samuel Taylor Coleridge*, ed. Ernest Hartley Coleridge, Oxford, Clarendon Press, 1912, p. 132.

14 'The Eolian Harp' in *Coleridge: Selected Poems*, ed. Richard Holmes, London, Harper-Collins, 1996, p. 37.

15 *Austin Farrer, Oxford Warden, Scholar, Preacher*.

16 Samuel Taylor Coleridge, *Confessions of an Inquiring Spirit* (published posthumously, 1853) published with *Aids to Reflection*, London, George Bell, 1904, pp. 325–6.

17 Here Coleridge developed a distinctive philosophical pattern in contrast to other 'rationalist' eighteenth-century writers. His 'polar logic' refers to his holding together of the objective and subjective. Cf. Stephen Platten, 'One intellectual breeze: Coleridge and a new apologetic', *Theology*, Sept. 2008, esp. pp. 324–6.

18 Coleridge, *Confessions*, p. 326.

19 Ibid., p. 295.

20 Farrer, *Glass*, p. 8.

21 See footnote 5 above.

22 Cf. here Austin Farrer, 'An English Appreciation' in *Kerygma and Myth*, ed. H. W. Bartsch, London, SPCK, 1953, pp. 22f and also David Brown, 'The role of images in theological reflection', in *The Human Person in God's World: Studies to Commemorate the Austin Farrer Centenary*, ed. Brian Hebblethwaite and Douglas Hedley, London, SCM Press, 2006, esp. pp. 89–96.

23 See, for example, Austin Farrer, *A Rebirth of Images*, London, Dacre Press, 1949, which is an imaginative commentary on the Revelation to St John the Divine. His monographs on St Mark and St Matthew use a similar literary approach.

24 Austin Farrer, *Reflective Faith*, ed. Charles Conti, London, SPCK, 1972. In the introduction, John Hick notes: 'Farrer argues that when we look at the world with the perceptiveness of the poet, not imposing our cultural categories upon it but letting it affect us in its own unique concrete particularity, our minds are led through the world by a rational path to its creator and sustainer' (p. xiv).

25 Coleridge, *Confessions*, p. 335.

26 Rowan Williams, *Christ the Heart of Creation*, London, Bloomsbury, 2018.

27 Maurice Wiles, *The Remaking of Christian Doctrine*, London, SCM Press, 1975.

28 David Galilee, 'The Remaking Defended', *Theology*, LXXVII, Oct. 1975, pp. 554–5.

29 Brian Hebblethwaite, 'Providence and Divine Action', in *Religious Studies*, 14(2), June, 1978.

30 Maurice Wiles, 'Farrer's Concept of Double Agency', in *Theology* Vol. LXXXIV, July 1981, p. 245,

31 Ibid., p. 247.

32 Ibid., p. 248.

33 David Galilee and Brian Hebblethwaite, 'Farrer's Concept of Double Agency: A Reply', in *Theology*, Vol. LXXXV, Number 703, Jan. 1982, p. 9.

34 Ibid., pp. 12–13.

35 Rowan Williams, *Christ the Heart of Creation*, London, Bloomsbury, 2018, p. 2.

36 Ibid., p. 3.

37 Farrer, *Glass*, p. 11.

38 Williams, *Christ*, p. 3.

39 Farrer, *Glass*, p. 33.

40 Austin Farrer, *Faith and Speculation*, London, A & C Black, 1967.

41 Cf. here esp. ch. VI 'Revelation and History', pp. 86–103.

42 Williams, *Christ*, p. 6.

43 Farrer, *Glass*, p. 2.

44 Ibid.

45 Farrer, *Glass*, p. 47.

46 Ibid., p. 14.

47 Ibid., p. 24.

48 John Habgood, *Being a Person: Where Faith and Science Meet*, London, Hodder and Stoughton, 1998, p. 45.

49 Farrer, *Glass*, p. 99.

50 Douglas Hedley, 'Austin Farrer's Shaping Spirit of Imagination', in *Scripture, Metaphysics and Poetry: Austin Farrer's The Glass of Vision with Critical Commentary*, ed. Robert MacSwain, Aldershot, Ashgate, 2013, p. 210. Also included in Hebblethwaite and Hedley, cf. note 22 above.

51 *Faith and Speculation*.

52 Austin Farrer, *The Freedom of the Will*, London, A & C Black, 1958.

53 Farrer, *Glass*, p. 8. Bracketed material is mine.

9

Language and Symbolism: Austin Farrer Meets Gregory of Nazianzus

MORWENNA LUDLOW

Images

In this chapter, I wish to explore some suggestive points of contact between Gregory of Nazianzus and Austin Farrer's theology of inspiration as set out in his Bampton Lectures, published collectively as *The Glass of Vision*. In the final two parts of my paper I will bring Gregory and Farrer more closely into conversation on the issue of the boundaries between inspiration and poetry – between divine and human acts of literary making. This is not to attempt to use Gregory to correct Farrer in some simplistic way, as if he has answers to questions which Farrer leaves unanswered. It is rather to suggest that Gregory prompts some questions which Farrer does not directly address in *The Glass of Vision*, but to which his concept of inspiration – however 'inexact' – might fruitfully be applied. The issue I wish to explore is what Farrer's ideas in *The Glass of Vision* might have to say about other, post-apostolic acts of Christian literary making. To narrow this down I will focus on the act of preaching: to what extent and in what ways is the preacher like (and unlike) an apostle and a poet?

In the third of the lectures which comprise *The Glass of Vision*, Farrer asks what should be looked for in Scripture, if one is to attend to God's voice.[1] He rejects the idea that one should read Scripture thinking that revelation is 'given in the form of propositions' – an assumption which he (very guardedly) attributes to pre-modern theologians (GV, pp. 37–8, 43). He is also critical of the view which separates revelation – understood as the person of Jesus Christ and events of his life—from Scripture which is a witness to them (GV, pp. 38–9). Such a separation of content from form tempts one to try to strip away the latter. But if one pursues such a strategy with Scripture, Farrer warns, the substance of revelation 'has an uncanny trick of evaporating once its accidents of expression are all removed' (GV, p. 38). Farrer's own approach is to see revelation as the dynamic interaction between God's self-revelation in Jesus Christ and the God-given images by which it is understood and interpreted.[2] Christ used such images as the Kingdom of God, the Son of Man and so on, to interpret his own words and deeds. Such images were inherited from Jesus' own scriptural tradition, but his own life and words gave them radically new meaning. Consequently, the interaction between event and images is mutual, so that 'the great images interpreted the events of Christ's ministry, death and resurrection, and the events interpreted the images; the interplay of the two is revelation' (GV, p. 42).

This doctrine of revelation as the interplay between event and images allows Farrer to affirm both that 'the revelation of deity to manhood is absolutely fulfilled in Christ himself' (a self-revelation 'by word and deed') *and* that 'the actions of Christ's will, the expressions of Christ's mind' are only 'the precious seeds of revelation' (GV, p. 41). The interplay of event and image begins with the life of Jesus Christ; these seeds are then taken up and developed by the apostles who, participating in the mind of Christ through the working of the Holy Spirit, 'worked out both the saving action and the revealing interpretation' (GV, pp. 40–1, 43). This process of 'working out' took place both in the life of the apostolic church in general and in the composition of the apostolic books in particular (GV, p. 51). Farrer is careful to balance the two of these, lest he diminish the life of the early church and commit what he calls 'the old biblicist error' that sees the Bible as the 'primary instrument of the Pentecostal Spirit' (GV, p. 51). As we have just seen, revelation for him is broader than the inspiration of the New Testament; the interaction of image and event can be experienced by believers now as it was by the apostles in, for example, baptism and Eucharist. The images thus continue to 'shape life as engagement with God'; believers 'can hope to know God's active presence', as they live by those images.[3] Nevertheless, Farrer's main interest in *The Glass of Vision* is Scripture. The focal point of his lectures seems to be an attempt to develop a coherent concept of scriptural inspiration, given the doctrine of revelation which has just been sketched out. It is this key focus that produces his core argument:

> In the apostolic mind ... the God-given images lived, not statically, but with an inexpressible creative force. The several distinct images grew together into fresh unities, opened out into new detail, attracted to themselves and assimilated further image-material: all this within the life of a generation. This is the way inspiration worked. The stuff of inspiration is living images. (GV, p. 43)

The biblical authors, then, experienced revelation (among other things) as the inspiration of the texts they composed. Because 'the stuff of inspiration is living images', the locus of inspiration is the human imagination.[4] But this is human imagination working beyond its natural limits. Divine inspiration is a supernatural form of knowledge which Farrer carefully distinguishes from the knowledge of God arising from natural theology (GV, Lecture V). As a supernatural act, this knowledge expresses both divine and human agency. Neither competes with the other; rather, inspiration opens up human imagination to the infinite, so that it is both continuous with, but transcends itself (GV, Lecture II, especially pp. 34–5).

This theological epistemology resonates strongly with that of Gregory of Nazianzus, especially as expressed in his so-called 'Theological Orations' (*Orations* 27–31 in the traditional numbering). In these, Gregory is arguing in particular against his opponent Eunomius, whom he accuses of believing that the statement 'the Father is ingenerate' is a true proposition that defines the divine nature. In response, Gregory argues that humans are limited in their knowledge of God not only by sin but also – and more fundamentally – by their creaturely nature. He points out that human mental activity is fundamentally embodied, while God is not; no proposition, no language is thus able to encapsulate the truth about the divine.[5] More than this: no human can even comprehend the divine nature.[6]

Gregory's condemnations of his opponents' 'complete obsession with setting and solving conundrums' resonates closely with Farrer's rejection of Aristotelian syllogisms as the stuff of theology: 'The believer in God must suppose that the mystery of God's existence is no mere puzzle, but a genuine mystery'.[7] Neither author is interested primarily with their opponents' actual philosophical sources; rather, they are concerned that once one claims that humans can have propositional knowledge of the divine nature, God's nature becomes a problem to be solved, not something to be worshipped. And, as with Farrer, Gregory's rejection of propositional knowledge of God leads him not to sheer apophaticism, but to the dual affirmation that humans can know God by faith/grace and that humans know what they know of God through faithful contemplation of images.[8] Just as Gregory rejects Plato's idea that language is a weak attempt to articulate a philosopher's non-verbalized (unimaged) knowledge of the divine nature, so Farrer rejects the idea that one could bypass theological images in order to access an imageless truth (GV, p. 93).

Gregory's frequently used archetype of the knowledge of God is that of Moses ascending Mount Sinai.[9] Moses' experience shows us, Gregory writes, that God is 'outlined' or 'sketched out' by the human mind, 'but only very dimly and in a limited way – not by things that represent him completely, but by the things that are peripheral to him, as one representation (φαντασία) is derived from another to form a kind of singular image (ἴνδαλμα) of the truth'.[10] Thus, as Christopher Beeley remarks, God is *truly* known, albeit not *completely* known, by the limited human mind ' through created images and ideas'.[11] Consequently, Gregory's famous definition of the greatest theologian is 'not the one who has discovered the entirety [of God's being] … but the one who has imagined (φαντασθῇ) more of it than someone else, and has gathered in him- or herself more of an appearance, or a faint trace, of the truth (τὸ τῆς ἀληθείας ἴνδαλμα, ἢ ἀποσκίασμα)'.[12] The role of the theologian, according to Gregory, is not to create these images, but to gather them, to sift them and use them wisely.[13]

Where do the images come from, according to Gregory? Farrer himself recognizes that the metaphysician and the natural theologian use analogies or metaphors; they are not just found in inspired Scripture. In particular, the philosopher might use analogy to try to express that which is absolutely singular, like the human soul or God. But the images of revelation are authoritatively communicated and supernatural, while the analogies used by natural theology and metaphysics are products of the natural imagination (GV, Lecture V, especially pp. 81–2).[14] Gregory of Nazianzus does not make such precise distinctions. Nevertheless, recent scholars (arguing against some earlier scepticism) have argued that Gregory asserts the scriptural origin of orthodox images of the divine.[15] His theology is grounded on belief in supernatural knowledge – illumination.[16] However, as Frances Young argues, the Bible was not just the epistemological but also the literary foundation of Christian theology. Figural representation is thus absolutely central to early Christian discourse: one of Young's key examples is Gregory's complex web of quotation, allusion and imitation (*mimesis*) of biblical themes, stories and images.[17] As Young writes: 'the language of the Bible is parable, sign and symbol, and Christian religious language remained metaphorical, even though it was the language of representation ... it is the figurality of Christian discourse which gives it power'.[18]

The point of remarking on these resonances is not to argue that Farrer was influenced by Gregory of Nazianzus, nor that Farrer was attempting to revert to a patristic conception of inspiration. Rather, my argument is that the resonances I have so far established suggest that there are enough commonalities to justify bringing the two into conversation. In what follows I will now suggest some ways in which Gregory's and Farrer's notion of images might illuminate and critique each other.

Poets, prophets, apostles and preachers

Austin Farrer makes a very careful distinction between natural and revealed knowledge – or the 'noble inspiration' of a secular poet and the divine inspiration of the apostle. The apostle responds to a supernatural event – the incarnation – which he interprets through divinely-given images: 'the apostles know that they are transforming images by referring them to Christ, or rather, that Christ has transformed them, by clothing himself in them and dying in the armour' (GV, p. 108). This is what makes it revelation. However, Farrer also notes that the 'noble inspiration' of a poet works just at the apex of the human faculty of imagination. It might be *experienced* as something beyond herself, even though it is not. By contrast, the inspiration which brings supernatural knowledge of God represents not the denial of the natural, but the 'opening of the finite to the infinite' (GV, p. 35). It functions in continuity with that apex, but just beyond it and, crucially, 'the boundary between the two need be neither objectively nor subjectively felt' (GV, p. 93).

Farrer's whole argument in *The Glass of Vision* circles around his suggestion that the apostolic imagination is in some ways similar and in other ways dissimilar to poetic imagination. But this is not the only analogy present in that work, for his argument proceeds through a succession of analogies in order to come closer to finding what apostolic inspiration is *most* like. Rhetorically, this method is very persuasive, but it also means that some of the boundary-lines between likeness and unlikeness are somewhat unclear. As Farrer himself admits, 'there is no question here of proper and exact statement, of a theory of poetry or of prophetical inspiration. All we can do is to distinguish certain real differences, and evoke the inscrutableness, even in our own minds, of the making word' (GV, p. 106). Gregory of Nazianzus raises this question of boundaries rather insistently, firstly in relation to the issue of inspiration (which I will treat in this section) and secondly, in relation to his own literary creativity (developed later).

As we have discussed above, Gregory believes that knowledge of God is grounded in divine inspiration or illumination. However, when one asks to whom such illumination is given, Gregory appears to assume that it is relatively uniform phenomenon, stretching across prophets, the apostolic authors of the New Testament and theologians like himself. The *content* of that revelation might have developed according to God's careful plan to reveal gradually; but the *kind* of thing which revelation is seems not to change. So, for example, in the first of the sequence of theological poems known as the *Poemata arcana* Gregory carefully sets himself in a tradition following from the great authors of the Old Testament:

> I shall set this word upon the page as a prologue, a word which before now godly men have uttered to bring fear to a harsh-minded people, those two witnesses of divine sayings, Moses and Isaiah ... Spirit of God, in your truthfulness, come rouse my mind and stir my tongue to be a loud-sounding trumpet, that all who are fused with the fullness of godhead may heartily rejoice.[19]

This persona of the author fully inspired by the Spirit, in line with the prophets, is also found in his prose. Thus, in one of his Easter sermons Gregory announces that he will take his stand next to the prophet Habakkuk; in another, his model is David.[20]

Gregory also expresses the concept of divine inspiration by invoking the Holy Spirit as a classical poet might invoke his Muse. Thus the opening to Gregory's great theological poems which we cited above in fact sets his composition in a double tradition: on the one hand he is like Moses and Isaiah; on the other, Gregory invokes the Spirit directly as a poet might invoke the Muse: 'O Spirit of God, may you then waken my mind and tongue as a loud-shouting clarion of truth, so that all may rejoice, who are united in spirit to the entire Godhead'.[21] At times Gregory's poetry alludes to the *Phaedrus*, that work in which Plato argued for a place for 'a truly rhetorical and persuasive craft' grounded, among other things, on divine inspiration.[22] Intriguingly then, for Gregory the inspiration granted to Moses, Paul or Gregory himself, seems to lie in some kind of continuity with that accorded to Plato's philosopher (as set out in the *Phaedrus*) and even with a classical poet.

So, Gregory has an expansive concept of supernatural revelation. The crucial point, however, is that he claims that it *includes himself* as poet and preacher:

> I subjected myself to the Lord, and prayed unto Him (Ps. 36 [37].7). Let the most blessed David begin my speech, or rather let Him Who spoke in David, and even now yet speaks through him. For indeed the very best way of beginning every speech and action, is to begin from God, and to end in God.

So long as Gregory subjects himself to God, God's speech through him is essentially the same as it was through David. On the one hand, this seems remarkably, even outrageously, bold. Unlike Farrer, who carefully tries to delineate the difference between the workings of God in the prophets and the apostles, Gregory claims continuity not only between them but between them both and himself.

On the other hand, Gregory's boldness prompts one to ask: what is happening in Christian preaching? If a sermon is to be more than an academic theological commentary on a text, or more than moralizing, if a preacher composes her words prayerfully and sincerely tries to subject herself to God – is there no sense in which the preacher participates in divine inspiration? Or, to pose the question more modestly: in what sense is the preacher like and unlike the prophets and the apostles? For an answer, we will turn again to Farrer's distinctions.

In order to persuade his audience to read the New Testament more poetically, Farrer needs to ascertain to what extent and in what sense they are poetic. He applies himself to this task in his last two lectures in which he seems to identify three closely related senses of the poetic.[23] The first sense is what we might call the basic poetic impulse which causes someone, as Farrer puts it, to 'move an incantation of images under a control' (GV, pp. 104–5). The second sense of the poetic applies to the quality of this poetic impulse, specifically as to whether it is free. The third sense of the poetic applies not to the creative emergence of images in the original response to the control, but rather to the production of secondary images under pressure from the primary set.

In Lecture VII, Farrer deals with the first two senses. Although he strenuously resists the idea that there is a two-stage process involved, or that form can be separated from content in the process, nevertheless, his argument seems to focus on what one might call two sides of the poetic process which he examines in order to delineate the difference between the prophet and the poet. According to Farrer, both prophet and poet are responding to something which they experience as an imperative or 'controlling pressure' – an *'ought'* (GV, pp. 102–3). For the poet, this 'ought' is 'the texture of human existence, or the predicament of man'; it is therefore thoroughly natural. For the prophet, the 'ought' is 'the particular self-fulfilling will of God' (GV, pp. 103–4). The other side of the process is the human response and herein lie the first two senses of the poetic. First, the response of both poet and prophet is 'poetic' in that their mode of response to the 'ought' is imaginative: there is no initial response to the 'ought' which is then 'translated' into images, no content which is then given new imaginative form.

However, the poet and prophet differ in their imaginative acts. The poet responds subjectively to her experience of the human predicament. She may feel that she could respond in no other way, for the images which she uses 'impose themselves with authority'; nevertheless, she alone is the author – the maker – of her response (GV, pp. 95, 98–9, 103). By contrast, the prophet is truly constrained by God's will: 'his control tells him exactly what to say, for he is not responding to the quality of human life, he is responding to the demands of eternal will on Israel as they make themselves heard in the determinate situation where he stands' (GV, p. 104). Consequently, Farrer expresses the contrast between poet and prophet in terms of freedom and subjection, respectively – a contrast which holds even though the poetic and prophetic acts might *feel* equally bound:

> For poetry arises in the imagination; and not under the direct control of fact, so that it should be the literal transcript of it. Yet it is not a silly or vain day-dreaming either; it is controlled by realities, but the control is looser or more elastic than in the case of literal description. The poet's inventions respond somehow to the deep nature of human existence, and give it an expression all the more powerful because inventive and free.[24]

In this second sense of the poetic, then, the poet is truly a poet – a maker (*poietes*) of her response – and the prophet is not.

In Lecture VIII Farrer applies these senses of the poetic to the apostles. Again, Farrer denies that humans first have an experience which is then translated into images: for both prophets and apostles, the creation of the images *is* their response. But there is a difference in the kind of images in play. On the one hand, the prophet's message is not 'a revelation of fundamental images'. Farrer seems to suggest that they have received those master images from their tradition, for the images 'stand behind' their oracles and have a fundamental power which means that they 'thunder and lighten' in the prophets' words (GV, p. 108). In the apostles, on the other hand, there *is* a new revelation: 'the great images of faith are being freshly minted and reborn through Christ's incarnation' (ibid.). Farrer concedes that it might be the case that the master images change their nature 'very gradually' in the prophets' oracles, but this is a supernatural process – 'the process of the incarnation preparing its own way' (GV, p. 109).

Even more strongly than with the prophets, then, one sees that in one sense the apostles are *not* poets in the second sense: God, not the apostles, is the 'maker' (*poietes*) of their images, for 'in the apostles we see the images already refashioned by the fingers of the divine potter' (GV, p. 109). However, both the prophet and the apostle are poetic in the first sense that their activity as inspired people is to weave a web of images under a divine source of pressure, just as the poet weaves her images in response to the stuff of human existence.

Farrer then introduces a further sense in which both apostles and prophets can be understood as 'poetic': not only do they use/produce certain master images, the key symbols of salvation, but they also produce 'subordinate images by which the master-images are set forth or brought to bear' (GV, p. 108). Hence there is a second-order pressure to which the biblical authors are responding: not only the divine 'ought', but also the master images resulting from that divine imperative.

Given these three senses of poetic, then, one might well ask *to what extent and in what ways* is the preacher like a poet? First, the preacher might well *feel* (at least on some occasions) that she is responding to some imperative and that her response consists not in an attempt to analyse and describe God in propositions, but rather in images arising in her imagination. To the extent that she is weaving images under a control, she is poetic and in this she is like the poet, the prophet and the apostle.

Second, it may be that she is responding, poet-like, to the warp and weft of human existence in her preaching – albeit responding to the stuff of existence in the light of her beliefs about Jesus Christ. Sometimes, then, her images might arise as her 'made' response, and not under some supernatural pressure. Then she will be more like a poet in being a maker of her images, even though she may feel as though she could articulate her response in no other way. But equally, sometimes it may be that she *is* responding to a divine 'ought', that she is subjecting herself to that kind of pressure which Gregory of Nazianzus so boldly describes as the Holy Spirit or God opening his mouth. But in this subjection is the preacher more like Farrer's apostle or prophet? On the one hand, one might want to preserve the decisively different character of the apostles' revelation: surely it would not be right to say God is refashioning images anew in today's preaching as God did in that first generation of witnesses to the incarnation? On the other hand, to assert that preachers today are like prophets might deny the sense in which all believers are part of the church to which the apostles belonged. Is there not a sense in which preaching, like the activity of the apostles, is partly an expository, partly a poetic act? (GV, p. 103) Is there not a sense in which, as later preachers wrestle with the biblical text, these images '[grow] together into fresh unities, [open] out into new detail, [attract] to themselves and [assimilate] further image-material'? (adapting GV, p. 43). Although preaching may be theologically-informed, the core of preaching is to let the images live and bear fruit, not primarily to analyse, critique, test and determine their sense (as Farrer describes the role of theology) (GV, p. 44). The preacher would seem to need to be that Bible-reader who, Farrer writes, 'will immerse himself in the single image on the page before him, and find life-giving power in it, taken as it stands'. Could it not be through preaching, as through the sacraments, that 'the shape of the mystery of our redemption ... possesses and moulds [our minds]' as it possessed and moulded the minds of the apostles? (GV, pp. 50, 53)

So, the preacher might well be poetic in the sense that in using images to express the ineffable she is responding imaginatively to some kind of control. With God's grace, she might also be allowing herself to be possessed and moulded by those images – in which case she is *unlike* a poet who is truly the maker of her own images. However, if the images continue to possess and mould the preacher's mind, then she is certainly working with secondary images under pressure from those master images. In it is this third sense that the preacher is probably most aware of being like a poet.

Working with one's materials

Farrer develops this third sense of the poetic in *The Glass of Vision* (applied to Mark) and in the essay 'Inspiration: poetical and divine' (applied to Revelation).[25] In the latter especially, Farrer compares the pressure of the master images on the apostle to the pressure of other controls on the poet. The poet's creativity is controlled by 'the bondage of the formal conditions they accept; the metre, for example, and the rhyme'. A poet does not have an emotional response to grief and then translate that into sonnet form; rather, authentic response arises as he *works with* the sonnet form. The complex interplay of the various elements which the poet allows to impose themselves on him 'challenge a writer's invention' but also 'help him discover what he wants to say'.[26]

This sense of a craftsperson's materials being a point of both challenge and creativity is a strong theme in modern writing on craft. The importance of the craftsperson developing an intense knowledge of her materials is stressed, alongside the idea that such knowledge is difficult, if not impossible, to encapsulate in propositional language. Many craftspeople articulate the experience of learning that it is precisely in working with the resistance of their materials that one experiences the greatest moments of creativity. In short, as Richard Sennett has argued in detail in his book *The Craftsman*, points of resistance might seem like problems, but they move craftsmanship forward.[27] As Dorothy L. Sayers has noted, this is as much the experience of the wordsmith as with other kinds of maker.[28]

Gregory of Nazianzus knew this experience of resistance. Anyone who has read his poetry will be familiar with agonizing over his verbal failings, especially his prolixity which in Gregory's mind is an obstacle to, rather than a vehicle for, divine words. Punning in Greek, he asserts that poetry forces him to set his words to a metre – that is, to set a measure or a limit to his words.[29] Rather than merely being ironic self-deprecation, this expresses precisely the experience of creative resistance we have noted above. It is precisely in working creatively with the constraints of metre that he is able to express his most profound theological thoughts. In Farrer's words, Gregory's poetic forms 'challenge [his] invention' but also 'help him discover what he wants to say'.[30]

But Gregory, as we have seen, is a poet who also claims that he is working under inspiration. In Farrer's terms, he is weaving images in an activity which arises from his imagination being 'possessed and moulded' by 'living images' (GV, p. 53). In a second order, he is weaving images under the control of those master images. But, for Gregory, that second order of poetic weaving is not just *analogous* to the poetic activity of composing under 'the bondage of the formal conditions they accept; the metre, for example, and the rhyme' – it is part and parcel of it. The two kinds of bondage are inseparable.

In *The Glass of Vision* Farrer comes close to making the interconnection between the two this tight. As a gifted and rhetorical speaker and writer himself he perhaps recognizes the controls inherent in the act of composition. He also recognizes that it is false to separate a moment of response to a control from a second moment in which it takes poetic form. But in his attempt to clarify that the apostolic writers were *like* poets (in our first and third senses), he perhaps is unwilling to admit that a writer might also *be* a poet – not in the second sense of being the free maker of her response, but in the third sense of being creatively constrained not just by the major images of salvation but also by her literary form.[31] Farrer perhaps comes closer to articulating this point in his later essay on inspiration. Nevertheless, in general his main purpose is to illuminate the biblical text, and his eye is more on the analogy between the apostle and the poet (which demands to be applied with caution) and less on that between the poet and present-day theological makers.

The lectures which comprise *The Glass of Vision* were given in a context where Christianity and its intellectual modes were being both attacked and vigorously defended. Mid-twentieth-century Oxford was an epitome of both movements and one of the places they collided. Farrer concentrates on the question of what one should look for in Scripture and how one should read it, if one is to attend to God's voice. This is his own very focussed form of apologetics. He seems less interested, in *The Glass of Vision*, at least, in arguing for the coherence of Christian discourse in general in the way that Gregory of Nazianzus was. Nevertheless, by bringing these two theologians into conversation, I have tried to show not only how they share sensitivity to the various aspects of poetic activity, but how Farrer might have much to offer a more far-reaching vision of Christian wordsmithery. Gregory's boldness about his own approach prompts theologians and preachers to ask some searching questions both of Farrer and of themselves.

Notes

1 Austin Farrer, *The Glass of Vision* (as in Robert MacSwain (ed.), *Scripture, Tradition and Poetry: Austin Farrer's The Glass of Vision with Critical Commentary*, London and New York, Routledge, 2016, p. 43). Henceforth referred to in the text as GV.

2 This is related to Farrer's belief that there is no such thing as uninterpreted experience. See Edward Henderson, 'Austin Farrer: The Sacramental Imagination', in *C. S. Lewis and Friends: Faith and the Power of Imagination*, ed. David Hein and Edward Henderson, London, SPCK, 2011, pp. 35–51.

3 Hein and Henderson, pp. 35–6.

4 Austin Farrer, 'Inspiration: Poetical and Divine', in *Interpretation and Belief*, ed. Charles Carl Conti, London, SPCK, 1976, p. 41.

5 Frederick W. Norris, 'Introduction', in *Faith Gives Fullness to Reasoning: The Five Theological Orations of Gregory Nazianzen*, ed. F. W. Norris, Leiden, New York, E. J. Brill, 1991, p. 33; Christopher A. Beeley, *Gregory of Nazianzus on the Trinity and the Knowledge of God: In Your Light We Shall See Light*, Oxford, New York, Oxford University Press, 2008, pp. 96–100.

6 Beeley, *Gregory of Nazianzus on the Trinity*, pp. 94–5, 100.

7 Gregory of Nazianzus, *Oration* 27.2, cited by Frederick W. Norris, 'Gregory Contemplating Beautiful: Knowing Human Misery and Divine Mystery through and Being Persuaded by Images', in *Gregory of Nazianzus: Images and Reflections*, ed. Jostein Børtnes and Tomas Hägg, Copenhagen, Museum Tusculanum Press, 2004, pp. 19–36. Norris, 'Introduction', pp. 20–1; Farrer, *The Glass of Vision*, p. 72.

8 F. W. Norris, 'Contemplating the Beautiful', p. 27.

9 Beeley, *Gregory of Nazianzus on the Trinity*, pp. 90–113.

10 Gregory of Nazianzus, *Oration* 38.7, cited in Beeley, *Gregory of Nazianzus on the Trinity*, pp. 102–3.

11 Ibid., p. 103.

12 Gregory of Nazianzus, *Oration* 30.17., cited in Beeley, *Gregory of Nazianzus on the Trinity*, p. 97.

13 Norris, 'Contemplating the Beautiful', pp. 27–8.

14 Austin Farrer, 'Poetic Truth', in *Reflective Faith: Essays in Philosophical Theology*, Grand Rapids, Michigan, Eerdmans, 1974, pp. 24–38.

15 Gregory of Nazianzus, *Oration* 31.31–3; see Norris, 'Introduction', pp. 41–2; Norris, 'Contemplating the Beautiful', p. 30.

16 Beeley, *Gregory of Nazianzus on the Trinity*, pp. 90–103, 112.

17 Frances M. Young, *Biblical Exegesis and the Formation of Christian Culture*, Cambridge, Cambridge University Press, 1997, ch. 5.

18 Young, *Biblical Exegesis*, p. 258, developing the work of Averil Cameron.

19 Poem 1.16–24, in *Gregory of Nazianzus, Carmina [Poemata Arcana]*, ed. Claudio Moreschini, tr. D. A. Sykes, Oxford, Clarendon Press, 1997.

20 Gregory of Nazianzus, *Oration* 45.1; 2.1.

21 Gregory of Nazianzus, *Poems*, 1.1.1:23.

22 See especially *Phaedrus* 269a-e and 271d-272b; quote 269d (tr. Fowler) and Gregory's allusions in, e.g. Poem 1.2.14 (tr. Gilbert,) Gregory of Nazianzus, *On God and Man: The Theological Poetry of Saint Gregory of Nazianzus*, Popular Patristics, Crestwood, NY, St Vladimir's Theological Seminary Press, 2001. On fourth-century Christian responses to Plato's programmatic statement, see Morwenna Ludlow, *Art, Craft, and Theology in Fourth-Century*

Christian Authors, Oxford Early Christian Studies, Oxford, Oxford University Press, 2020, ch. 11.

23 Here I am delineating them in a way which Farrer does not and in the process may be forcing distinctions which are not clearly there in Farrer's text. The concept of the two sides of a unified poetic process is also my interpretation.

24 Farrer, 'Inspiration', p. 42.

25 See also Austin Farrer, *A Rebirth of Images: The Making of St John's Apocalypse*, Westminster, Dacre Press, 1949; *A Study in St Mark*, Westminster, Dacre Press, 1951.

26 All quotations from Farrer, 'Inspiration', p. 51.

27 Richard Sennett, *The Craftsman*, London, Penguin Books, 2009, chap. 8. See also Peter Korn, *Why We Make Things and Why It Matters*, London, Vintage, 2017, p. 50.

28 Dorothy L. Sayers, *The Mind of the Maker* (2nd edn), London, New York, Mowbray, 1994, chap. XI.

29 'On silence at the time of fasting', lines 10–12; 'On writing in metre' (Poem 2.1.39), line 35, both in Gregory of Nazianzus, *Autobiographical Poems* (tr. C. White), Cambridge, Cambridge University Press, 1996.

30 All quotations from Farrer, 'Inspiration', op. cit., p. 51.

31 Although I have used the example of poetry in regard to Gregory, I assume that prose too has its creatively constraining forms – many of which are very evident in the sermon.

Doctrine

10

'A Society of Two'?
Austin Farrer on the Trinity[1]

ROWAN WILLIAMS

It is a pity that, in his most sustained essay in introducing Christian doctrine, Austin Farrer committed himself to the statement that the 'revealed
parable' which determined the Christian notion of God was 'a story of
two characters', and that the God so revealed was 'a society of two'; that
the Holy Spirit was referred to as a person on the same footing as the
others could only be explained as an accident of the Latin language.[2] A
pity, because this can so easily be taken as almost a *reductio ad absur-
dum* of what is still commonly thought to be the typical 'Latin' form of
trinitarian doctrine, in which the subsistent reality of the Holy Spirit is
somehow overshadowed by the Spirit's role as a 'bond' between two much
more obviously solid and 'personal' agencies – a doctrinal position often
associated by Eastern Christian theologians with the Western adoption
into the Nicene Creed of the statement that the Spirit 'proceeds from the
Father and the Son' (*filioque*). In this reflection on some of Farrer's writings
on the Trinity, I want to explore both what Farrer might have meant by
these undoubtedly rather odd and provocative formulations, and whether
he does justice to the full subtlety of his own trinitarian thinking. As usual
where his strictly doctrinal thought is concerned, he does not make it easy
for the interpreter: there are several short pieces that pertain directly to
trinitarian theology, but they all exhibit Farrer's telegraphic and condensed
style at its most tantalising. It is not surprising that discussions of the theme
are sparse in the literature.[3] But I shall argue that the wording which I
began by quoting needs to be read with care against a much broader background, and that a more nuanced account of what Farrer might be saying
about the Holy Spirit in particular can be distilled from other works.

It is certainly the case that Farrer sees trinitarian doctrine as rooted in
the nature of Christian prayer, splendidly described thus in a Christmas
sermon: 'What else is it to pray, but this: that we live for a little while in the
Son of God.'[4] To pray to God in 'filial' mode and so to experience what it is
to be God's child is the heart of the insight that unfolds itself as trinitarian
doctrine. To believe in the Christian God *is* to accept that a relationship
is offered and opened to us with the source of all that is characterized

by something like what we call 'friendship'. As we explore it further, we recognise that it is – necessarily – a relation of utter dependence (we are finite and created, God is not, so this relation must be wholly asymmetrical), yet one in which we are invited into unrestricted intimacy; the relation of adoptive filiation, becoming a child of God by grace. The argument, as found in several places, especially in a very important broadcast talk published in 1953, 'The Trinity In Whom We Live',[5] in the luminous little essay, 'Very God and Very Man'[6] (probably written at around the same time or slightly earlier), and in the 1961 sermon on 'Thinking the Trinity',[7] might thus be summed up roughly in these terms. The effect of the life, death and resurrection of Jesus is such that we now know ourselves to be the objects of God's limitless valuing of us. What we apprehend God's love for us to be is analogous to friendship; but friendship entails an equality that is at first sight unthinkable where creator and creature are concerned. But what if we concluded that God is always already both giving and receiving love? There can be no qualification of the perfect equality of this relation, so that the receiver receives all that the giver has to give; so that if there is love given and received in the divine life, there is a relation of equality there – *dependent* equality, we should have to say, but nonetheless a relation in which there could be no disjunction, no less or more or before and after. This is the mystery we call the divine Son; and because there is a divine Son, there is, as we might say, a model for how we can be 'equal' with God, true friends of God, if we are assimilated to the life of this eternal Son. Such assimilation will necessarily be imperfect with regard to us (*quoad nos*): as finite and temporal beings, we grow toward its fullness rather than enjoying it timelessly and fully, but it is nonetheless *there* at the heart of our redeemed being. And our prayer is the act by which we deliberately inhabit that space which is the Son's life, exercising the freedom we have received from him: 'To pray is to give God back the mind of God, coloured with our own. But we must first be given the mind of God.'[8]

The 1953 talk sums this up concisely: 'God extends to us … what belongs uniquely to his co-equal Son. If God's love for us were all the love there was, then divine love would never have been.'[9] It is a version at first sight of the old apologetic argument (often associated with Richard of St Victor[10]) that for God to be truly love there must be both an 'object' and a 'subject' of love eternally; but Farrer in fact offers a rather different perspective in his stress on the experiential basis of such reasoning. If we confess that our life as believers is a life animated by the gift not only of creation itself but of 'friendship', the awareness of being immeasurably valued by our Maker as if we were truly capable of being the creator's equal, we need to read the events of salvation history as laying open to us the reality of an eternal 'condition' for our welcome into such a relation – the eternally co-equal recipient of divine love, the prototype of our own destiny and calling. 'The sonship is spread to embrace us.'[11]

What then of the third 'person'? Farrer does not at any point say or imply that the Spirit is in any way less eternal or less really distinct than the Father and the Son, but the basic pattern he has sketched has difficulties in finding appropriate language for the identity of the Spirit. The starting point is the acknowledgement that the Son receives from the Father all that the Father is: 'We receive from the Father all we are, he alone [the Son] receives from the Father all the Father is.'[12] But just as we need to receive from the Father the act and power to love in return, so in some sense the eternal Son must likewise receive from the Father the power of responding without reserve. For us, 'the Lord who is the Spirit' (as in 2 Cor. 3.18) conveys into us the mind of Christ, the responsive love of the incarnate Son toward the Father; but even in the Godhead, if the Father bestows on the Son all that is intrinsic to the paternal identity, the Father bestows the power to will and act in and through another. Thus the Spirit is what makes the Son live *his* life in and for the otherness of the Father, and also in and for the otherness of the world he will redeem. Hence in the later discussion in *Saving Belief*,[13] Farrer can describe the Spirit as 'God the self-bestowing or indwelling, God finding scope of action in the being or action of another.' God the Father gives the life that is his, which involves the giving of his freedom to be 'outside' himself; in giving his identity, we might say, he gives more than the identity of an atomised individual agency, because he is never such an agency. To give what he is he must give more than he is. And lest we should think that the Son in some sense needs his life 'supplemented', or augmented by the gift of the Spirit, we should remember that the same holds in this case: the Son does not respond to the Father as an individual who subsists at some sort of distance from or in some sort of independence of the Father, but depends on the Father for that capacity to love the Father wholly and selflessly which is the distinctive gift of the Spirit. And finally, '[t]he Spirit is not imperfectly real through being the completion of another's life: he enjoys perfection in being perfectly bestowed on a perfect recipient by a perfect giver.'[14] There is a related but less carefully worded formulation in a later sermon,[15] where Farrer speaks of the way in which 'the substance and life of Godhead [is] constantly poured from the Father into the Son – the Holy Ghost.'

The proposed structure seems to be this. The Father, in eternally giving divine life to the Son as source, gives a divine life that is always 'exceeding' anything we should be able to define as individuality: the Father has no identity that is not an identity for, with and in an Other. Consequently, when the Father generates the identity that is the Son, what is generated is a life that is *equally* an identity for, with and in an Other. The Son would not be the Son at all – would not *be* at all – unless he had received this other-oriented and other-dependent dimension of divinity. But this implies that the 'other-oriented and other-dependent dimension' is not identical with *either* Father *or* Son. It is that dimension of inseparable divine act that cannot be defined as either the act of generating or the act of receiving generation. The implication is that the Father 'already' (we must take it for granted that temporal language is inappropriate, but it is hard to avoid) has a sort of 'other' not identical with the Son, but in some sense the base or condition of the Son's life: 'the whole Spirit of the Father pours into the Son, and in so doing becomes the Son's own Spirit',[16] or, more startlingly, 'Holy Ghost means the divine life communicated or bestowed ... the first and proper being of the Holy Ghost is in the Eternal Son.'[17] As Robert MacSwain rightly observes in his comments on Farrer's *Glass of Vision*,[18] Farrer aligns himself pretty plainly with the Eastern Christian rejection of the *filioque*, and in effect replaces it with a *spirituque* for the Son. The Son comes from the Father *and* that which is already somehow 'with' the Father in eternity. God as Source, God as generative – the unbegotten begetter, in patristic idiom – must be more than simply begetter:[19] the particular kind of otherness that is the *filial* relation of the Logos to the Source is the 'effect' (once again the scare quotes cannot be avoided) of this logically prior self-othering that we call 'Spirit'.

Even the most irreproachably orthodox theologian is not on oath in a sermon, and the language of the Spirit as 'substance and life of Godhead' – which, as it stands, would identify the Spirit with the single divine *nature* – should be taken not as an attempt at strictly doctrinal definition but as a rhetorical flourish to convey the wholeness or integrity of the Father's self-gift in begetting the Son. The primitive or basic reality we are dealing with in trying to talk about the Trinity is, so Farrer implies, the self-dispossession that is fundamental to divine life. If this is the starting point, it makes sense to say that the begetting Father is never any kind of isolated divine individual; but rather than taking this as immediate grounds for speaking of the divine Son, Farrer interposes another kind of otherness, not itself filial but the ground of filial response and reciprocity. To the extent that we could say that self-giving or self-bestowal or self-communication were intrinsic to God's being *God*, we could just about defend the language of 'substance and life' in describing what it is that the Father communicates to the Son. But the language is painfully strained here; Farrer is pushing against the limits of what is intelligible (as one does in trinitarian theology, needless to say) and is constantly on the edge of implying that the Spirit is almost a *principle* (of selflessness or self-bestowal) that needs concretising in the Son. Indeed, his defence against the conclusion that the Spirit is 'imperfectly real', quoted above, suggests that he knows quite well where the pressure point is in his account of the divine relations: he insists here that it is entirely proper to see the Spirit as precisely that which 'completes' the relation of Father and Son, and that this is the perfect reality appropriate to the Spirit's identity and in no way a reduction or subordinating of the Third Person. Vogel, summarizing some of Farrer's discussion in the third of the Bampton Lectures, says that, for Farrer, 'the Spirit never emerges into view'.[20]

But this – surprisingly – echoes a theme found in some twentieth-century Eastern Orthodox theology. Vladimir Lossky, in his classic work on *The Mystical Theology of the Eastern Church*, makes a similar point about the relative 'anonymity' of the Spirit: for Lossky, the *kenosis* of the Holy Spirit lies in the fact that 'while He manifests the common nature of the Trinity, [he] leaves His own Person concealed beneath His Godhead. He remains unrevealed, hidden, so to speak, by the gift in order that this gift which he imparts may be fully ours ... [T]he Holy Spirit effaces Himself, as Person, before the created persons to whom he appropriates grace', and in the eschaton the 'face' he shows will be the faces of all the innumerable host of the redeemed.[21] In other words, we should *expect* the 'personal' reality of the Spirit to be elusive and resistant to any kind of image such as we might have of the Father and the Son; but for Lossky it is crucial that the Spirit should originate directly in the life of the Father, and not in the Father together with the Son. The Spirit does not direct us *toward* the Son (as if the Son were in himself the object of our devotion, over against us) but brings the life of the Son into being in us, first through the bare fact of our participation in Christ's body, and then in the realisation in every unique created person of the distinct mode in which the likeness of God is to be shown in them – this latter being the work of the Spirit strictly as a person in its/her/his own right. Lossky's schema – which has also had its critics – like Farrer's, treats the creation in us of a 'Christomorphic' life as central, and preserves the scriptural focus on prayer to the Father as the first datum of trinitarian thought; and in insisting, like Farrer, that the Spirit's identity is integrally such as to efface any image or imaginable 'personal' presence as the Spirit realizes in active and distinct human hypostases the divine-human hypostasis of the Son, he actually provides Farrer with a rationale for that unhappy formulation about 'a society of two' with which we began this essay. The filial response to the gift of the Father must not be in any way the act of an 'independent' agent, it must itself be in some sense *given* to the respondent – yet not in any way that would intrude another presence claiming attention: the Father's gift is simultaneously the gift of the freedom to respond, and as such presupposes something that is communicable between Father and Son, not simply identical with either. Lossky speaks of this in terms of the 'witness' of the Spirit to the Son in the economy of salvation;[22] Farrer struggles to find a way of 'mapping' this on to the divine life as such, so that the Son's receiving of the Father's gift is the remote analogical source of how we understand our own assimilation into filial love. In either context, it would be fundamentally wrong to think of the Spirit as adding some *other* dynamic to the divine life or to the redeemed life beyond the fact of filial response; yet the filial response cannot be fully grasped without the always-already different procession of the Spirit from the Father, always elusive, never before our eyes because always animating what and how we see or know Father and Son.

So Farrer's 'society of two' formulation can be given *some* kind of theological respectability if understood as a strong statement of what Lossky thinks of as the Spirit's *kenosis*; the difficulty in his work – and the difficulty which Lossky avoids – is in the implication that, because of the quirks of

Latin patristic vocabulary, what we mean by 'person' is different in its application to Father and Son on the one hand and Spirit on the other. I don't think Farrer quite means to say this, but the unsympathetic reader might well draw such a conclusion; as they might from the language elsewhere apparently assimilating the Spirit to the divine life as such. Perhaps the most salient phrase in the problematic wording of *Saving Belief*, though, is the reference to the 'revealed parable' from which we begin. *The Glass of Vision* includes, early on,[23] a quite complex discussion of how one might identify trinitarian theology in the text of the New Testament. Farrer dismisses three possible methods of grounding the doctrine in the biblical text – the search for propositions that would logically imply the orthodox teaching, the accumulation of threefold formulae in the text, and the appeal to three distinct modes of religious experience or encounter. To all of these he opposes his own preferred method, 'to look for the image of the Divine Trinity'.[24] This means tracing how certain pre-Christian images, especially the Isaianic list of gifts of the 'Spirit of the Lord' bestowed on the messianic king (Is. 11.1–3), and the hallowing of the eternal Father's Son by a voice from heaven in the (possibly) intertestamental *Testaments of the Twelve Patriarchs* are reworked in Christian Scripture – in the Marcan narrative of the baptism of Jesus and in the images in Revelation 4 and 5 of the seven-fold lights burning before God's throne, the seven eyes of the sacrificed Lamb and the seven 'spirits of God' sent out from the Lamb into the world: 'The sevenfold light of the Holy Ghost burns before the Father's majesty, it blazes also in the eyes of the mystical Lamb.'[25] This, Farrer argues, is how the seer of Revelation presents the Trinity – the eternal God with the seven spirits before his throne and the crucified and risen Jesus, in whom the seven spirits live, as in the very beginning of Revelation (1.4–5). This is not a speculative structure, though it fuels speculation in due course ('Later theology was to conclude that there is no real meaning in the absolute priority and essentiality of Christ's sonship, if he is himself a creature').[26] Patristic theology, says Farrer, mangles the logic of the image, reading John 1.4 as affirming the dependence of the Spirit on the Logos ('What arose through him was life' – this life being identified with the Spirit) instead of seeing that 'Spirit' is in Scripture always a designation for 'the life of the Godhead as bestowed'.[27] If so, this life must be there to be bestowed on the Logos by the Father.

The nub of the argument is as it is in later and briefer treatments: the Spirit is what is given to the Son in order that the Son may *be* the Son; the Spirit is God as self-communicating. What this discussion does, however, is to illuminate something of why Farrer consistently approaches the grammar of trinitarian doctrine as he does. He is concerned that we should not lose touch with the 'revealed parable' – that is, with the *images* in which the doctrine is primordially conveyed. The shape of those images is, for Farrer, clearly one in which divine 'Spirit' is first and foremost that dimension of divine life which is distinct from the Person of the Father to the extent that it can be given away by the Father as that which establishes not only the hypostatic being of the Son but the specific freedom to give back to the Father what is received – to live and act in selfless filial love, the light blazing in the eyes of the Lamb, in Farrer's characteristically wonderful phrase. Because the entire argument of the Bampton Lectures has to do with images as the primary vehicle of revelation and thus the primary data for theology, it is important that this most determinative of Christian doctrines should be anchored in scriptural imagery. In short, Farrer's own justification for the idiosyncratic features of his trinitarian vocabulary would have been in this fundamental methodological point. The picture, the narrative revealed is of the Father's generating and naming and (could we say?) 'capacitating' the Son: two 'characters', then, but a necessarily triple-textured account of their relationship.

But this is, it has to be said, an eccentric passage in the Bamptons. The average theologically literate reader of the New Testament would surely turn for trinitarian structures neither to mere triple formulae nor to ideas about diverse religious experiences but to what Farrer himself most regularly uses when he wants to elaborate on why the doctrine is so fundamental. They might turn to the account of the shape of Christian prayer found in Paul or John, our incorporation in the heavenly prayer of the eternal Word through the gift of the Spirit whereby we call God *Abba*; to the complex dynamic of the Johannine Farewell Discourses, the mutual indwelling of Christ and the Father, and the witness to and actualization of this by the Paraclete; or to the trinitarian shape of the baptismal narratives in the Synoptic Gospels,[28] the narrative that arguably establishes in the first place the structure of Spirit-filled filial life given over to the Father as the shape of identity in Christ. The dramatic 'staging' of the heavenly court and sanctuary in Revelation does indeed offer opportunity for some spectacular midrashic reworkings of familiar Jewish material, of the sort that Farrer as exegete excels in. And there can be no doubt – thanks to the work of scholars like Margaret Barker[29] – that the images of heavenly liturgy were of far more theological significance for the first Christians than we have normally supposed in the past. But the solid and recurring themes of adoptive filiation through the Spirit's work are far more visible witnesses to what prompted the development of speculation about the threefold life of God. And the flawed patristic exegesis Farrer refers to in regard to the Spirit's derivation from the Son is by no means a dominant reading in the early Christian period (it is not to be found in Origen's Commentary on John, for example); the whole section of this lecture has an uncomfortable feel of shadow-boxing – forcing text and argument, rather as he accuses the Fathers of doing in their exegesis, so as to establish once and for all the ground of doctrine in revealed image – and a very specific revealed image in this instance. Had Farrer concentrated his argument on the structure of the Farewell Discourses, the emphasis there on the Paraclete as witness and remembrancer might have helped him avoid the awkward drift toward a depersonalizing of the Spirit that his language facilitates. The idiom of the Fourth Gospel is no less a set of narrative images than the apocalyptic idiom on which he concentrates; but it at least evokes a fully active triplicity in a way which his more usual terminology rather fails to do – which is no doubt why Lossky, with all his convergences with some of Farrer's concerns, is so much more committed to the idea of the Spirit as 'independent' witness (independent in the sense of not being a joint product of the Father and the Son).

So there is a good deal to be said in Farrer's defence; he is not after all a simple binitarian, and he has strong methodological grounds for focussing our attention on the nature of the 'revealed parable' from which trinitarian theology starts. The problem is with a narrow and idiosyncratic version of that parable which leaves out of account so many of the texts which in practice he draws on so effectively in his account of trinitarian prayer. There are some hints that he was aware of some unfinished business in respect of his trinitarian speculations, as a couple of sermons on the subject preached in 1961 seem to be struggling to offer a version of the doctrine less directly dependent on the 'revealed parable' as presented in the earlier writing. The sermon on 'A Father's Begetting'[30] is a – somewhat elusive – meditation on what it is to be begotten, to be 'authored', as he puts it, reflecting on the various levels at which human fatherhood can be said to generate life in a child. What distinguishes heavenly fathering is the simple fact that there is nothing the Father does not or cannot give the Son: the earthly father is physically responsible for a child's existence, but this is a bare causal relation; more important is the way a father talks a child into talking, communicates what it is to think – and in a relation marked by grace, a father can also begin to introduce a child to the knowledge and love of God. The heavenly Father is no transient physical cause but an unceasing wellspring of life, never replaced (as an earthly father is in some sense replaced in the process of our own growth into maturity and parenting in turn); and (to pick up a phrase we have already noted) what is given in this fathering is 'the substance and life of Godhead'. 'The earthly pattern of father and son is a duality, the heavenly pattern is a blessed and indivisible Trinity. This is so, because the Father of the heavenly Son is *not only his father, but his God*.'[31] What exactly is being claimed here? Presumably the point is that the relation of the eternal Word to the Source cannot be simply the effect of a cause, since the continuous gift of life is what actively sustains the person of the Word; and the way in which God gives life is unique. It is the communication of what makes the Father *God*, but not what makes the Father *Father* – and that 'what makes the Father God' seems to be identified with the Spirit. Once again, we face the awkward implication that the Spirit simply is the divine essence – not indeed in quite the way that Eastern Orthodox polemicists accuse Westerners of implying, that the Spirit is nothing but an abstract quality shared between Father and Son, but nonetheless a dimension of the divine life that is hard to conceive as hypostatically subsisting in the same way as Father and Son. Farrer does not, I think, succeed in clarifying what it means to say that earthly fathering is a twofold and heavenly fathering, a threefold pattern; somewhere in this difficult sermon there is a recognition that what makes the difference must be in whatever it is that makes the heavenly relation more than just the process of formation that one human subject exercises on another – though the intimacy of a really creative parenting relation may give us one of the best imaginative clues as to why we use such language of the divine life. But what remains unclear is why this does not amount to a more intense form of unity-in-duality rather than a trinity.

Some of the same difficulty attends the sermon preached in Trinity College chapel in the same year, 'Thinking the Trinity'.[32] Here too, there is a more direct appeal to human experience and interaction, in this case looking to the nature of mental life itself. 'Mentality always was a social, not a solitary, thing'[33]: so if we are to follow another central Farrerian methodological principle, the belief that in some measure we know God by knowing the nature of active intelligence in ourselves,[34] the sociality of our human intellection tells us something of God. We learn to talk by being talked to (an echo of the other 1961 sermon just discussed), and so we come to think, to 'talk silently to the images of the absent, or we can pretend to be our own twin, and talk to ourself'.[35] But God's 'thought' is not some kind of projection of an imagined twin: 'the self with whom he speaks, and who takes the responsive part, is a dear and real person, the Son of his love'; and what they exchange is 'the whole mind and heart and substance of their godhead.'[36] For us as finite subjects, there is a difference between the way mind is matured in discourse and interaction and the way it grows in solitary reflection (a telling word in this context); the challenge of 'thinking the Trinity' is to hold these together, so as to recognize that anyone 'who has the character to be either a thinker or a friend lives the Trinity in some fashion'.[37] What is distinct in us is inseparable in the divine. And in God, what the persons love in each other is 'the perfect truth of eternal godhead'. What in our relations is 'the bond of mutual liking' is in God the work of the Spirit.[38] Father and Son recognize in each other, so to speak, the identical love that makes them divine.

Yet again, despite the freshness and vividness of Farrer's development of the analogy of mental life, the Spirit seems to be slipping frustratingly toward assimilation to divinity-as-such. Yet Farrer's own finely-tuned accounts of Christian prayer in the Trinity certainly seem to presuppose something more of an active and 'personal' – even if occluded – role for the Spirit. The powerful and poetic sermon 'Pentecostal Fire'[39] evokes the energy and agency of the Spirit as a presence hidden in all human spirits, informing and directing our longing for God – 'the ground of your heart, the fountain of your true desire'.[40] It is the spring of true human spontaneity, the true becoming-ourselves that God wills and effects for us by implanting this urgent presence in our depths. Nothing in this or comparable texts suggests that the Spirit is simply a notional divine essence. There is a genuine tension in Farrer's thought here, and both the biblical and the self-reflective or anthropological models he deploys sit uneasily with the exuberant formulations of trinitarian spirituality which so characterize his preaching and devotional writing. Is there any way of reconciling these elements in Farrer? A theologian of his stature, we might well say, deserves the benefit of a certain amount of doubt – or at least an attempt to see what might be made of his language once we have allowed for the effect of what I have suggested is the narrow focus of his exegetical emphases.

So, retrieving some of the points noted early in this essay, we might attempt a version of his approach less vulnerable to the criticisms that have been advanced. Begin with the idea that no trinitarian subsistent can be considered as a self-subsisting individual; no divine person exists in any way at all independently of the subsistence of the entire Godhead, the three hypostases. The Father is never anything other than the Father of the Son, and has no identity that is not the identity of Father. But – so Farrer suggests – that identity as Father is equally unimaginable without this identity being simultaneously the identity of a God who is free simply to bestow the life that is his as if it were 'other' to him. He can *be* the eternal begetter because he is, as divine agent, eternally reflecting his personal nature as giver: he breathes out that giving character and it informs the filial response of the Son, in that the Son is given not only 'divine life' in general, but the specifically *interpersonal* character of self-bestowal and self-emptying that is always already real in the Father's outbreathing of Spirit. The Father cannot be Father of the Son without this 'second difference', as it has been called[41] – that which makes the intradivine relations something more than a plain 'reproduction' of the Father by the Son, a simple and exhaustive mutual symmetry. The critique of the *filioque* needs some fine-tuning if we are to do justice to the biblically-grounded belief that the Spirit is never other than the Spirit *of the Son*; but this is the place to introduce Lossky's emphasis on the Spirit as kenotic witness, the hypostasis which remains unseen in the sense that it/he/she is always generating filial union with the Source in and through the agency of the Son, and thus (in the economy of salvation) manifesting or proclaiming the Son, activating the Father's affirmation or vindication of the Son (the Son who is 'raised in the Spirit'; Rom. 1.4; 8.11, 1 Pet. 3.18) – acting 'on' the Son, we could say, and directing creation to the Son, an agency that cannot be reduced to the primordial self-bestowal of the Father in generating the Son as if that were the act of an individual begetter rather than of a begetter who is 'already' self-bestowing. Thus what is given to the Son is not simply 'divine life' in the abstract sense of those grammatical properties (immutability, omniscience, etc.) that constitute God's essence, but the character of divine life as self-sharing – something not constituted exclusively by the generation of the Son. In this sense only we might say that the Spirit is that which communicates the 'mind and heart and substance of godhead.'

If something of Farrer's perspective can be reconstructed along these lines, and if we make allowances for the problematic language of the Spirit as the substance and life of 'Godhead', there are significant insights still to be developed here. The value of Farrer's inchoate thoughts on trinitarian theology is primarily in its consistent dynamism, its stress on the Trinity as that which makes sense of the actuation and direction of redeemed life (and in fact of created life in general). The fundamental point about love and friendship with which the 1953 essay begins, the conviction that God can make friends of us because he is eternally generating responsive equality in his own life, remains significant for him, and opens up a rich field of further exploration into friendship and equality as characteristic of the Body of Christ. And there is no ambiguity at all about his commitment to the belief that the Spirit is the divine agency by which we are assimilated to the liberty and love of the eternal Son through the eternal Son's enactment of filial devotion in the historical conditions of our humanity. The attempt to connect the Trinity with the very nature of mental life is tantalizing, but needs more development. Thus in the context of the 'Thinking the Trinity' sermon, for example, we should have to elaborate just how the self-reflective mind, in imagining and imaging its own otherness ('pretending to be its own twin'), posits a third term that is *neither* subject *nor* 'twin': if I as thinking subject project an interlocutor, I implicitly acknowledge that the content of what I have thought is not straightforwardly identical with my act of thinking but something that can be set at a distance from my own bare subjectivity before it can become the matter of my inner dialogue with the projected 'twin'. Not a fruitless direction of speculation, but it is a formidably complex question, requiring a more sophisticated phenomenology than Farrer offers in this connection.

This very preliminary survey of Farrer's trinitarian theology has brought into focus some serious tensions around how we speak of the Holy Spirit – though they are hardly unique to Farrer: as Lossky's treatment of the Spirit shows, even the most careful attempt to avoid depersonalizing the Spirit still has to acknowledge that there is an unavoidable reticence, the recognition of a certain aporia in what we can say, expressed by Lossky in terms of the Spirit's *kenosis*. Some of Farrer's formulations can be read as nudging us in this direction ('The Spirit is not imperfectly real through being the completion of another's life', for example; though for this to help as much as it might, it would have to be balanced by similar statements about the other two hypostases); but we have seen that, in this particular context, Farrer's two central methodological insights prove problematic. He is profoundly concerned to interpret the doctrine as, like so much of our doctrinal language, the outworking of a set of scripturally given images – the realm of 'revealed parable.' And he consistently seeks to ground talk of God in general in our awareness of ourselves as intelligent and willing subjects. But the way in which both these determining methodological moves are deployed here leaves a great deal of unfinished business; I have suggested that the first is adversely affected by some eccentric exegetical choices, and the second by a lack of detail as to how we are to conceive the eternal 'other' of the primordial willing/intelligent personal life as itself an agent of will and intelligence rather than a passive 'content' to be transferred from one agent to another. Neither of these weaknesses necessarily invalidates the methodological perspective; but we may take warning that these perspectives need some refining and extending if they are not to land us with an unsustainable pneumatology. Farrer's contribution to a theology of Christian prayer grounded in the reality of adoptive filiation is so rich and generative that we might well say that he deserves the tribute of carrying forward the work needed to anchor it more effectively in a trinitarian model that more successfully resists the binitarian shortcut that his language perilously skirts. I hope that this exploration of his thinking may prompt some more of that work, as a mark of gratitude for Farrer's exceptional inspiration.[42]

Notes

1 Farrer's works are referred to by the following abbreviations in these notes:
'Trinity': 'The Trinity in Whom We Live', *Theology* LVI, no. 399, September 1953, pp. 322–7.
LB: *Lord I Believe: Suggestions for Turning the Creed Into Prayer*, London, Faith Press, 1958.
SS: *Said or Sung: An Arrangement of Homily and Verse*, London, Faith Press, 1960.
SB: *Saving Belief: A Discussion of Essentials*, London, Hodder and Stoughton, 1964.
FS: *Faith and Speculation: An Essay in Philosophical Theology*, London, Adam and Charles Black, 1967.
CF: *A Celebration of Faith*, London, Hodder and Stoughton, 1970.
RF: *Reflective Faith; Essays in Philosophical Theology*, ed. Charles Conti, London, SPCK, 1972.
EM: *The End of Man*, London, SPCK, 1973.
IB: *Interpretation and Belief*, ed. Charles Conti, London, SPCK 1976.
SMP: *Scripture, Metaphysics, and Poetry: Austin Farrer's The Glass of Vision with Critical Commentary*, ed. Robert MacSwain, Aldershot, Ashgate, 2013.
TSH: *The Truth-Seeking Heart: Austin Farrer and His Writings*, ed. and intr. by Ann Loades and Robert MacSwain, Norwich, Canterbury Press, 2006.
2 *SB*, pp. 128–9.
3 Brian Hebblethwaite's chapter on 'The Doctrine of the Trinity' in his study of *The Philosophical Theology of Austin Farrer*, Leuven, Peeters, 2007, pp. 107–15, surveys the basic texts, and comes to a rather critical verdict. J. Vogel, 'A Little While in the Son of God: Austin Farrer on the Trinitarian Nature of Prayer', *Scottish Journal of Theology* 64: 4 (November 2011), pp. 410–24, is more sympathetic, a good and clear introduction to the fundamental insistence in Farrer's trinitarian thought that doctrinal construction must be built upon and around a doctrine of the nature of Christian prayer. This insight is developed in a reading of Farrer's own work and explored by means of a comparison with the theology of Sarah Coakley, a comparison that unfortunately somewhat misrepresents a key aspect of Coakley's argument by suggesting that she somehow uncouples her pneumatology from the filial vocation of creatures in the eternal Son. An earlier article by Robert MacSwain ('Above, Beside,

Within: The Anglican Theology of Austin Farrer', *Journal of Anglican Studies* 4.1 (June 2006), pp. 3–57) has a good, though brief, summary and discussion of several of Farrer's texts on the Trinity (pp. 46–52).

4 SS, p. 29.

5 'Trinity', pp. 322–7.

6 IB, pp. 126–37.

7 CF, pp. 72–7. These three pieces on the Trinity are all reprinted in whole or in part in TSH, pp. 148–54, 102–10 (the second part only of the original text) and 155–60.

8 'Trinity', p. 324.

9 Ibid.

10 Richard of St Victor, *de Trinitate*. III, PL 196, 915B-930D; see, e.g., John Burnaby, *The Belief of Christendom: A Commentary on the Nicene Creed*, London, SPCK, 1963, pp. 212–13. Richard's argument is strictly from the logic of ascribing perfect *caritas* to God. Farrer ('Trinity', p. 326) actually repudiates the idea of any speculation on 'the necessary nature of the Godhead', which suggests that he would not have wanted to follow Richard.

11 IB, p. 137.

12 'Trinity', p. 325.

13 p. 87.

14 Ibid.

15 EM, pp. 69–70.

16 SS, p. 114.

17 LB, pp. 21–2.

18 *SMP*, p. 49, n. 20.

19 Cf. ibid. p. 49: 'The act of paternal love is twofold – to beget and to bestow.'

20 Vogel, 'A Little While in the Son of God, p. 421.

21 Vladimir Lossky, *The Mystical Theology of the Eastern Church*, Cambridge and London, J. larke, 1957, p. 168; cf pp. 161–3, 172–3.

22 Ibid., pp. 158–60.

23 SMP, pp. 44–50.

24 Ibid., p. 45.

25 Ibid., p. 47.

26 Ibid., p. 48.

27 Ibid., pp. 48–9.

28 Mentioned by Farrer in SMP, p. 47, but characterized as clarifying only the economy of revelation rather than the eternal life of the Godhead.

29 See, e.g., Margaret Barker, *Temple Theology: An Introduction*, London, SPCK, 2004.

30 EM, pp. 67–71, delivered in Keble College Chapel.

31 p. 70; my italics.

32 CF, pp. 71–7.

33 Ibid., p. 74, cf. SB, pp. 49, 51: 'Mind is a social reality ... mentality, as we know it, is plurifocal.'

34 See, for example, the essay, 'Does God exist?' in RF, pp. 39–47, and at greater length, FS chs 3, 7–10.

35 CF, p. 74.

36 Ibid.

37 Ibid., p. 75.

38 Ibid., p. 76.

39 SS, pp. 101–5.

40 Ibid., p. 104.

41 See John Milbank, '"The Second Difference": For a Trinitarianism Without Reserve', *Modern Theology* 2 (1986), pp. 213–34; cf. Rowan Williams, *On Christian Theology*, Oxford, Blackwell, 2000, chs 8–10, esp. pp. 123, 140–1, 164–5.

42 I must acknowledge gratefully the very helpful comments of Robert MacSwain on an earlier draft of this essay.

II

Farrer on the Atonement

RICHARD HARRIES

Central to Farrer's thinking is his conviction that God is a God who saves; who redeems us. Although he engaged with philosophers at the highest level, like Pascal his God was not primarily the God of the philosophers. His one systematic exposition of Christian belief is tellingly entitled *Saving Belief*.[1] The Faith as set out in the book is not just for the assent of rational minds, but to save those rational minds. If we ask what it is that God saves us from, Farrer, uncharacteristically, gives us no clear general answer. Perhaps it was a question he felt each one of us had to answer for ourselves in terms of our own self-knowledge. But I think he would have been sympathetic to a line of thought in the sermon at the funeral of a priest friend of mine. The priest had had a ministry among people who were to some extent on the margins – sensitive, wounded people – and they filled the church. The preacher suggested that each of those present was there because the priest had saved them from their own self-destruction. In each of Farrer's sermons there is some insight into ways in which we self-destruct, and how we might be drawn out of ourselves into the light of Christ.

The ironic humour that Austin Farrer deployed, and the playfulness shown in the occasional whimsical aside, should not disguise the fact that he was in deadly earnest in what he said or wrote. This utter seriousness came into its sharpest focus in his sermons. It is easy to be seduced by these sermons, the skill with which he engaged the listener, the sheer brilliance of the language, the ease with which he set forth fundamental Christian truths. So it is all too possible for the reader to admire rather than pay attention to the message. In fact one can imagine C. S. Lewis's Screwtape writing to a lesser devil urging him to lure readers into doing just that.[2] What all Farrer's writings, but most obviously these sermons, express, is a deeply serious wrestling for souls. They bring to mind Lancelot Andrewes even though the rhetoric of the two divines was so different.

This seriousness is particularly evident in a sermon on forgiveness. Farrer begins by having some fun at the expense of a colleague who asked examinees to write an essay on sin before he went on to define sin as 'What I do to God'. It is not what I think about myself. It is not primarily feelings of guilt or shame from which we might want to be released. And if we have no such feelings it does not mean we are free of sin. As he wrote:

Sin is what I do to God, wilfully violating his majesty and flouting his good pleasure. He meets me everywhere in so many forms, and specially in his breathing image, the human form divine. Again and again I trample him down. My sin is what I do to God; whether I am conscious of doing it or whether I am not, I do it; and there it is, and if I become conscious of God I shall not remain unconscious of my sin.[3]

We might shrug our mental shoulders and think with Voltaire that God will forgive because 'That's his job' and meanwhile ask to be left alone. But God does not leave us alone. If he did we would fall out of existence. We only exist because moment by moment he holds us in being. So, as Farrer continues:

> To get sin out of the world I must get God out of the world, and I cannot. He is about my path and about my ways; his love is on the road before me opening up those good works in which he predestines me to walk, and standing in the way of those follies to which I incline.[4]

The church did not invent the idea of sin, argues Farrer; rather it is an inevitable concomitant of defining what is good. To teach people to tell the truth, for example, so essential for our life together, is inevitably to bring into focus its opposite, which is lying. Our relation with God is inescapable for we draw our very existence from him. It is not something we are free to ignore. 'We violate his will if we do not follow it, we are starved of our supreme good, if we do not embrace it.' So, 'If we are not reconciled to God, we are spoiling the music, not just letting music alone.' This depends on some consciousness of God however, as he admits, and we can only be judged in relation to the extent of that consciousness.

There is a revealing sentence in this sermon on forgiveness, for in a sudden turn Farrer writes in the first person:

> I have sinned. I have offended against the majesty of God by contempt of his love and by violation of his will. And I have incurred blood-guiltiness, for I have left poor Lazarus covered with spiritual sores to perish in the street.[5]

Any other preacher would have referred to the physical poverty of Lazarus, as does the parable itself. But Farrer speaks of 'spiritual sores'. It reveals the seriousness with which he took his role as priest/scholar. Amid all the wonderful distractions of Oxford, intellectual and social, he reminds himself that the undergraduates whom he taught, preached to and conversed with were covered with spiritual sores which it was his task to heal.

So, sin is taken with great seriousness. In order to understand Farrer's teaching on what God does about this it is essential to see his answer in the wider context of some of his key ideas.

First, fundamental to all Farrer's thinking is the conviction that the distinctions we make between thought and word and word and action do not apply to God. What God thinks he speaks and what he speaks he enacts, so it is only in and through God's acts that we know him. God said, 'Let there be light' and the world came into being. We know him in and through that world. In a human court a judge might find an accused not guilty and order him to be released. The words of the judge and the release are separate. But in God they are one act. God's forgiveness and the step he took to release us are a unity. God acts and we know him in the effects of his action. He does something about our sin and we know him in what he does.

God's will is not a law or rule but 'God himself in action, and God is always in action'. If I go against this, 'I go against what Omnipotence is doing with me, would I but let him'. This means that there is a real battle of wills between God and sinners and it is God's good purpose to break down our enmity. However often we may turn our backs on God he forgives me, for:

> he takes my head between his hands and turns my face to his to make me smile at him. And though I struggle and hurt those hands – for they are human, though divine, human and scarred with nails – though I hurt them, they do not let me go until he has smiled me into smiling: and that is the forgiveness of God.[6]

A second fundamental idea for Farrer, of course, is Divine double agency, discussed more fully elsewhere in this book. This is the view that God always works by fully respecting the autonomous operations of his creatures. So in the case of the natural order God does not just make the world, he does something much more wonderful, he makes the world make itself.[7] In the case of us human beings this means that God works with and through our freely chosen actions. It is God who works but he works in and through us. For God is not another thing competing with our space. It is not the case that the more of him the less there is of us. On the contrary the more of him there is the more there is of us.[8] So it comes about that we can own an action as fully ours and at the same time say that it is the grace of God working in us, a claim which most Christians, like St Paul, would want to attest to.

And how can God best work with us in such a way that he fully respects our self-determination? By coming among us and relating to us without power or prestige as person to person. This again is fundamental for Farrer. Philosophy can indicate what might be meant by the word God – the infinite and underlying first cause of all secondary causes – but we know this God only as God has made himself accessible to us in human terms, in Christ.

Against that background it is then possible to consider Farrer's understanding of the incarnation, which again is integral to his understanding of redemption. For here, he admits, he follows an Eastern rather than a

Western understanding in making the incarnation rather than the cross fundamental to his theology. He approaches the uniqueness of Christ from two angles. First, there can be different degrees of relationship between creature and creator. At the lowest level, there is complete externality, as in God's relationship to the natural world. With human beings there can be a relationship in which we are conscious of inspiration, as when we pray for 'Thoughts higher than our own thoughts, prayers better than our own prayers, powers beyond our own powers'. In the case of Jesus the mutual interpenetration of the divine will and the human will was so complete and perfect that we can talk of identification. But this in itself is only half the picture. Jesus could have lived out his life of complete identification with the Father as a village carpenter. But he didn't because his vocation was to proclaim the Divine kingdom, the rule of God in human affairs, and to call people to live under that rule. This was because in and through him God was redeeming the world. In a characteristically brilliant passage Farrer wrote:

> The very action of Jesus is divine action – it is what God does about the salvation of the world. In the common case of a good human life, humanity supplies the pattern and God the grace. In Jesus, divine redemptive action supplies the pattern, and manhood the medium or instrument. A good man helped by Grace may do human things divinely. Christ did divine things humanly.[9]

Jesus lived a truly human life. He was shaped by the Judaism and limited cultural outlook of his time. He believed factual things which we now know to be mistaken. But in doing his father's will of proclaiming the kingdom he lived out his life as a son in perfect obedience to his father. He revealed what divine sonship meant in human terms. He did not live out eternal sonship as it exists in the life of the Trinity. He had no access to what that meant. He was the human embodiment of that relationship, his humanity being limited in the way all human lives are. In his case however he lived in perfect filial dependence and obedience as he carried out the work of divine redemption.

That redemption meant bringing people into the kingdom and so into the same relationship with the father that he eternally enjoys. He revealed the divine life and shared it with his followers so that they too were caught up in it and inspired to live it out. They too were taken into the life of the Trinity and called to work it out in their particular vocations. But the vocation of Jesus was unique, to act as the supreme agent of God's redemptive purpose, and in carrying this out the degree of mutuality was so complete it amounted to personal identification.[10]

This is not only God's redemptive act but the process in which God became man, or what Luther called 'The Proper Man'. For though God became flesh (*carnus*) at conception, he became man at his death. When we learn we have to unlearn previous ways of doing things. When we learn the good we unlearn the vice. Christ did not have to unlearn but he did learn and grow. When did this growing finish? His whole life is a birth and this is consummated in the empty sepulchre. In this process, he became who he was, a true human being.[11]

Farrer is deceptive in a number of ways. Widely recognized as a person of deep personal piety with a clear desire to help people enter the faith or understand it at a deeper level, it was easy for people to overlook the ferocity with which he rejected some traditional theological ideas. He was not attacked as a liberal for watering down or undermining the faith, but his views were in fact unequivocal in their criticism of what some, then and now, regarded as fundamental. About the cluster of ideas which make up a penal substitutionary view of the atonement, for example, he wrote that, if this is taken as a piece of solid theology,

> It is monstrous enough. The theologian will be bound to ask what he is to make of a debt to a Supernatural Bank of Justice. The idea is utterly meaningless; and if we try to give it substance by personifying the Bank as God himself, we merely exchange nonsense for blasphemy.[12]

Farrer strongly rejected the idea that Paul taught that Christ propitiated God. He offered expiation, the spiritual cure for our sins. He equally strongly rejected the idea that Paul taught that God poured his wrath on Christ or cut him off from grace as a substitute sinner on the cross. 'Nothing of this sort is to be found in the Bible.' If we ask what then did God do for our salvation the answer is that:

> In the saving action of the incarnation God came all lengths to meet us, and dealt humanly with human creatures ... He came among them, bring-ing his kingdom, and he let events take their human course. He set the divine life in human neighbourhood. Men discovered it in struggling with it and were captured by it in crucifying it. What could be simpler? And what more divine?[13]

As though recognizing that this would leave many people dissatisfied, he then analyses the line in Mrs Alexander's famous hymn 'There was no other good enough to pay the price of sin'. Over several pages he care-fully probes what this metaphor might or might not mean. It is easy to see that our redemption has been brought about *at* a price. God's forgiveness is God embracing our hostility, but this means embracing an armful of spears. He is the person carrying the flag of truce who gets shot. But what about the idea that our redemption is achieved *by* a price? He gives the analogy of a father and son who are estranged. Imagining the son to be entirely to blame, he is the one who ought to bear the humiliation involved in making up. But in fact it is the father who makes the overture and suffers the arrogance of the son and disappointment until he succeeds. The father bears what ought to have been borne by the son, in the case of Jesus this means crucifixion.

In another sermon, 'Christ's atoning death', Farrer asks what it means for Christ to have died *for* us. He is indeed the proper man and he died a perfect death, handing his life over to the father without flaw or qualification. But in what way is this for us? In answering this he explores the meaning of death. We are not just animals for whom death is simply a physical fact. For us it has a spiritual purpose, the casting off of a lower nature with all its corruptions and the hold that sin had on us through it. Death is ideally a death to sin, but we alas cannot die this death. Our body dies but our spirit cannot cast off sin and flesh together, for our heart is given to our fleshly self and not to God. But of Christ it can be said 'the death he died he died to sin once and for all: the life he now lives, he lives to God'.[14]

This death of Christ is not just there for us to imitate. Because it was an act of God it had in it an infinite power, to the radiation of which no limit can be set. All we have to do is consent and adhere to him, for he carries us through life and death. So Christ dies our death and achieves our life for us, and we die our death and enter into life through him. And this happens because on his side God is in him, and on our side we take hold, adhere or believe.[15]

Farrer is quite clear however that this does not let us off the hook. We still have to abandon a false attitude, sacrifice our pride and make amends to anyone we have wronged. These things are not remitted to us. We have all these things to do but his initiative set us in motion.

It was not necessary for Jesus to die for God to forgive us. We distinguish an attitude from an action, for example a grudge which we need to set aside in order to forgive someone. But God has no such grudges. We also distinguish forgiveness from reconciliation. But for God they are one movement. The embracing of us by Christ is the forgiveness which elicits our turning to him. For him forgiveness and reconciliation are one action.

Another key idea of Farrer which we need to take into account if we are to fully understand how he understands redemption, is the fact that for him membership of the church is not an optional extra, something which a professed Christian might or might not choose to take up. For as God gives himself to us through his incarnate life and death, that life and death comes to us only through his body on earth, the communion of Christian believers united with one another through their union with Christ. So it is that in his sermon on forgiveness he refers to the story of Christ healing the paralytic man not just to make the point that the forgiveness of God comes to us through Christ, but Christ and his forgiveness comes to us through his appointed ministers. Farrer focusses on the wonder of the crowds that God had given such power to forgive to men – not just to the Son of Man but to men in the plural. Building on this he quotes the texts in which

Christ gives his church authority to forgive, and suggests this is done not just through a general confession and absolution but as individuals confess their own sins to God before a priest and that priest in the name of Christ offers his forgiveness. There is a dual connection. First between God and Christ incarnate. We know God in and through Christ. Secondly between the incarnate, risen and ascended Christ and his continuing presence on earth in his body, the *koinonia* of Christian believers. There is nothing vague, wispy or merely philosophical here; all is embodiment, all is made real in flesh and blood.

This, you might say, is applicable to the individual believer but what about the belief that Christ achieved something decisive for the whole of humanity, indeed the whole of creation? God's act of universal forgiveness is the whole train of action he set working through Christ, the Spirit and the Church toward the reconciliation of all. 'And of this great process Christ's blood was, once more, the cost.'[16]

Farrer's argument is that men in this life make themselves into such people as will, or will not, respond to him in heaven. But in heaven they see not a solitary Christ but Christ in and through all those who are incorporated into him, who are part of his body. All salvation comes through him and without him there is none, but those who have not known him in this life have a chance in the next when they see his glory in those who are his.[17] Farrer did not argue either for or against universal salvation, saying that he was unwilling to look into the fate of the impenitent. But he did believe that all people would have a chance after death to see the glory of the incarnate Christ in those he had made his own. Bonhoeffer once defined the church as 'Christ taking form in the body of believers'. For Farrer it is Christ in that body of believers whom others will see, or fail to see, not only in this life but in the life to come.

Austin Farrer says that Paul was fortunate in having the myth of Adam to hand to bring out its universality, but we cannot use that myth in the same way. He argues that God acts in two ways. First, he acts in creation as the source of our wills where 'he creates men who create themselves'. Then, secondly, he influences one person through the impact of another creature. In particular he influences men through the man of glory, the creature Christ. This accounts for how God impacts on believers but what about the mass of humanity, how does Christ's death affect them? Not, says Farrer, by a diffused Christianity but through those who have been taken up into his body.

Here Farrer draws on three crucial aspects of his thought. Firstly, the central importance of Christian belief in heaven. He did not, like some modern Christians, sit light to it. For him it was a fundamental of the faith which could not be denied without bringing the whole house tumbling down. Secondly, his emphasis that heaven is still part of the *created* order. Most Christians, if they think about it at all, would think of heaven and God as being on the same level, a supranatural order beyond our ken. No, says Farrer, heaven is just as much part of the created order as is the world of flesh and blood. The created order is not identical with the physical world. The big divide is between God the uncaused creator of all that is, and what he has made and that includes heaven as well as earth. Then, thirdly, when Christ is seen in glory, he is seen 'with his saints' as the New Testament states. In heaven they see not a solitary Christ but Christ in and through all those who are incorporated into him, who are part of his body. These themes were particularly developed in *Love Almighty and Ills Unlimited*, his key contribution to theodicy. There he wrote:[18]

> Christ shone in his transfiguration, but it was a single episode and not the basis of the Gospel. The divine life which radiated through him took effect in words, deeds and sufferings; a saving action developed in discourse and in mutual dealing with friends and enemies; more especially with friends. The Christ of the Gospels can only be known through what he did and in the doing of it. And how shall Christ of Advent be known, but through what he has done and in the possession of it? If Christ's glory and godhead were first manifest in the saving of men, and in the men he saved, how shall these things be manifest at last, but in the men he has saved, and in their being at one with him?[19]

This is nothing less than:

> The completion of Christ's incarnation. Christ is made whole in head and members; this is the Israel of God, the core and substance of heavenly being, a reality sufficient to act as the touchstone of judgement for all the souls of men, assimilating to itself and embodying in its own life those who are found able to respond – and in this way the universal efficacy of Christ takes effect.[20]

So, in more devotional mode:

> When we meet him, and see in his hands the impress of the force with which we hammered his nails, we shall be in hell. But he will draw our eyes to his, and then we shall be in heaven. For we shall see them warm with welcome, alive with exultation ... then we shall share his joy for under the eyes of Truth himself we shall not have the hypocrisy to grieve at what he is most happy to have done: and looking on his wounds again we shall find them terrible no more.[21]

Farrer, to a remarkable degree, combined a sceptical mind with a devout temperament. One of the effects of this was to lead him to get right back to first premises and to start his thinking from there. This had the further effect of leading him to seek maximum clarity in what he wrote. In relation to the subject of this chapter, it led him to seek and state quite clearly what Christ had done for us. He liked to use a range of biblical images to bring out the spiritual force and implications of Christ's death. He was also willing to deploy the imagery associated with traditional theories of the atonement for the same purpose, to highlight some aspect of our redemption. But he thought that to rest content with this, simply using all the theories and images to explore a mystery beyond any of them, led to an ultimate scepticism. He believed something clear and definite had to be said and could be said. If that was done the images and metaphors could be deployed to bring out the spiritual and emotional aspects, but there needed to be a hard core to which they could relate. Hence his statement, so definite and clear, already quoted:

> In the saving action of the incarnation God came all lengths to meet us, and dealt humanly with human creatures ... He came among them bringing his kingdom, and he let events take their human course. He set the divine life in human neighbourhood. Men discovered it in struggling with it and were captured by it in crucifying it. What could be simpler? And what more divine?

This means that the incarnation, as argued earlier, was his key belief in thinking about our redemption, the setting of divine life in human neighbourhood. This was an actual event, with historical consequences, something objective. It led to the cross and this had the effect of raising a large question mark against every self-evaluation, and so to the breaking down of all barriers for the first followers of Jesus; and this had the further effect of bringing into being a community of believers. This too was an event, something achieved in history. As argued earlier, Farrer did not believe that the effects of the incarnation were limited to time and space. Whether in time or out of time all would have the opportunity to recognize Christ in his people. His work of redemption, breaking down all barriers and reconciling them to the fount of their being, was not only objective but had universal significance. But he sees this objective, universal significance not in mythical terms but in the actual working out of the incarnation within time and beyond time.

Notes

1 Austin Farrer, *Saving Belief*, London, Hodder and Stoughton, 1967.

2 C. S. Lewis wrote a book in which the chief devil advises lesser devils on ways of leading humans into sin, *The Screwtape Letters*, London, Fount, 1977.

3 Austin Farrer, 'Forgiveness of Sins' in *A Faith of Our Own*, World Publishing, Cleveland, OH, 1960, pp. 66–7; Austin Farrer, 'All Souls' Examination,' *Said or Sung*, London, Faith Press, 1964, p. 58.

4 Ibid., p. 66.

5 Ibid., p. 73.

6 This and the words in the previous paragraph, ibid., p. 68.

7 The phrase comes originally from Charles Kingsley's *Water Babies*.

8 This is a main emphasis, with due acknowledgements to Farrer, of Rowan Williams in *Christ the Heart of Creation*, London, Bloomsbury, 2018.

9 *Saving Belief*, pp. 74–5.

10 On incarnation see Edward Henderson, 'Double Agency and the Relation of Persons to God' in *The Human Person in God's World*, ed. Brian Hebblethwaite and Douglas Hedley, London, SCM Press, 2006, pp. 65ff.

11 This was the theme of one of the four Holy Week Addresses given at Cuddesdon Theological College in 1963 and notes taken at the time by the author.

12 *Saving Belief*, p. 103.

13 Ibid., p. 99.

14 'Christ's Atoning Death', in *A Faith of Our Own*, p. 23; 'Atoning Death', in Austin Farrer, *The Essential Sermons*, ed. Leslie Houlden, London, SPCK, 1991, p. 45.

15 Ibid., p. 24.

16 *Saving Belief*, p. 107.

17 This paragraph is also based on the Holy Week lectures Farrer delivered at Cuddesdon Theological College in 1963 and notes taken at the time by the author.

18 Austin Farrer, *Love Almighty and Ills Unlimited*, London, Fontana, 1966.

19 Ibid., p. 129.

20 Ibid., p. 130.

21 Austin Farrer, *Lord I Believe*, London, Faith Press, 1958, p. 68; US edition, Cambridge MA, Cowley Publications, 1989.

12

Theosis, Godmanhood and Double Agency: Berdyaev, Farrer and the Divine-Human Relationship

GREGORY PLATTEN

'There is no end to God's making of man.'
Austin Farrer, 'The Potter's Clay'

'... the mystery of Christianity is the genesis of God in man and man in God.'
Nicolas Berdyaev, *The Meaning of the Creative Act*

The turbulent twentieth century, with its unprecedented human tragedies and advances, provided fertile soil for theologians whose research focussed on the divine-human relationship. This chapter brings together two very different theologians: Austin Farrer (1904–68) and Nicolas Berdyaev (1874–1948) for whom that relationship was central, and whose thought, it might be argued, shares some characteristics of the Patristic concept of *theosis*. Quite how much contact these two had has not yet been established. We do know, however, that both were directly associated with the pioneering work of the Fellowship of St Alban and St Sergius, based in Oxford. Berdyaev was a regular contributor to Fellowship conferences,[1] and Farrer was known as an occasional speaker at the House of SS Gregory and Macrina.[2] This Fellowship, whose membership included leading Russian émigrés fleeing Lenin and Stalin's persecution, was a novel place of encounter between the Western Catholic tradition (largely Anglican) and Eastern Orthodoxy.

This chapter is both a contrast and a comparison of Berdyaev and Farrer, which seeks to explore whether their understanding of the divine-human relationships might be understood within the broad, Patristic notion of *theosis*, which is perhaps best translated as 'deification'. Berdyaev and Farrer are neither natural intellectual nor cultural bedfellows. An attempt to suggest that they reach the same conclusions, or even that they follow the same route map, would be strained and foolhardy: the influences on their thought, their own personal and intellectual backgrounds, and even their styles, could not be more radically different. It is, however, arguable that they share a common desire to retain human agency alongside the invitation to participation in the divine life. There are other points at which their conclusions share common ground: they both foresee a creative, dynamic relationship between God and humanity, and they both show humility in the face of the theological complexity of this idea. Despite their obvious differences, they share some common elements and these common elements are fundamental to speaking about human freedom and the incarnation. In order to do this, it is necessary to offer a thorough introduction to Berdyaev, who has become something of a Cinderella at the theological ball – despite a fascinating biography and exercising considerable influence upon the intellectual culture of his time.

It is important first to introduce briefly the notion of *theosis* (θέωσις): as a term, it is first recorded in the pre-Christian works of the Greek-Cyrenian Callimachus (*c*.310–*c*.240 BC). It enters the Christian theological lexicon, in the way that we currently understand it, to mean 'deification' through Gregory of Nazianzen's writings, although interestingly it is one of the rarest terms for deification used by the Greek early church writers.[3] Later used by both Pseudo-Dionysius and Maximus the Confessor, it is used to describe salvation, understood in terms of the union of the divine and the human, through the salvific act of Christ. The Orthodox theologian Vladimir Lossky describes it thus:

> Christian theology is always in the last resort a means: a unity of knowledge subserving an end which transcends all knowledge. This ultimate end is union with God or deification, the θέωσις of the Greek Fathers. Thus, we are finally led to a conclusion which may seem paradoxical enough: that Christian theory should have a pre-eminently practical significance and that the more mystical it is, the more directly it aspires to the supreme end of union with God.[4]

As we explore Berdyaev and Farrer, it is my contention that (in their different ways) both writers are exploring the idea of the human incorporation into the divine, which is described by this word *theosis*. Indeed, Berdyaev wrote 'the realisation of beauty is the *theosis* of the creature, the revelation of the divine in the human personality'.[5]

Introducing Nicolas Berdyaev

In his time, Berdyaev's influence was considerable[6] but his profile today is arguably negligible. Berdyaev's biography can broadly be understood in three phases: his early life as an atheist activist in Russia; his exile from Russia; and finally his conversion to Christianity and life as an émigré among many other Russian émigrés in Paris. His personal and spiritual life are inextricably intertwined.

Berdyaev was born in Kiev (then in Russia) in 1874 to a father from the Russian elite and a mother from minor French nobility. Although nominally Orthodox, his mother kept faithful to her Roman Catholic roots, while his father (Berdyaev recalled in his autobiography) was a Voltairean free-thinker with a 'vaguely deistic' sympathy. Even as a young child, Berdyaev believed that he was seeking freedom, as 'from the very beginning I was aware of having fallen into an alien world'.[7]

Although a mediocre young pupil, he eventually matriculated into the University of Kiev, reading Natural Sciences – a modish course of study within Russian universities at the time. At the same time, Berdyaev became an active socialist and his pamphleteering led to arrest, imprisonment and subsequent exile. It was during his exile (where he stayed in an hotel in Vologda and had his own butler!) that Berdyaev's existential journey continued, his fascination with freedom at its heart. During this time, his thought attempted to elide Marxist and Idealist ideas, and this resulted in his being cast out by his Marxist and Idealist colleagues alike. His ongoing dissatisfaction betrayed an inner conviction of 'the prospect of a spiritual revolution'.[8]

Following his imprisonment, Berdyaev began further to explore this spiritual revolution, travelling to Germany and Switzerland, and immersing himself in Kantian ideas under the influence of Wilhelm Windelband (1848–1915). Returning to Russia he came under the spell of the so-called 'New Religious Consciousness', which he recalls had Dionysian elements, early Sophiology and Nietzschean philosophy, as well as encountering the extraordinary couple Dmitri Merezhkovsky (1865–1941) and his wife Zinaida Gippius (1869–1945). He calls this period a 'hothouse with no door or window to the fresh air'.[9] His marriage in 1904 to Lydia Trudasheva, herself a religious and political woman, strengthened his nascent spiritual hunger and turned his thinking in an explicitly religious direction.

Arguably, it is in the early years of the twentieth century that Berdyaev's thinking becomes Christian, without losing any sense of freedom's primacy and revolutionary nature. Indeed, in a testy letter to Zinaida Gippius, he actively criticizes 'God seekers' who do not take Christ seriously:

If I once was not with you because I did not know whether or not I was with Christ, and you did not know whether or not I would be against Him, now I will not be with you, but rather against you, if I feel that you are against Christ, but I do not doubt Him and never will.[10]

From this moment, Berdyaev begins to formulate a Christology, taking seriously his obsession with freedom, seeing it best manifested within the divine–human relationship. Berdyaev's thought does not sit easily within the Orthodox Church's mainstream tradition, although he absolutely regards himself as Orthodox.[11] At the same time, Berdyaev does not shrink away from criticizing the Orthodox Church in Russia. An article written in 1913 resulted in Berdyaev's exile some five years later. Criticizing the church (and by default the Imperial government) for attacking monks on Mount Athos with gunboats in a dispute over the Holy Name of Jesus, Berdyaev was facing a death sentence.

In an ironic twist, the Russian Revolution saw the end of Tsarist rule and also the end of Berdyaev's prosecution, although Lenin's accession to power brought about a desire to remove those members of the intelligentsia perceived to be a threat. Berdyaev was on that list of intellectuals. There were various theologians, philosophers and politicians exiled on what have become known as the Philosophers' Ships by Lenin's personal fiat.[12] Exiled first to Weimar Germany and then to Paris, Berdyaev would spend the remainder of his life there alongside other exiles, including his friend Sergei Bulgakov. It was during this period that Berdyaev began fully to formulate his thought on freedom, and Christ, and Christ's relationship to humanity. It is to this that we now must turn.

While Berdyaev has often been read philosophically, he is rarely read theologically. His obsession with human freedom has been the focus of the majority of studies, and such studies have led to him being described as the 'philosopher of freedom *par excellence*'.[13] While arguably freedom is a *leit-motif* for Berdyaev, it can only be understood through his understanding of Christ, and divine-humanity, or *Godmanhood* as Berdyaev calls it.

For Berdyaev, creation emerges from a primal freedom and this freedom reaches its full realization in the outworking of Godmanhood, a co-creative divine-human relationship. This idea of a primal freedom comes from Berdyaev's reading of the sixteenth-century mystic, Jakob Boehme, who speaks about an '*Ungrund*', which is best described as a 'no-thing' and is perhaps synonymous with the nothingness from which God creates the world. Berdyaev is attracted to this mystical notion of the *Ungrund* with what he calls Boehme's 'antinomic' approach, although he acknowledges that he 'does not claim to be true to Boehme in every respect'.[14]

Berdyaev describes his understanding of freedom and the *Ungrund* in primordial terms. Whereas for Boehme *Ungrund* might well be understood as the *nihilo* void of the Creation Narrative (Gen. 1.2), Berdyaev defines it rather more radically as 'it lies outside God, outside of being, is pre-existent to being which is already determined'.[15] For some this conclusion is fatal for the whole of Berdyaev's work, exemplified in the writing of Berdyaev's own friend, Evgeni Lampert, who wrote that this is the most 'disastrous conclusion in his whole philosophy ... and one which seems in fact in no way unwarranted'.[16] More recently, Rowan Williams criticized Berdyaev's approach, arguing that 'It's all very exciting but I am not sure what you are supposed to do with it ... there's an emptiness behind it.'[17] It is, however, possible to offer a defence of Berdyaev's thought. Indeed, Berdyaev acknowledges his own inconsistencies and contradictions, but he also argues that his thought is 'fragmentary and aphoristic not ratiocinative: it belongs intuitively with life.'[18] He is, he writes, a 'homo mysticus.'[19] He writes that he is seeking to 'speak of the unspeakable and ineffable apophatic mystery of God's life'.[20] For one espousing an apophatic approach, however, Berdyaev could occasionally be criticized for being too aphoristic – arguably too cataphatic in explaining his apophasis! At the same time, while noting his problematic style, in his outworking of Godmanhood,[21] one can see how Berdyaev is attempting to reconcile human freedom, redemption and the divine-human life beyond full human explication.

Freedom

Freedom was not simply an abstract obsession to Berdyaev, it was core to his incarnational understanding, which he calls his 'Christological anthropology'.[22] Both Christ and humanity emerge from this freedom. Let us briefly explore first Berdyaev's understanding of Christ, and how humanity relates to Christ, in order fully to understand how divine-humanity – or Godmanhood – is a process which results in a co-creative relationship.

Berdyaev's Incarnational theology is a mixture of tradition and novelty. Recalling once more how he saw his 'vision' (his own self-description) within the tradition of Orthodoxy, he roots his vision in the Second Adam typology of Paul (1 Cor. 15.22). Christ is, he writes, 'the spiritual Adam'.[23] In an article on Jakob Boehme he goes on to allude to Athanasius' *De Incarnatione* when he writes:

> Christ became the God-Man and Adam and Abraham in Christ a man-god [Berdyaev is quoting from Boehme's *Mysterium Magnum* vol. 5]. This means also, that God was incarnated, became man, so that man might become divinised, become deified … In Boehme can be found an aspect of that teaching about God-manhood, which in Russian thought chiefly was developed by Vl. Solov'ev.[24]

Christ the Second Adam, in this vision, restores humanity's lost freedom, the freedom from which all creation emerged and to which all creation seeks to return. The freedom of the first Adam and the freedom of Christ in the Second Adam are different. Using John's Gospel (8.32), he goes on, 'The truth shall make men free, but they [humans] must freely accept it and not be brought to it by force.'[25] Likewise, Berdyaev affirms the deifying and liberating necessity of Christ who 'has taken upon himself the sins of the world, and He can take away our sin and forgive it'.[26]

The root of freedom, shared by both Christ and humanity, means that salvation has to be voluntary. Indeed, the voluntarism of the human will is central to Berdyaev's Incarnational model. He is strongly influenced here by Nietzsche, of whom he is both fond and critical. Berdyaev is clear that humanity must have the power to come to Christ but also, radically, to be in partnership with Christ. He describes Nietzsche (usually regarded as atheistic in approach) as a 'forerunner of a new religious anthropology'.[27] It has been recently and convincingly argued that Berdyaev takes Nietzsche's concept of the *Übermensch* and fuses it with Athanasius' and Gregory of Nazianzen's Christology to reimagine Christology in terms of the God-man and *Godmanhood*. Grillaert argues that Nietzsche's *Übermensch*

> embodies the particular qualities Berdiaev finds missing in traditional Christian anthropology, specifically a focus upon faith in the human's creative powers which for him is where the religious dimension of Nietzsche's thought lies.[28]

The *Übermensch*, adopted and adapted by Berdyaev, is a human being with freedom of the will to become divine. He traces this anthropological history, which is in many ways a historical anthropogony, or human self-creation. From that initial *Ungrund* freedom borrowed from Boehme, Berdyaev traces the becoming of humanity, and Godmanhood from the early church writers to the crowning moment of Nietzsche. Berdyaev writes:

> ... the primal foundations of the world rest upon a certain irrational and wilful principle, and the whole essence of the world process consists in the illumination of this dark irrational principle in cosmogony and theogony ... I believe that this primal drama and mystery of Christianity consists in the genesis of God in man and man in God.[29]

Through Christ, but also through humanity's freedom to become like Christ, humanity becomes incorporated into a unique divine-human relationship. Each human has the power through 'will' to become divinely incorporated and realize this vocation. The failure of this relationship or this becoming, Berdyaev argues, introduces the idea of a tragedy to the heart of the divine-human relationship, and a sense of suffering for both humans and the divine. The notion of a tragic or 'suffering' Christ is a theme of Berdyaev's writings that would come to influence later theologians, including Jürgen Moltmann.[30] Paul Fiddes writes that Berdyaev's Christ 'longs for one who can reciprocate his love, and he knows tragedy'.[31] Quite clearly the God-man, Christ, experiences rejection at the hands of humanity. Through the absolute freedom of creation, which is embodied in the human will to choose partnership, rests the truth that humanity is equally free to reject and to crucify the God-man. Berdyaev writes: 'it [freedom] reveals tragedy in the Divine life itself. God Himself, the Only Begotten Son, suffers, and is crucified, an innocent sufferer'.[32] It is a suffering that humanity must also endure if it is indeed to be at one with the God-man and experience Godmanhood. George Pattison describes Berdyaev's approach well, when he writes:

This process of divine self-creation ... is understood as revealed within and through the interdependence of the divine and human. In other words, it is precisely in and through the creative transformation of suffering and creative contestation of the history of nothingness that is exemplified in the Passion narrative and encountered in innumerable instances of creative living that God 'becomes' Creator.[33]

Tragedy might be one possible outcome of the freedom of the human will, given in God's creation out of nothing. But there also remains the possibility of what Berdyaev calls the 'Creative Act', or the 'Eighth Day of Creation.' In this scenario the human will chooses to ally itself entirely with the divine – through Christ. Berdyaev also views the 'ethic of creativity' in terms of movement, as an 'act' that marks the inauguration of the final stage of freedom. This 'act' is the full, free, creative union of the divine and the human and what Berdyaev calls the 'eighth day'; he suggests it as another dimension, an extra day within the scheme of creation described by the Book of Genesis. It begins with Christ's manifestation in the world. He writes:

> The positive, creative purpose and content of freedom could not yet be conceived at that stage of creation, the seven-day stage, since in creation there had not yet been revealed the Absolute Man, the Son of God, the revelation of the Eighth Day.[34]

The creativity that Berdyaev is describing includes artistic and literary creativity, which he sees as rooted in the divine-human relationship which he also sees (in part thanks to Hegel's influence) as a process heading toward perfection. Indeed, he describes at length the way that the divine has been both illuminated and obscured in different periods of art, architecture and literature. Creativity, though, is more than human-divine inspired activity, it implies the complete transfiguration of the cosmos in which this creative act can 'leave the heaviness of the world behind'.[35] This must begin in daily life, and demands that humans choose to

> act as though you can hear the Divine call to participate through free and creative activity in the Divine work: cultivate in yourself a pure and original conscience, discipline your personality, struggle with evil in yourself and around you – not in order to relegate the wicked to hell and create a kingdom of evil, but to conquer evil and to further a creative regeneration of the wicked.[36]

This divine-human creativity has interesting implications for the whole gamut of human life, and Berdyaev explores the implications for politics, economics, peace and war, justice, and even technological progress (of which he is no fan!). In his musings he remains pessimistic about the world, in part no doubt influenced by living in a Europe in the midst of rapid, terrifying and turbulent change. In all of these aspects, though, it remains clear that radical change can be affected in the here and now through the divine-human relationship of Godmanhood, even as we await the final eschaton for its absolute fulfilment.

The implication of Berdyaev's 'Creative Act' is eschatological and refers both to the ethical renewal of the current world order but at the same time an age to come – the full transfiguration of the world. The creativeness of the present is the Holy Spirit at work whereby humans in union with Christ through their actions are precursors of the full transfiguration of fully realized divine-humanity that is yet to come. This time-to-come, this is the divine-human Creative Act which is what Berdyaev calls the 'Eighth Day'. This fulfilment is the restoration of man following the Fall, by which the process of divine-human creativity will be complete, and the union restored:

> When Christianity has reached its full development this antithesis [between creator and created] will be resolved and there will be a positive revelation of God-Humanity, the union of the two movements, the uniting of Christianity and creation.[37]

At this point, the incarnation will be fulfilled, as humanity and divinity transform the existing world. It remains unclear, however, whether Berdyaev understands this to be a temporal transformation or the beginning of an entirely new order. In the end, his imprecision in this regard is unhelpful. It reflects a paradox (of which he is aware) throughout his thought, as it veers between his extensive cataphatic, rhetorical and descriptive interpretations of divine-humanity alongside his ultimate belief that no one can 'speak of the unspeakable and ineffable apophatic mystery of God's life'.[38]

Austin Farrer

As we shall see, Farrer too accepted that humility was needed in the face of any substantial intellectual engagement with the Godhead and that, in the end, words will be inadequate, and one has to engage with an element of paradox. At the same time, Austin Farrer's style and approach could not be further from Berdyaev's aphoristic and kaleidoscopic approach.

Austin Farrer is better known to contemporary theology than Berdyaev, and his work is once again being recognized for its extraordinary depth and clarity. Indeed, he has recently been described as 'the foremost philosophical theologian of the Church of England in the mid-twentieth century' by Rowan Williams (arguably himself Anglicanism's finest contemporary theologian).[39]

Farrer, like Berdyaev, concludes that the very 'object of religion is to establish a proper relation between men and their creator'.[40] A great deal of Farrer's writing is devoted to exploring the relationship between the Creator and created humanity, describing a relationship that is free, and reciprocal: the inextricable knitting of wills. The analogy that he uses to describe this relationship in *Faith and Speculation* is that of a personal friendship, a relationship of promise and covenant ground but where there exists also a 'free mutuality'. Freedom, both in the abstract, and 'freedom of the will' is at the centre of Farrer's divine-human understanding and writing and underlines his concept of 'double agency'. There are arguably aspects of broad, thematic agreement between Farrer and Berdyaev, even if they part company in terms of how those themes are explored. For example, Farrer – like Berdyaev – is interested in freedom, although not in abstract terms but specifically understood in terms of the freedom of human will. Christology, too, is a theme both within his sermons and his philosophical theology – and, specifically, how God interacts in the world through humanity. Finally, Farrer explores paradox, and the ultimate inexplicability of the divine in human terms and language. Nevertheless, leaving the broad thematic similarities aside, Farrer's conclusions are often, unsurprisingly, very different.

Freedom as free will

Although he does not cite any names, in his criticisms of Continental Existentialism, Farrer could be offering a sharp critique of Berdyaev in his Gifford lectures:[41] 'Certain existentialist thinkers on the Continent have carried self-creation to the limit and have boldly proclaimed ... that liberty is so absolute, it topples over into absurdity.'[42]

The Freedom of the Will is a thorough refutation of determinism, and a clear attempt by Farrer to chart a path for human freedom that allows for the divine will and human freedom to coexist. Farrer continuously asserts the notion of human free will, while avoiding overly abstracted understandings of primal freedom, such as Berdyaev's abstract *Ungrund*. Mocking the Continental Existentialist's 'libertarian battlecry', which he caricatures as imprisoning, he writes, 'Thank heaven I have not to meditate *in vacuo* on what to make of myself'.[43] In so doing Farrer rejects an entirely voluntarist and existential approach to freedom in the abstract.

At the same time, he accepts that there remains an inherent paradox in being free and created by God. Farrer comes to describe this as the 'paradox of creative and creaturely wills'; it is concisely summarized when he writes about the 'paradox of two agents to a single activity, one finite, the other infinite' which 'cannot be confined within the limits of personal and moral existence'.[44] This 'paradox' is at the root of his incarnational theological writing, in which the human being has free will, but remains a natural creature: 'nature is a divine ordinance, and all natural effects, so far as they have a positive end, are the handiwork of God'.[45] He writes in *Interpretation and Belief*: 'the paradox of human existence is that man becomes an object to himself; he is concerned with realising what he is: this is the mystery of the will'.[46] For Farrer this paradox of finite and infinite is rooted, crowned and resolved in the God-Man, Jesus Christ.

Christology

While more conventional in his approach than Berdyaev, Farrer's creativity and insight must not be understated in any attempt to protect his perceived orthodoxy. Indeed, Farrer's theology and philosophy around the incarnation was, writes Rowan Williams, 'unusual and fertile'.[47]

For Farrer, Christ is 'very God and very man'; in an essay bearing that title he defends an orthodox Christological understanding, writing that: 'Christ is both God – the eternal Reason himself – and man, a common or garden rational animal like you and me'.[48]

A seemingly clear and simple declaration hides within it a deeper complexity – as much of Farrer's writing often does. Indeed, Farrer is clear that what he is hinting at in this remark is far greater than repeating a dry theological formula. It is to describe how the Infinite Godhead comes *to be* in *one* finite human being – it is a way of describing the fundamental core of the divine-human relationship. God is manifest both in the finite and infinite in Jesus Christ. He writes: 'God is that life ... that an eternity of exploration will not exhaust ... and God the Son on earth is a fullness of holy life within the limit of mortality'.[49]

In this unique relationship humanity is incorporated into the divine being; but in the relationship of the Son to the Father, we see finite and infinite in perfect symbiosis. Using a typically simple Farrer analogy, he explains that an orthopaedic surgeon knows how to repair the broken leg, because he knows the form and the function of the bones and muscles in the leg. So, by analogy, 'knowing how to be the Divine Son in earthly flesh involved ... a practical, contemplative and, shall we say, a mystical, knowledge, of the Father'.[50] Or as he puts it in an Ascension Day sermon with economy and depth: 'the earthborn Jesus rises into the native heaven of that divine life which has become man in him'.[51]

This perfect and mystical union of finite and infinite is, of course, the core of Farrer's own understanding of the wider divine-human relationship, which he understood in terms of 'double agency'. It is through this relationship that God continues to act in the world. Just as one man in Christ Jesus is in perfect relationship to God the Father as the Son, so every human being is capable of being in such a relationship of union too. While he believed that this new creation in Christ promised a 'world beyond this world', he also believed that through Christ's unique bond between finite and infinite, God was able to act in the world without either being interventionist in the classical sense, or being affected in the inner Godhead.

God is at work in and through humanity. Farrer uses Jeremiah's image of the potter working clay (Jer. 18): 'those hands did not make us once, like magic toys, and turn us free to run; the house of Israel is still clay in the hands of God, neither is there any end to the shaping of them'. Far from seeing us as play things in the hand of a puppet-master potter, he makes clear that God is a very different sort of creator: 'for the clay in which God works is free will, and though he gave us life, it is free'.[52] God works with our free will, as a potter works the clay. Edward Henderson describes it thus: 'God acts ... by acting in the actions of creatures in a way that preserves their natural modes of operation and their integrity as creatures enjoy a being of their own'.[53]

The analogy of the clay as free will reminds us that *will* is central to Farrer's notion of double agency. As Jesus Christ's will knitted absolutely with God the Father, so God is able to act in the world through human beings whose free will also voluntarily knits to the divine will. There can be no force upon the will: 'nothing results ... by mere force of hand, unless the clay is fit and responds' but 'if we love his will, we take the shape of it'.[54] Just as Jesus Christ was 'very God and very man' so any human being who knits her will to God's, enables God's will to be enacted in the world; an act of human and divine will as one. In *The Science of God*, Farrer explains that God is related to us:

As the will which underlies our existence, gives rise to our action and directs our aim ... we cannot touch God except by willing the will of God. Then his will takes effect in ours and we know it: not that we manipulate him, but that he possesses us.[55]

Paradox

There is, of course, a paradox at the heart of Farrer's 'double agency', of which he was acutely aware. Unity between the divine and human comes from a unity of humans freely 'submitting' to the will of God and in such we see the paradox of free submission: here we identify the paradox of a being that is *created, given freedom*, then later to be given the 'free' option to surrender that freedom.

We might compare the paradox of freedom proposed by Farrer with that of Nicolas Berdyaev. He too identifies a paradox, albeit from his perspective of 'absolute' freedom. He seeks to affirm a universal salvation (apocatastasis) rooted in the Ungrundian, original freedom. He stops short, however, because he realizes that a human soul born of absolute freedom cannot (by definition) be saved through any universal force. It is clear that the sort of radical freedom that Berdyaev proposes is curtailed in Farrer's model, and yet paradox remains. In Farrer's model, humans are given free will to determine future and self, and yet the goal Farrer wills for humanity is their total incorporation into the Godhead: 'God's action is encountered in one's own action in the embrace of the divine will as one's own will'.[56] While Farrer's approach to freedom, humanity, salvation and God is diametrically opposed to Berdyaev's model, he still accepts that paradox remains.

Farrer accepts that this paradox of the human will's submission to the divine also renders complex the relationship between divine and human action. When is an act divine, and when is it human, when is it divine-human? Quite where the 'causal joint' is between the divine and the human is not defined, and must remain unknowable. Farrer argues that this is because it is 'no concern of the activity of religion' but only a 'by product of the analogical imagination'. Double agency is to experience and not *to understand*:

> Turn from symbolism to action, and the problem vanishes' because 'We can … experience the active relation of created energy to the Creator's action. Everyone who prays knows that the object of the exercise is a thought or an aspiration or a caring which is no more ours than it is of God in us.[57]

Through the ascent of our divinely created but *free* will, to the action of the divine will, double agency takes place. For Farrer this is nothing other than incorporation into the trinitarian divine life. Here human action and the divine action become mysteriously and paradoxically one: divine-human action (double agency) becomes a single action of the divine. We are incorporated into the divine: 'it is the completion of Christ's incarnation. Christ is made whole in head and members'.[58] When we have reached that point of wills in unity, where we are so outside ourselves as to be fully in God, then we become incorporated into the Trinity, in what Farrer calls the 'fourth ecstasy':

> It was by being outside himself – by being ecstatic in the literal sense of that word that Jesus brought the life of the Blessed Trinity into our world; for it is in ecstasy and in mutual indwelling that the marvellous life of the Godhead consists … It is the fourth ecstasy, when creatures of God go out of themselves to be in God who indwells with them.[59]

We are reminded of Berdyaev's co-unity of the divine and human in the notion of Godmanhood: Farrer's 'fourth ecstasy' might have some similarities to Berdyaev's 'Eighth Day of Creation', although Farrer expresses his co-creative union in terms of humanity's free submission to the divine will that created it, the fourth ecstasy of the Holy Trinity.

Conclusion

In many ways, Farrer and Berdyaev are dimensionally different. Berdyaev's rhetorical, apophatic-speculative approach could not be more different from Farrer's carefully argued, logical Thomism.

At the same time, however, both are concerned to maintain the definitive freedom of the human while acknowledging the radical human-divine cooperation born of the incarnation. Both are also clear that, through a divine-human relationship, humans participate in the creative acts of God. While Berdyaev, at times, suggests a radically unorthodox parity between the divine and the human, Farrer writes about the meeting of wills, while making clear that humans are, by virtue of their being created by God, inferior to God and 'men live and act under God'.[60]

In the end, both admit to the inadequacy of words, and the ultimate unimaginable nature both of God and the divine-human relationship: 'as God himself is unimaginable, so also must be the dependence of his creatures upon his power'.[61]

Likewise, Berdyaev speaks of the 'unspeakable and ineffable apophatic mystery of God's life',[62] and the co-creative divine-human relationship as being best described as a 'fundamental drama of love and freedom.'[63]

Both are firmly convinced that the only way to understand the divine-human relationship of co-creativity, is through paradox. Farrer writes of the 'paradox of two wills in one existence, the perfect and the imperfect'.[64] In strikingly similar words, Berdyaev writes 'creator and creature, grace and freedom present an insoluble problem, a tragic conflict, a paradox.'[65]

It is not only in paradox that these two strikingly different theologians meet again. Both are clear that the divine-human relationship of co-creativity is never going to be rationalized and resolved in the mind. Rather, it will be apprehended and comprehended in experience and Christian life alone: 'What we lose in imaginative clarity is made up in actuality' writes Farrer, 'just where we cease to conceive our dependence on God, we begin to live it'.[66] Likewise, Berdyaev is clear that one can only fully comprehend the mystery of Godmanood, or divine-human creativity in terms of experience, which he explains is behind all his thought and writing.

Despite their acceptance that we cannot fully rationalize any understanding of divine-humanity, these two very different theologians do suggest that the salvific outworking of the Christian faith is nothing less than the ultimate union of the divine and the human. As such, it is arguable that both Farrer and Berdyaev are describing, in their unique ways, some notion of *theosis*, or the 'ultimate end of union with God, or deification', as Lossky describes it above, and which has long been a crucial theme of Christian theology.

Both Farrer and Berdyaev were practising theologians whose work, far from being an attempt to delineate invisible phantoms or score abstruse philosophical points, was in fact attempting to describe the divine-human relationship at the heart of their faith and being. Both accepted that the core of their faith resides not in the head alone, but in the heart. The divine-human relationship and its inherent paradox is comprehended fully not in reason alone, but in full *living relationship* to God.

Notes

1 S. D. Filippos, *The Fellowship of St Alban and St Sergius*, Newcastle-upon-Tyne, Cambridge Scholars Publishing, 2018, p. 42.

2 I am very grateful to Metropolitan Kallistos Ware who, in correspondence, recalls attending one such talk in the House of SS Gregory and Macrina in the early 1960s, adding: 'He was a remarkable thinker, and it was always interesting to listen to him.'

3 For an excellent exploration of the 'deification' in Early Greek writers, see Norman Russell's *The Doctrine of Deification in the Greek Patristic Tradition*, Oxford, Oxford University Press, 2004. Especially helpful is his second appendix exploring 'the Greek Vocabulary of Deification', pp. 333–44.

4 Vladimir Lossky, *The Mystical Theology of the Eastern Church*, Cambridge, James Clarke, 1957, p. 9.

5 Nicolas A. Berdyaev, 1937, *The Destiny of Man*, London, Geoffrey Bles, p. 248.

6 It is worth noting that Berdyaev's *The Russian Revolution* is quoted in the front matter of Aldous Huxley's *Brave New World*. Orthodox writer Oliver Clément attributes his conversion to Berdyaev who 'allowed me to glimpse not a moralizing Christianity – as my parents and many others imagined – but something profoundly liberating ... [it] changed my life' (quoted from Rafael Mathieu, *Olivier Clément, philosophe de la lumière*, http://www.page sorthodoxes.net/theologiens/clement/olivier-clement-intro.htm#mathieu (accessed 5.12.2011) – Mathieu records the centrality of Berdyaev's thought to Clément's conversion to Christianity).

7 Nicolas A. Berdyaev, *Dream and Reality: an Essay in Autobiography*, London, Geoffrey Bles, 1949, p. 1.

8 Ibid., p. 108.

9 Ibid., p. 141.

10 Donald A. Lowrie, *Rebellious Prophet*, London, Victor Gollancz, 1960, p. 98.

11 Nicolas A. Berdyaev, 'The Truth of Orthodoxy', *The Student World*, July (XXI), pp. 249–63.

12 For an interesting and readable account of these exiles, see Lesley Chamberlain's *The Philosophy Steamer*, London, Atlantic, 2006.

13 Philippe Sabant, 'Débats', in *Colloque Berdiaev*, Paris, Institut d'Etudes Slaves, p. 73.

14 Nicolas A. Berdyaev, Iz ètiudov o Iakov Beme, Ètiud II. *Put*, Vol. 20, pp. 47–79.

15 Berdyaev, *The Destiny of Man*, p. 18.

16 Evgeni Lampert, *Nicolas Berdyaev and the New Middle Ages*, Cambridge, James Clarke, 1945, p. 53.

17 Todd Breyfogle, 'Time and Transformation: a conversation with Rowan Williams,' *Cross Currents*, Fall 1995, 45(3), https://pdfs.semanticscholar.org/9f18/e857a05026bb839 9739cf45113804d4753fe.pdf?_ga=2.249691782.1691981341.1575468460-775567410. 1575468460 (accessed 18.9.2019).

18 Nicolas A. Berdyaev, *The Beginning and the End*, London, Geoffrey Bles, 1952, p. v.

19 *Dream and Reality*, p. 289.

20 Ibid., p. 99.

21 The term *bogochelovek* in Russian (*bogochelovachestva* – Godmanhood) is used by Berdyaev to describe his incarnational approach. Aloys Grillmeier argues that it has its roots

in the Greek *theanthropos* ('Gottmensch' in *Reallexikon für Antike und Christentum*, ed. Theodore Klauser, Stuttgart, C. Clope, 1983, p. 315). Some have argued that it is a confected term created by Russian philosopher Vladimir Soloviev (1853–1900), a figure who influenced Berdyaev's thought. But Solovyev scholar Oliver Smith counters this: 'far from being a heterodox innovation or a Gnostic borrowing, the conceptual cluster *theanthropia – theandria – theandropos*, from which it is all but certain Solovyev derived the exact Russian counterparts Богочеловечества and Богочеловек ... [they are] encountered throughout Patristic writings, *Vladimir Solovyev and the Spiritualisation of Matter*, Brighton, USA, American Studies Press, 2011, p. 297.

22 Nicolas A. Berdyaev, *The Meaning of the Creative Act*, London, Geoffrey Bles, 1957, p. 91.

23 Nicolas A. Berdyaev, *Freedom and the Spirit*, London, Geoffrey Bles, 1944, p. 128.

24 Nicolas A. Berdyaev, Iz ètiudov o Ja.Beme, Ètiud I. Uchenie ob Ungrund'e i svobode, *Put*, Vol. Feb, pp. 47–79, p. 47.

25 Nicolas A. Berdyaev, *Dostoevsky*, London, Meridian Books, 1957, p. 69.

26 Berdyaev, *The Destiny of Man*, p. 108.

27 Berdyaev, *The Meaning of the Creative Act*, p. 91.

28 Nel Grillaert, *What the God-seekers Found in Nietzsche: The Reception of Nietzsche's Ubermensch by the Philosophers of the Russian Religious Renaissance*, Amsterdam, Rodopi, p. 224.

29 Nicolas A. Berdyaev, *The Meaning of History*, London, Geoffrey Bles, 1936, p. 56.

30 Jürgen Moltmann writes of Berdyaev's thinking on tragedy in *The Trinity and the Kingdom of God*, London, SCM Press, pp. 42ff.

31 Paul Fiddes, *The Creative Suffering of God*, Oxford, Clarendon Press, 1992, p. 73.

32 Berdyaev, *The Destiny of Man*, p. 41.

33 George Pattison, *Crucifixions and Resurrections of the Image*, London, SCM Press, 2009, p. 58.

34 Berdyaev, *The Meaning of the Creative Act*, p. 147.

35 Berdyaev, *The Destiny of Man*, p. 139.

36 Ibid., p. 298.

37 Berdyaev, *The Meaning of the Creative Act*, p. 283.

38 Berdyaev, *Dream and Reality*, p. 99.

39 Rowan Williams, *The Vocation of Anglican Theology*, London, SCM Press, 2014, p. 91.

40 Austin Farrer, *Faith and Speculation*, London, Adam and Charles Black, 1967, p. 53.

41 It is interesting to note that at the time of Farrer's Gifford Lectures Berdyaev's writings were at the peak of their popularity, and almost all of his works would have been published in translation. Farrer was bound to have come across them, or people who were reading them. Farrer's friend and colleague, the biblical scholar Christopher Evans, recalled in a conversation with the author how Berdyaev was, at this point, 'almost a second Bible to some of us'.

42 Farrer, *The Freedom of the Will*, New York, Adam and Charles Black, p. 299.

43 Ibid., p. 300.

44 Ibid., p. 312.

45 Farrer, *Faith and Speculation*, p. 55.

46 Austin Farrer, *Interpretation and Belief*, London, SPCK, 1976, p. 88.

47 Rowan Williams, *Christ the Heart of Creation*, London, Bloomsbury, 2018, p. 1.

48 Farrer, *Interpretation and Belief*, p. 126.

49 Ibid., p. 135.

50 Ibid., p. 136.

51 Austin Farrer, 'The Potter's Clay' in Leslie Houlden, ed. *Austin Farrer: The Essential Sermons*, London, SPCK, pp. 16–19, 70.

52 Ibid.

53 Edward Henderson, 'Double Agency and the Relations of Persons to God', in *The Human Person in God's World*, ed. Brian Hebblethwaite & Douglas Hedley, London, SCM Press, 2006, p. 38.

54 Farrer, 'The Potter's Clay', pp. 17–18.

55 Farrer, *The Science of God*, London, Geoffrey Bles, 1966, p. 107.

56 John Eaton, 'Divine Action and Human Liberation' in *Divine Action: Studies inspired by the Philosophical Theology of Austin Farrer*, ed. Brian Hebblethwaite & Edward Henderson, London, T & T Clark, 1990, pp. 211–30, p. 219.

57 Farrer, *Faith and Speculation*, p. 66.

58 Farrer, *Love Almighty and Ills Unlimited*, London, Collins, 1962, p. 130.

59 Farrer, *A Celebration of Faith*, London, Hodder & Stoughton, 1970, p. 103.

60 Farrer, *The Freedom of the Will*, p. 313.

61 Ibid., p. 315.

62 Berdyaev, *Dream and Reality*, p. 99.

63 Berdyaev, *The Freedom of the Spirit*, p. 189.

64 Farrer, *The Freedom of the Will*, p. 311.

65 Berdyaev, *The Destiny of Man*, p. 34.

66 Farrer, *The Freedom of the Will*, p. 315.

Prayer and Preaching

13

Farrer, the Oxford Preacher

JANE SHAW

Austin Farrer was, above all, an Oxford preacher. The university was the environment of his student, priestly and academic life, apart from a short period as a curate in Dewsbury. Balliol College, where he read Greats as an undergraduate from 1923 to 1927; Cuddesdon College, just outside Oxford, where he spent a year training for ordination; St Edmund Hall, where he was Chaplain from 1931 to 1935; Trinity College, where he was Chaplain from 1935 to 1960; and Keble College, where he was Warden from 1960 until his death in 1968: these were his immediate contexts. His sermons are full of casual references to the culture of collegiate university life; many begin with an Oxford-based story, or object. Some may think this makes his preaching either parochial or unworldly. His friend Basil Mitchell, the philosopher, commented that Farrer had little interest outside his university life: 'it was difficult to get him to take seriously the organized activities of any body intermediate between the college and the cosmos'.[1] Guy de Moubray, who read PPE at Trinity just after the war and had served in the army from 1944 to 1946, had philosophy tutorials with Farrer and described him as 'not of this world'.[2] Farrer's lack of worldliness must have seemed especially sharp to a man such as de Moubray who had served in the Intelligence Unit in India and then gone on to liberate Singapore at the end of the war.

But what if the Oxford stories and details are, in fact, key to the ways in which Farrer constructed and composed so many of his sermons? Leslie Houlden, in selecting Farrer's 'essential' sermons for an anthology in 1990, 'avoided sermons which relate very closely to the life of an Oxford college and assume an affinity with its structures and customs'.[3] In this article I will take the opposite tack from Houlden, looking especially at some of the sermons that relate closely to daily Oxford life with the purpose of doing two things: firstly, to see how Farrer's use of stories, illustrations and objects from his immediate culture may have enabled him to be an effective communicator with his congregations; and, secondly, to examine his understanding of the relationship between university and church, scholarship and faith, the life of the mind and the life of the spirit. I will then conclude by looking at responses to Farrer's preaching at the time, and his published sermons since his death.

Farrer's Oxford

Farrer's Oxford is woven throughout his sermons. We can piece together many biographical details of his life there just by reading the sermons. From them, we learn that he was an undergraduate at Balliol; he became an Anglo-Catholic at St Barnabas in Jericho, where he was moved as an undergraduate by 'the incense and lights, the music and the silence'[4]; of his chaplaincy at St Edmund Hall (brief, in the early thirties) we hear nothing, while the chaplaincy at Trinity College, stretching over a quarter of a century, is the backdrop to many of his sermon illustrations. Weekday tutorial discussions in theology and philosophy open up into Sunday sermons. 'Pearls of Great Price', a sermon preached at Trinity College in 1957, opens with the words: 'This is not really a sermon, but a tutorial discussion broken loose. We all know that tutors must not preach at their pupils. But ... the sermon suppressed in the study may be permitted to break out in full spate on the chapel floor.'[5] The fabric of everyday life in shared meals and common rooms is called upon to draw the listener in. For example, a visiting preacher's sermon on predestination 'discussed in hall at the scholar's table' led to the theme of Farrer's sermon the following week.[6] We learn that during his time as a fellow of Trinity he lived in a house with a large garden, where he grew vegetables and fruit throughout the war, sustaining his family and friends in a time of rationing. As Warden of Keble he saw all 100 students in his first term (and subsequently in every Michaelmas term, as heads of house do) and had a deep sense of the distinctive history of Keble College, as well as the importance of the man after whom it was named. Many of these things about his life we learn by chance (or *apparently* by chance) because they are told as a way of opening up a theme in a sermon.[7]

Farrer's preaching was largely confined to Oxford; he disliked going much beyond his natural habitat to preach – despite the fact that he received invitations and was much in demand, and he did go to preach in major places of worship such as Westminster Abbey, St Paul's Cathedral and the Temple Church, as well as local parish churches and Pusey House chapel in Oxford. *Said or Sung*, published just as he was moving from being Chaplain of Trinity to Warden of Keble, contains 30 sermons, all but one preached in Oxford. As he notes in the Foreword: 'Most of the sermons were preached in Trinity College chapel, and only one of them outside the university.' So immersed is he in his context that he does not mention that the university is Oxford; that is a given.[8] Furthermore, he did not really believe in inviting celebrity preachers as an attraction for the students ('mackerels to catch sprats' as he put it[9]), preferring to do the bulk of the preaching himself.

Farrer's preaching context was very different from today's Oxford chapel life in several ways. At Trinity College, chapel attendance was no longer compulsory when Farrer was chaplain; it remained part of the fabric of college life, especially on Sunday evenings, though the College President for much of Farrer's time at Trinity, John Weaver, was moved to remind people of the 'corporate obligation to all resident members of college' to attend the main (non-communion) Sunday chapel service during World War Two. He was aware that the chapel service could not compete 'in outward impressiveness with those of some other colleges, which are able to afford professional choirs' but he put forward the appeal 'on the grounds of preserving and handing on a good college tradition'.[10] Nevertheless, as a rule, the 'home preacher' Farrer could rely on a steady, weekly connection with the congregation of students and fellows, especially once his reputation was established and he settled into being chaplain at Trinity. Secondly, the college was much smaller then than now; when Farrer arrived in 1935, there were approximately 110 in residence, which dropped to the mid-90s during the war years. There was then a 'bulge', with ex-servicemen arriving after the war, and numbers peaked at 289 in 1948. By the mid-1950s numbers settled at around 200 (and rose to approximately 230 by the 1960s, when Farrer had left).[11] This means that there was a deeply shared collegiate culture – images and events taken from collegiate life would have a resonance with all. Finally, the college was all male; there was a homosociality in which all kinds of assumptions about behaviour, culture and expectations could be made. And to this we might add homogeneity: a largely white student body, mostly Christian, mostly Anglican, with a high proportion of students who had been privately educated.

Farrer's Oxford sermons

Farrer was a delicate rhetorician with an unerring sense of the arresting opening image or story taken from his – and his listeners' – immediate context. Others have commented on this central feature of Farrer's preaching. As John Barton puts it: 'The opening anecdote or image is no "sermon illustration" for Farrer ... but an integral part of the argument which is a single whole.'[12] Richard Harries has written: 'The pattern of Farrer's sermons is always the same. They begin with some odd or amusing everyday incident told in a straightforward conversational style. They end some ten minutes later as an inspired invocation of the majesty of God.'[13]

Farrer draws the hearer in with that which is familiar, and then he gives them the message. Take the opening sentence of the sermon 'Made to Order' inspired by a delivery van at the time of a college ball.

> The sermon I am going to preach to you came to me readymade – it drove into the Front Quadrangle where I happened to be standing – drove in on four wheels, and came to a stop in front of my nose: a brisk little van with this inscription painted on its doors, 'Crosses and wreaths made to order'. The driver jumped down, opened the doors, and began getting out

the stuff for the College ball; and it struck me that a preacher might act in the same way – might play the part of a delivery man, and simply open out what is concealed behind these extraordinary words, 'Crosses and wreaths made to order.'[14]

This prompts him to ask: what it would mean if we could pre-order our crosses and wreaths? We would likely be cautious: we would be modest in choosing our wreath (our crown), and correspondingly cautious in ordering our crosses, planning 'small heroisms' and carrying them out to our own admiration. But in truth, we cannot really choose our crosses or our wreaths and, in any case, God measures our actions not in 'poundage of each particular weight' but rather by 'the love with which they are carried'. For our crosses are small but 'Christ unites them with his own cross'. In other words, Christ has already made up for our shortfall by his work on the cross, and we are invited to share in that; we are partakers of that sacrifice via the Eucharist, and we go out into the world from that table 'to be made a reasonable, holy and living sacrifice, and to be taken up into the one sacrifice of Jesus'.[15] By the end of this sermon, we could not be further from the van making a delivery for the college ball, and yet we have been taken on a vast spiritual and theological journey by that initial episode.

Farrer's images and turns of phrase are also selected to conjure up everything one needs to know about a situation. In 'Keble and his College', which he preached one Foundation Day when he was Warden, he speaks of those who founded the college, especially 'all those clergymen's widows, going without marmalade to pay for their rooms'. In this simple but perfect phrase, we immediately understand that this is a different sort of college, not least in its foundation, by those who were faithful to a vision of a college that would be open to all men, regardless of wealth or church party, at a time when 'the man of moderate means could not study here [the University of Oxford] on a basis of social equality with the rest'.[16] This college is, then, a far cry from those founded with the spoils of medieval episcopacy.

Nowhere is the drawing in of the listener perhaps more startling than in his sermon titled 'All Souls Examination'. The opening story is perhaps unpromising – especially for those who think that the rituals and communities of Oxford colleges are both elitist and esoteric – as he tells the story oft-repeated around the university (maybe an urban myth; maybe not?) that fellows at All Souls College used to be selected on the basis of what they did with the cherry stones when served cherry pie at dinner. 'If they spat the stones they were disqualified for boorishness, and for smoothness if they swallowed them. The serious competition lay between those who, with various degrees of elegance, got the cherries into their throats and the stones into their spoons.' Candidates now have to write an essay on an assigned topic, he goes on to say, and tells his congregation that recently that topic was sin. The seemingly irrelevant story is a way of introducing a thoroughgoing sermon on a central topic of the Christian life: sin, forgiveness, and life in the love of God. But the sermon is also, subtly, about more than that. It raises a theme that we find throughout Farrer's sermons: the wisdom of Christ and its relation to the learning of the university. As he puts it: 'I cannot help thinking that the All Souls' examiners would have done better to stick to ordeal by cherry pie. For what in the world could they expect a lot of young men more clever than wise, and more wise for the most part than Christian, to make of sin?'[17]

Farrer uses the images of daily Oxford life to question the assumptions of his twentieth-century student listeners about holiness of life. In 'Pentecostal Fire', preached in Trinity College chapel, he describes the visible Pentecost event as 'a roomful of sober, earnest-minded citizens bundling out into the street and shouting as if they were drunk'. His student listeners, he imagines, might well say this is exactly how a man, usually sober, behaves at a rowing dinner in college: 'Well, really, just think of old Peter, or whoever it is, some worthy candidate for Holy Orders, on an occasion like a bump-supper night, balanced on the top of a roof and yelling his head off.' It is the invisible power of the Holy Spirit made manifest in the people gathered that he wants to get the students to understand, and he does so by puncturing their assumptions – that might go something like this: 'What a party, thought the citizens of Jerusalem. And so would the members of this College have thought, if they had been present.'[18]

So how are we persuaded that *this* is how God works – through a party, or at least the energy that makes a party? Surely a party is all about the uncorking of the human bottle, so it does not burst? 'And so,' he says to the students, 'on certain privileged nights in the university year you uncork yourselves. Like the wicked men in the psalm, you grin like dogs and run about the city.' And the assumption is that when the student uncorks the bottle 'the spirit you expect to come out is anything but holy'. Uncorking cannot therefore take up too much time, so the spirit goes back into the bottle when the party is over. 'And religion, you are quite clear, has to do with corking up, not with uncorking.'[19]

But what if the true uncorking were everything that Christianity is about, the voice of the Spirit, the events of Pentecost: in short, *who you are*? So 'says the voice of the Spirit, I am you; I am the ground of your heart, the fountain of your true desire. I ask nothing of you but to be yourself.' To begin to know that, then we have to listen. 'Stop asking, "What ought I to do, what do they expect me to do, what will they admire me for doing, what will it amuse me to do, what am I greedy to do, what is it pious to do?" and ask, "What do I want with all my heart and mind?"'[20] The uncorking of Pentecost is all to do with that.

The sermon perfectly encapsulates Farrer's theology of aligning our will with God's, and he gives his listeners hints on how to do it. We may not experience the uncorking of Pentecost with the rush of words as the first-century disciples did, but he is confident we can know it. Farrer advocates prayer-kneeling, not rushing; this is needed to 'clear away all the rubbish of superficial pleasure and equally superficial duty that lies on the surface of your mind, recognizing that it is there, but reminding yourself that it isn't really what you want. Be quiet, wait until your living will begins to move, and to long for the will of God.' This can lead to unexpected experiences (like the events of Pentecost); it is the 'spring of spontaneity'. But most of all it leads to becoming fully who God made us, fully who God calls us to be: 'And once this you is alive by God's grace, what wonders it performs!'[21] In other words, appealing to a group of male undergraduates that may have been sober at that moment in chapel, but liked to drink and go to parties, he suggests that there is another way of becoming uncorked all the time; that the energy thrown into and generated by a party is what we need to live fully and for the good of the world.

In 'Nice and Worldly' he turns his attention once again to the potential tensions between the life of faith and the life of the world. It opens with reference to 'a Christian mission being preached in the University' – an event in which a prominent figure would have delivered a series of sermons and addresses, probably in the University Church, accompanied by small prayer and discussion groups in the colleges. Farrer was not keen on such University Missions in general, and opened another sermon with the following lines: 'Someone has just said to me, "I hope you saw the effect of the mission in your early Chapel this morning." "Yes, certainly," I replied, "the congregation was down by a third." "Oh," said my interlocutor, "that's not the answer I expected." "Maybe not," said I, "but it was the result that I anticipated."'[22] His somewhat sceptical attitude is implicit in this sermon as the following passage illustrates: 'The mission preacher paints the world white and black, he bids us detach ourselves from the kingdom of darkness and adhere to the kingdom of light; and while we are under the spell of his words we see that light shining, as it were, from the missioner's head.

Farrer understands that many of us have, in the moment of the missioner's sermon, seen 'a clearness of life' that contrasts sharply with our 'muddle of aims, our self-indulgence, our meanness and our vanity'. And then we leave the mission and bump into a friend – Farrer calls the friend 'Robin Johnson' – who invites us for a drink, and we join in, and the idea that our easygoing, good-humoured, drinking companion belongs to the missioner's unconverted world of wickedness seems rather ridiculous. The moment of 'a clearness of life' has quickly passed even while an uncomfortable tension remains.[23]

Farrer's brilliance lies in his capacity to get inside the mind of the undergraduate who is trying to reconcile what he has heard at the university mission with his everyday life. For that undergraduate both the missioner and his drinking friend have something to offer him, and so Farrer asks: 'how can you make room for both?' While it is clear that Farrer – as preacher, as chaplain, surely he must? – ends up on the side of the converted life, and preaches a thoroughgoing sermon on what it means to be a servant of Christ, nevertheless he sees in that a role for acknowledging 'Robin Johnson' in the very nature of that redeemed life. As he comes to the end of his sermon, in one fell swoop he removes the seemingly impossible dichotomy faced by the student, removes the judgementalism of a simplistic faith (the 'black and white' of the missioner), and reminds us of the Creator God's grace to all.

> May God give me more of that holy fire, so that I may not wait for another life before I begin to find and love and serve my only true good, my merciful creator. May God give me grace not to run from this fire, nor to throw away the cross; but may he give me grace besides to recognize his handiwork in all men; to acknowledge that converted or unconverted, he made them, and filled them with all sorts of excellences.[24]

This sermon illustrates Farrer's capacity to tackle the issues with which his student congregation was wrestling and offer, in response, an implicit apologetics. He opens up to the students a tolerant and generous faith: the overall message of the sermon is that God wants us to 'grow, live, expand, enrich our minds and our imaginations, become splendid creatures'.[25] Farrer preached this sermon during his time at Trinity, and therefore before the 1960s and 70s mood of 'Free to be me, free to be you' had fully emerged, but we can imagine how his message could have been received in any context in which students were trying to discover themselves.

As a scholar and a priest, Farrer also understood the potential tensions between the Christian life and the academic path. 'Narrow and Broad' opens with his acknowledgement of the potential tension between the two: 'Living in a university as I do, and even venturing from time to time to hear essays from beginners in philosophy, I cannot help being aware of the sort of tortures faith suffers from contemporary criticism.'[26] In 'Candour' he notes that 'intellectual integrity is praised in universities, as I suppose that steadiness of nerve is praised in the army'. About halfway through the sermon, he lets the students know that tutors know when they have done very little work, and thereby also allows the dons in chapel a moment of fellow feeling (though we might today regret the gender assumptions at work in this passage):

> Many of you think that the academic side of your Oxford life is a game of cheating played against the dons. It is a game which does you little good. You ought surely to regard it as a Christian duty not to write your essays as though your tutor were a girl at a sherry party whom you hoped to impress, but to tell us simply and plainly what you have read and what you have not, what you think and with what you disagree, when you understand us and when we are being unintelligible. For if it is the honour of a don to make a straight job of research, why should it not be the honour of a student to make a straight job of study? But I do not find you to be very tender on that point of honour.[27]

This turns out to be not so much an aside as a lead-in to the key point, for Farrer wants to reconcile integrity in academic life with integrity in the Christian life and show that they are not so separate. In both, making 'an honest job of it' is important: don't avert our eyes from anything, and tell the truth as we see it. But we need God's help to do this. To have true integrity we need to combine 'intellectual thoroughness' and 'intellectual standards' – which are not enough alone – with 'an unforced candour, a simple objectivity of view, which is of another kind' and (says Farrer) found in saints if you can find them. He asks: 'What stands in the way of honest vision?' The answer is 'Myself'. And so he concludes, 'Integrity of mind may seem a secular virtue, yet however it may be with other men, I cannot hope to have it without divine salvation. For I cannot save myself from myself."[28] He knew from his own experience the need among his listeners (his fellow dons and students) to integrate the academic life with the life of faith.

In negotiating the potential tension between the life of the mind and the life of faith, Farrer offers his implicit but distinctive apologetics, giving students and dons the tools for adopting the life of faith in the midst of their world of intellectual enquiry. In his sermon 'Keble and his College' mentioned earlier, he notes that 'it is commonplace to say that many things are acceptable in faith, which are not accessible to certain knowledge'. But, he reassures his listeners, 'this is only true as far as it goes'. He continues: 'We do not want people going about with a sheer appetite for indiscriminate believing.' What is really important is that 'faith, in the Christian sense, is the twin of love. And love, with its inexhaustible appetite for what deserves loving, sees beyond evidence, sees the soul behind the body, and God behind all.' But even if faith and love go beyond absolute evidence, 'they are not blind'. Preaching in his capacity as Warden of the college, he gives to his colleagues and students the authority to discern their path as people of faith in a university context:

> After all the detection of shams, the clarification of argument, and the sifting of evidence – after all criticism, all analysis – a man must make up his mind what there is most worthy of love, and most binding on conduct, in the world of real existence. It is this decision, or this discovery, that is the supreme exercise of a truth-seeking intelligence.[29]

The tropes and routines of college life were employed by Farrer to draw his listeners in. This makes his preaching akin to that of Jesus, especially in the parables. The agrarian images of Jesus' preaching may not resonate so deeply with the urban-dwelling Bible readers of today as they did with Jesus' first-century hearers, but the images still draw the reader in. Likewise, Oxford collegiate life may not be of relevance to all the readers of Farrer's sermons now, but the nature and rhythms of close-knit collegiate life are immediately grasped and appreciated, even as the particulars are not necessarily understood. The reason for this is, surely, that Farrer's appeal to the everyday occurrences of his context was entirely authentic. He did not try to be or write or preach as someone he was not.

How were Farrer's sermons received?

Early in his time as chaplain at Trinity College, Farrer was (understandably) somewhat uncertain, and according to one of his students – with whom he remained in contact to the end of his life – not so memorable as a preacher. R. Howard Williams came up as a scholar in 1936 to read Greats, very soon after Farrer had himself arrived. Williams was a pious young man (he later went on to train for ordination as an Anglican priest and then became an Eastern Orthodox monk) and had been accustomed to beginning and ending every day with prayers at school. On his arrival at the college 'One of the first things one was told to do as a freshman was to acquire a curious white linen garment, open at the front but fastening at the neck, which went by the name of "scholar's surplice". This gave the impression that the chapel was to have an important place in the lives of all of us.' He was soon 'surprised that non-attendance at chapel was taken for granted.' The main problem was that the daily offices of morning and evening prayer 'were rendered by the President' (Herbert Blakiston, the head of Trinity College, who was ordained and had himself been chaplain in the late 1880s) in a 'characteristically dry manner' and with 'great rapidity'.[30] Farrer himself found this very difficult and wrote to his father that he had dropped his 'attempt to induce attendance at daily chapel because the chaps do find it quite sincerely farcical and irreligious as the President will have it done.'[31] (Things improved after 1938 when Blakiston stepped down: the new President, John Weaver, was a devout Anglican and was more supportive of Farrer's way of conducting services and organizing chapel life.) Williams persisted with daily attendance at chapel – although later had little memory of it – along with his tutorial partner and friend Denis Grey; they were on weekdays the only two people present at services besides Blakiston and Farrer.

Sunday Evensong was better attended, but Williams did not remember much about the preaching except Farrer's 'diffident delivery. He even seemed to stutter at times.' Williams could recall very little about the content of Farrer's preaching, except for one sermon:

> My sole remembrance from those sermons is that on one occasion Farrer spoke of the jinn [genie] of the stream where Jacob wrestled (Gen. 32:22–32). Presumably the point was that Jacob wrestling is a parable of our own wrestling with God in prayer, as we struggle with him, not allowing him to go until he blesses us. Unfortunately only the jinn impressed itself on my memory, and the point of Farrer's sermon was missed. Somehow

he did not command my attention. Mea maxima culpa. Nothing led me to suspect that in his maturity he would be a great preacher.[32]

Not all students warmed to Farrer as either chaplain or tutor. Guy de Moubray, the student who thought of Farrer as 'not of this world', did not comment on Farrer as a preacher, but he described a feature of philosophy tutorials with him vividly. 'Whilst we were reading our essays, Farrer was in the habit, in the summer months, of throwing a sixpenny piece into the fire grate and listen to it tinkling down the hearth!' He also found Farrer unable to help in his own quest to bridge the study of philosophy and his questions about faith. 'My own personal problem in moral philosophy was how it could be possible to be truly altruistic if one was in fact motivated by the desire for salvation. Farrer could not help me.' This fits with the assessment of Farrer's biographer, Philip Curtis, that 'To the average undergraduate at Trinity Farrer continued to be a remote and rather daunting figure, "a brain on a stalk" as he once put it.'[33]

Yet others were deeply impressed by Farrer. Mark Morford, a scholar who came up to Trinity in 1948, just as de Moubray had graduated, wrote that 'At Trinity Austin Farrer alone engaged in challenging discussion, and I remember well his prescience in discussing a lecture by a visiting neuroscientist which had questioned the need for a god who, as the scientist made clear, would at best be only a god of the gaps left in scientific knowledge. Richard Dawkins, nearly 60 years later, is asking the same question.'[34]

Indeed, Philip Curtis suggests that the post-war years were 'golden years' for Farrer when he 'came to his full stature as chaplain, preacher and divine'. Curtis writes: 'The whole religious life of the College seemed to come alive ... His delight in people, in life and in thought was transparent. Its source was the daily discipline of prayer.' He delivered the Bampton Lectures to large numbers in 1948 (published as *The Glass of Vision*) and was becoming better known through his writings. In 1952, he even published some of the short homilies he preached at the Sunday morning Eucharist, under the title *The Crown of the Year*. By Hilary Term 1955, some 20 years after he had arrived as chaplain, attendance in the chapel was really good (as it was across most college chapels in this period): 'there were usually about 30 at the Sunday Mass, the weekday congregation at Evensong was steady at 16 to 20, and the chapel was packed at Sunday Evensong.'[35] Once he moved to Keble, he preached regularly in the college chapel.

Since Farrer's death, he has been much lauded as a great preacher. Charles Hefling notes that he 'was no ordinary preacher. He has been called one of the great preachers of his generation, and his sermons can be read without evaporating; often a second or third reading offers fresh riches.'[36] This statement opens up the question of Farrer the preacher versus Farrer the 'sermon artist' – the author of perfectly framed and constructed sermons that delicately balance theology with the spiritual life. John Austin Baker, who has described Farrer as one of the great preachers of any generation, says of Farrer that in his rhetoric 'he aimed to move his hearers, to play upon them, not for any false effect, but so they might see and perceive, hear and understand, turn again and be healed.'[37] This is his assessment of Farrer as the *deliverer* of sermons. But others suggest that Farrer was never a great orator: John Barton, who was at Keble as an undergraduate when Farrer was Warden and was taught by him, is a great admirer of his sermons but notes that Farrer could never make himself heard in Keble chapel, and that he was no great deliverer of lectures either. 'Farrer's sermons were indeed masterpieces of composition, but sadly this was not always apparent when you heard them because, in Keble chapel with, in those days, no sound system, they were in fact very difficult to hear. Farrer had little capacity for voice-projection, and the words rose up into the roof. One soon learned to sit very close to the pulpit.'[38]

It has become increasingly difficult to publish collections of sermons, on the grounds that they do not translate well from the pulpit to the written page, and in any case no one reads them any more; and yet, remarkably, the written texts of Farrer's sermons – as art forms in themselves – remain vibrant and appreciated. While it is usually thought that sermons should be heard rather than read, there is something about both the composition and the eloquence of Farrer's sermons that has enabled them to endure as short pieces to be read. Robert Titley sums this up: 'Sermons, says Rowan Williams, are written in water: if you preach *in order* for it to be published you probably won't preach very well. Even so, many of Farrer's did and do find their way into print, and are wonderfully at home in this different medium.'[39] John Austin Baker regards Farrer as belonging to 'the tiny company of preachers of genius' for whom 'the text of a genuine sermon as actually delivered should satisfy the criteria of the literary form as well'.[40]

The images and occurrences taken from Farrer's daily life and immediate context in Oxford drew listeners in when he preached. In the published sermons, these images and events, despite being from another period and for many another world, remain essential parts of the structure of the sermon: these images and events take us to Farrer's theology and his exposition of holiness of life. They also invite the reader into Farrer's life as he knew and experienced it, and thus they let us know that he wrestled with what it meant to live faithfully. We can only ever do that wrestling in the contexts in which we find ourselves: Farrer's context was Oxford, and his appeal to that which was all around him gives the sermons a deep authenticity. It is then, paradoxically, the very particularity of those examples that enables the reader to transcend their context and grasp the spiritual and theological wisdom that Farrer lived, preached and taught.

The author thanks John Barton and Robert Titley for conversations about Farrer's preaching, and Clare Hopkins, the archivist of Trinity College, Oxford, for her assistance.

Notes

1 Basil Mitchell, 'Austin Marsden Farrer', in *Austin Farrer: A Celebration of Faith*, ed. Leslie Houlden, London, Hodder and Stoughton, 1970, p. 14.

2 Guy de Moubray, 'Memoir', written for the Trinity College Oxford archive. Trinity archive DD370 de Moubray, p. 73.

3 *Austin Farrer: The Essential Sermons*, selected and edited by Leslie Houlden, London, SPCK, 1991, p. x.

4 'Human and Divine Habitations' in Austin Farrer, *The End of Man*, London, SPCK, 1973, p. 163.

5 Farrer, 'Pearls of Great Price', in *The End of Man*, p. 39.

6 Farrer, 'Craggy Doctrine', in *Said or Sung: An Arrangement of Homily and Verse*, London, The Faith Press, 1960, p. 17.

7 For full biographical details of Farrer, see Philip Curtis, *A Hawk Among Sparrows: A Biography of Austin Farrer*, London, SPCK, 1985.

8 Austin Farrer, *Said or Sung*, p. 7.

9 Leslie Houlden, 'Introduction: Farrer the Preacher', in *Austin Farrer Words for Life: Forty Meditations Previously Unpublished*, eds Charles Conti and Leslie Houlden, London, SPCK, 1993, p. xi.

10 J. H. R. Weaver, President of Trinity College, Chapel Letter to all members of college, October 1942, DD308 Eve, Trinity Archive.

11 With thanks to Trinity College archivist, Clare Hopkins, for providing these statistics from the College Reports.

12 John Barton, 'Austin Farrer as Preacher', in *The New Testament and the Church: Essays in Honour of John Muddiman*, ed. John Barton and Peter Groves, London, Bloomsbury, T & T Clark, 2016, p. 162.

13 Richard Harries, 'Introduction' to *The One Genius: Readings through the Year with Austin Farrer*, London, SPCK, 1987, p. xii.

14 Austin Farrer, 'Made to Order', in *Said or Sung*, p. 22.

15 Ibid., pp. 24–6.

16 Farrer, 'Keble and his College', in *The End of Man*, ed. Charles Conti, London, SPCK, 1973, pp. 153–4.

17 Farrer, 'All Souls Examination', in *Said or Sung*, p. 57.

18 Farrer, 'Pentecostal Fire', in *Said or Sung*, pp. 101–2.

19 Ibid., p. 104.

20 Ibid.

21 Ibid., pp. 104–5.

22 Farrer, 'In Season and Out', in *The End of Man*, p. 168. On Farrer's discomfort with such University Missions, see Curtis, *A Hawk Among Sparrows*, p. 136.

23 Farrer, 'Nice and Worldly', in *Said or Sung*, pp. 11–12.

24 Ibid., pp. 15–16.

25 Ibid., p. 13.

26 Farrer, 'Narrow and Broad', in *Said or Sung*, p. 139.

27 Farrer, 'Candour', in *Said or Sung*, pp. 173–4.

28 Ibid., pp. 174–5, 177.

29 Farrer, 'Keble and his College', pp. 156–7.

30 R. Howard and S. Williams (Brother James of Longovarda), 'Memoir' (1992), pp. 10–12. DD139 and Williams, Trinity archive.

31 Quoted in Curtis, *A Hawk Among Sparrows*, p. 111.

32 Williams, 'Memoir', p. 13.

33 Curtis, *A Hawk Among Sparrows*, p.127.

34 Mark Morford, P.O. 'Trinity College in 1948', p. 1, Trinity Archive DD436 Morford.

35 Curtis, *A Hawk Among Sparrows*, pp. 125–7.

36 Charles C. Hefling, Jr., *Jacob's Ladder: Theology and Spirituality in the Thought of Austin Farrer*, Cambridge, MA, Cowley Publications, 1987, p. 3.

37 John Austin Baker, 'Introduction', *The End of Man*, p. ix.

38 John Barton, 'Farrer as a Preacher', p. 160.

39 Robert Titley, 'A Poetic Discontent – why it's good to listen to Austin Farrer', unpublished paper delivered at CLUB at the Athenaeum, 19 February, 2009, p. 7. Several collections of Farrer's sermons were published after his death.

40 John Austin Baker, 'Introduction' to *The End of Man*, p. ix.

14

Until Their Hunger Is Their Mind:
Farrer's Theology of the Eucharist

JEFFREY VOGEL

One of the truly compelling features of Austin Farrer's theological writing is the way in which it inhabits the tension between receiving and doing in the Christian faith, sacrificing the will to the good and willing the good, grace and works. On the one hand, Farrer makes the will the primary analogue between God and humanity. This voluntarism has been highlighted as one of his chief contributions to modern Christian thought.[1] Just as we are actors, so, too, is God – or rather, because God is an actor we also are. Though the difference between God's will and our own is an infinite one, we nevertheless have a foothold for beginning to think about divine activity in the world through consideration of our own agency.[2] More significantly, Farrer emphasizes that we know something of God only in the course of doing something about God. Ideas aren't grasped unless they are tried out. Dogma must be prayable. Even in the midst of profound theological reflection, Farrer is never far away from utterly practical exhortation. Saints are put forward as the closest thing we have to a demonstration of God's existence.[3]

On the other hand, Farrer insists that the will must be put to death, that Christianity is no natural wisdom because it calls its followers to come and be hanged.[4] Only those who have surrendered their wills to God can truly be said to be free, for only then does God will in and through them. Christ alone achieves this completely – is the perfect coming together of God and humanity – because he yields his will entirely to the Father's. The temptation he faced in the desert was precisely to act on his own initiative. Those who choose to follow him must open themselves to God's activity in their lives as he did. And thus, the life in Christ is not first and foremost one of doing but of undoing, of giving up one's will.

Doing and receiving, moving and being moved, acting and contemplating. While certainly not in contradiction with one another, these dual notes of the Christian faith tend to drift apart in much theological writing, with one coming to dominate and the other falling into the background. Farrer brings both to the fore in equal measure. Wherever one looks in his writings, one is struck by his insistence on the Christian life as a task, as ethical demand. There is no escaping into the world of ideas with him. After all, he is by his own admission the least mystical of men.[5] And just as frequently one finds him urging – often in the most provocative language – the necessity of sacrificing the will, of putting the self to death. It is perhaps no surprise that the latter act, if one can call it that, is for him the necessary condition of the former.

The place in Farrer's writing where these two emphases come together most clearly is his theology of the Eucharist. Here we have an act that is first and foremost a receiving. Here we have a mystery that eventuates in the most practical acts of doing. It is not without reason that Farrer says of the Eucharist: 'This sacrament is not a special part of our religion, it is just our religion, sacramentally enacted.'[6] The Eucharist is a ritual of receiving that commits one to giving of oneself to others. It makes present to the faithful Christ's sacrifice on behalf of the world, yes, but Christ includes the community of worshippers in his offering to God, makes them a part of his sacrifice, such that in the very act of receiving from him they are transformed into actors in his name.

In what follows, I will show how Farrer's eucharistic theology holds these notes of receiving and acting together. My hope is that this approach will shed fresh light on some of the more familiar themes in his work – for, within the secondary literature on Farrer, there is comparatively less about his eucharistic theology. This is perhaps because his treatment of it occurs almost exclusively in his devotional writings – his sermons, his meditations, his texts intended for use in prayer and worship. And yet, his writing on the Eucharist illuminates many of the ideas that garner the most attention among scholars of his work: the concurrency of the divine and human wills in our activity; the nature of the person and work of Christ; the trinitarian character of his spirituality; the role played by images in our knowledge of God. In addition, it reveals him to be attentive to the role of the body in Christian life and practice, thereby anticipating an emphasis in much contemporary theological work.

To begin my salvation with my body

In his biography of Farrer, Philip Curtis explains Farrer's conversion to Anglicanism from the Baptist tradition of his youth partly in terms of his preference for order and ceremony.[7] This preference for order comes out particularly clearly at the beginning of his collection of eucharistic texts, *The Crown of the Year*, which consists of a series of written paragraphs to be read during the celebration of the sacrament. Farrer believes some such guidance is necessary, for the Eucharist is a rite in need of explanation, but he expressly denies the benefit of an overly long exposition of the act or one that is characterized by freewheeling speech. The rite itself is to be the main thing, and anything that detracts from its centrality is for him only a hindrance. The Eucharist is the reason why the church gathers, he says, the 'element of our Christian life, as air is the element of our physical being'.[8] He also expresses uneasiness about excessively elaborate approaches to the ceremony surrounding the sacrament, preferring instead to emphasize its plainness, its familiarity.[9]

In general, Farrer does not devote a great deal of attention to the question of how Christ comes to be present in the elements of the Eucharist. It is enough, it seems, that it is by Christ's own creative word that the bread and wine are made to be his body and blood.[10] A far greater emphasis in his thinking is the significance of the sheer bodiliness of the sacrament. A short essay at the end of *The Crown of the Year* demonstrates this well:

> By virtue of my body I am founded in time and place, through it I am inserted in my environment. Jesus, conceived by the Holy Ghost in the womb of Mary, established in the world a body joined uniquely to the life of God, and our bodies are to be united with his body in one extended body, the mystical Church. Our state of redemption, like our existence, like his incarnate existence, is to begin with the body.[11]

Christ inserts himself into our environment by means of the bread and the wine. At the meal with his disciples on the night before he was killed, he took bread that was shared between himself and his followers, a common bread, and declared it to be his body. Farrer perceives a kindness to the disciples on the part of Christ in using what was also their own, what was quite natural to them, to unite them to the life of God. Christ does nothing but what is human, and yet does such human things divinely, in a way that transforms them and imbues them with an altogether other significance. By his declaration, Christ made the elements of bread and wine his body and blood and those who ate and drank of them were 'annexed' to him, becoming an extension of his body in the world. The same is true of those who participate in the ongoing celebration of this meal in the church.

There is, of course, a spiritual meaning intended in the idea of the church as the body of Christ – a community of people united in faith, hope and love, a community that shares the mind of Christ – but the physical basis is primary. Indeed, the idea lacks a certain reality if this community is not manifested in bodily form. Farrer uses this fact at times to exhort his congregants to more frequent attendance at church services, comparing the neglectful absence of certain members of the community to a maiming or an amputation.[12] He says: 'Can we say that the incorporation of Christians together in one mystical body is likewise a bodily fact? We could not say so, if the links between the several members were mental only. But they are not merely mental, Christ will not have them to be so.'[13] Salvation is a bodily reality from start to finish.

Part of the significance of this for Farrer is that salvation precedes any willed activity. Our bodiliness is the most basic form of our presence in the world, the sheer fact of our being here. It is the given that is prior to, makes possible, all subsequent effort and activity. It depends on no choice, is not subject to any decision. Perhaps we range past our bodies in thought and action, Farrer says, but we remain rooted in a time and a place by virtue of our embodiment. That this aspect of our existence would be taken as the means by which we are joined to Christ is for him the truest evidence of grace. As he puts it:

> It is the mercy of Christ to begin my salvation with my body. This me, the mere opaque bodily fact, the me which is there before my will, and whether I will or no ... Christ takes this me, and annexes it to himself by bodily bonds, without waiting for the sanctification of its acts and uses.[14]

There is certainly the decision to be a part of the Christian communion, to be at the altar in the first place, and therefore a kind of willed activity that precedes this annexation. But in a more profound sense the basis of communion between Christ and Christ's members depends on no activity of their own at all – no activity, that is, other than receiving itself. The acts of eating bread and drinking wine have no inherent moral component to them. They cohere with what we do already by necessity, by virtue of being finite creatures dependent on sustenance from without. And thus the communion between Christ and Christ's members requires nothing of those who seek it other than a desire to be fed by him, a recognition of need. As I will show a little later on, even the idea of preparing oneself for receiving the Eucharist becomes, for Farrer, the means by which the faithful are shown their insufficiency and thus broken of their habit of self-dependence. One can bring nothing to this communion beyond the openness to take Christ in.

In consuming the eucharistic elements, communicants take Christ's body into themselves. The food becomes part of their body; Christ comes to dwell in them. At the same time, Farrer says, drawing on an ancient tradition, the consumers are themselves consumed. They are brought into Christ. Farrer is equally comfortable saying that Christ lives us and that we live Christ, for the identity that results from the sacrament is a real one. The faithful are taken into heaven with Christ, offered there as a delight. They are incorporated into the lively concourse of Father, Son and Spirit. And the faithful are the presence of Christ in the world, united with all other consumers of the sacrament in a mystical body. This body, unlike other organizations, is not the result of a truce between competing interests. Its unity consists in the will of God alone, the will that is now in them by virtue of their identity with Christ. As Farrer writes of this body, 'Either it is nothing, or it's a divine society, a new creation of the divine will, not the by-product nor even the sublimation of human concerns and interests.'[15]

No body but what he sacrificed

Farrer retains the language of sacrifice in talking about the Eucharist that has been the source of much contention between the various Christian communions since the time of the Reformation. It is of the utmost importance for him that the bread and wine consumed in the Eucharist are the body of the sacrificed Christ, but he veers utterly away from the idea of the sacrifice as substitution. What matters is how Christ's sacrificial will comes to characterize those who participate in the sacrament. The entire thrust of his thought is toward inclusion of believers in Christ's action, the practical living out of Christ's will in their lives. Just as dogma is to be prayable, so, too, are sacraments to be liveable. They have no relevance to us if they do not transform us in our thought and action.[16]

The heart of Christ's sacrifice consists in the giving up of his will to God. Indeed, this yielding to God is the very essence of Christ's divine sonship, which Farrer describes most succinctly as an 'active openness of heart'.[17] Christ lives with this openness throughout his earthly life, holding nothing of himself back from God, submitting to God uninterruptedly, presenting no obstacle to God's will but allowing it to dwell in him fully, to act in and through him. He seals this openness to God on the cross, submitting to the Father's will in spite of his own desire to be saved from death. For Farrer, this openness to God's will on the part of Christ is the very thing that reveals him to be fully God. From start to finish, in his living and in his dying, the will of God is fully present in him, and thus he communicates God to those who draw near to him. At the same time, the unhindered activity of the divine will in him makes him to be fully human, more truly human, in fact, than we, because, as Farrer sees it, human beings are most truly themselves when they will what God wills, when they will with the will of God.[18]

The relevance of this in the current context is that it is to this will that those who participate in the Eucharist are joined. In taking Christ into themselves, they themselves are brought into his sacrifice. Farrer says this in a variety of ways but claims, most simply, that Christ offers those who partake of his body and blood to the Father along with himself, including their sacrifice in his own.[19] The gift of the sacrament, the offering of bread and wine, the sacrificed body of Christ, is also a gift of themselves. And thus, in their very receiving they yield themselves to the will of the Father. Farrer wonders if the import of this was understood by the original disciples:

> Ah, but do the disciples understand the nature of the bond? Jesus has blessed his food, to be the body he will offer in his sacrifice; do they know that they are committed to membership in such a body as that? A body flogged, crucified – see, he crumbles the loaf before their eyes. Do they perceive the new meaning in the ancient custom, the breaking of the bread? Are they willing to be parts of such a body, are they willing that his body, with its sacrificial destiny should be theirs?[20]

He goes on to answer that they were not yet willing but came to be over time. And the same is true of all who partake of this meal in his view. However unworthy, they are taken up into sacrificial being by their participation in the sacrament, a participation that they must renew repeatedly throughout their lives. As a result, the will of Christ takes root in them and begins to transform them. God delights in them, according to Farrer, regardless of the pace of this transformation, because God delights in the will of Christ that is at work in them. Just as God delighted in Christ's obedience on the cross, so too, does God delight in those who are nailed to Christ's sacrificial will.

This emphasis on the true identity between believer and Christ in the sacrament, such that it can be said that Christ 'lives us', is a unique feature of the Christian religion in Farrer's view. Other religions capture well the holy otherness of God, the divine transcendence that disallows any confusion between Creator and creation, but Christianity alone makes the further move of saying that God chooses to identify with us wholly amid this difference.[21] For Farrer, this idea of identity is no mere theological talk. 'There are no fictions with God,' he says.[22] The faithful are incorporated into the Son, and though they continue to be characterized by sinfulness, God sees the will of Christ that is within them.

The union of Christ with believers takes place by means of a physical act. But the physical act is ultimately the means by which the will of Christ comes to be present in them. It serves as the basis of a transformation of their entire being. More specifically, it completely unmakes them. In Farrer's view, we misunderstand the sacrament if we suppose that it is for the purpose only of a little help, some encouragement along a way that we are already walking.[23] It is rather the nailing of one's own will to the cross, the judgement and death of the self-reliance that causes one to be separated from God and others. But if we learn anything of God in Christ, Farrer says, it is that what judges ultimately redeems.[24] The death of the will, its being taken up into the will of the divine Son, ultimately leads to new life with God and with others.

The stuff of my being

Just as Christ is raised to new life by the Spirit of God that is within him, so, too, are those whose lives are included in Christ's sacrificial death raised up as a new creation by the Spirit. Farrer's theology is trinitarian throughout. His account of the economy of salvation, his description of the act of prayer, his account of the sacraments – all describe a movement of incorporation into the Son by means of the Spirit that unites one to the Father, a being taken up into the relationship between Father, Son and Spirit. And yet, once again, this thick theological description eventuates in purely practical activity. As he puts it:

No one supposes that, when the Spirit indwells us, he takes up a local habitation in some corner of us, like a lodger in a house – No, what is meant is that his action becomes the soul of our action, his mind the soul of our thought: he shapes himself to us, so that he may shape us to himself.[25]

In general, Farrer is unimpressed with enthusiastic displays of religion or accounts of the divine indwelling of believers that do not involve real doing. Those who live in the Son of God live as he lives. Those whom the Spirit indwells move out toward others because that is what the Spirit does. The Spirit shapes the faithful by bringing them into the attitudes of Christ to God and others.[26]

Whereas the 'darling self' is guided by its own interests, attempting to annex God and others to its own plans and projects, those who have died through participation in Christ's sacrifice and have come to be indwelled by the Spirit are characterized above all by other-directedness. It is typical of Farrer to present the work of the Holy Spirit in this way, that is, not as a power that draws attention to itself but one that directs it away, not as an experience of God or as an object of thought, but as the transformation of our power of experiencing, thinking and acting to include others.[27] The Spirit is hidden at the root of the will, known only by the works of love that it inspires. And these works, Farrer says, are the manifestation of the very being of those who have the Spirit of God within. He writes:

> What is the gift of charity ... Not only doing the decent and helpful thing, for, says Christ's apostle, I might go to the extreme of visible generosity, I might give all my goods to feed the poor, and yet lack charity. Still less is it mere tolerance and a show of amiability. It means that a caring for God and my neighbour becomes the stuff of my being, the mainspring of my will, not something joined on from outside. God does not have love, he is love, and to have love we also must become it.[28]

Farrer describes the love of God elsewhere as the 'pure act of inexhaustible self-giving'.[29] There is no end to this self-giving in God. Likewise in those whom the Spirit indwells. It becomes the stuff of their being. Consequently, the communion of believers has a 'divine' quality about it. Its members relate to one another in peace, with the coherence of a single body. Their own will is dead and they have the will of God within them.

For Farrer, this description of believers being united to the will of Christ by the Spirit within them is simply true. He can be found at times reminding his parishioners of this fact about themselves, urging them first and foremost to believe it, and secondly to adhere to it more closely in their life and deeds, exhorting them not to be a contradiction – or worse, a sacrilege. And therein is the paradox of the ontology of the Christian believer – dead to oneself, lived by Christ, moved at the root of one's being by the Holy Spirit, and yet still with the imperative to act in accordance with this reality.

Unlike Christ, who has no natural resistance to the Father's will, those whom the Spirit indwells as a result of being united to Christ are never completely free from resistance. There are such things as saints, but most of us are not like them – and even saints are simply those who have tested the divine patience to the end and yet remained. It is the sinful who participate in the sacrament, and thus the sinful into whom the Spirit comes to dwell. Consequently, the death and resurrection of the will within them occurs only over time. The Spirit takes root in them slowly, over the course of their lives. Farrer puts it this way, 'But as the Holy Spirit grows in us, it is not he but we who grow. He does not grow up and leave us behind, we grow up into him. He becomes the spring and substance of our mind and heart.'[30] This growth must be constantly fed. It is not guaranteed simply to progress on its own, without constant, vigilant effort. The crucifixion of the will must happen again and again and again: hence the necessity of repeated participation in the sacrament. By being joined to the body and blood of Christ, the faithful are empowered to 'live Christ for another week',[31] at which point, Farrer thinks, they must come and make the sacrifice again. It is an endless transformation that is begun in them, and thus one that they must never cease to renew.

Farrer places significant emphasis on the importance of the failure of the faithful to manifest Christ in their lives in making this transformation possible. At times, it even seems that failure is given a positive role in God's work of salvation in their lives. For in failing to be charitable, in proving incapable of willing with the will of God or acting in accordance with the reality that they have become, the faithful are shown the insufficiency of their own wills. Awareness of this has the potential to break them of the self-reliance that ultimately prevents the will of God from dwelling in them more fully. As Farrer puts it, 'For we do not learn what dependence on God is, except through having our self-dependence broken in the mill of life, slowly and painfully. Many tears, much shame, continual repentance, this is the lot of those who pledge themselves to God. A paradoxical pledge; we learn to keep it by breaking it.'[32] The reality of one's inability drives one to seek the grace of God once more.

It seems a paradox: the Spirit enters into those who participate in Christ's death and resurrection through the sacrament, empowering them to will with the will of God. And the presence of this will within them is known by the practical deeds of charity in their lives. And yet, as important as the sacrament in enacting the surrender of will necessary to live in this way is the failure to do it well, the realization that the will has not been surrendered at all. In Farrer's mind, this draws one closer to God, causes one to flee to the saving action of Christ once more, and thus creates within one the openness of heart characteristic of divine sonship. 'He [Christ] by desert, but we by mercy, through the breaking of our world, the breaking of our heart, receive the adoption of sons.'[33] This is the ultimate goal for Farrer, the incorporation of the faithful into the Son of God. They are brought into the life of the Son by means of participation in his body and blood; they are driven to come back to it by their inability to remain there. Their wills are sacrificed in the Eucharist, for in taking Christ into their bodies they are made a part of him, such that his action becomes their own. And those same wills, never very far away, rear their heads in moments of failure, thus shattering their self-sufficiency once more. And in this strange way – this cycle of receiving and acting and receiving once more – God works for their salvation.

Until their hunger is their mind

With paradoxical language such as this, Farrer seeks to inhabit the tension in Christian thought between receiving the life of God and extending it to others, manifesting it in one's life and continually failing to do so. One can intend to give oneself to God without taking back, Farrer says, but one cannot actually do it. 'What I give with part of my mind, and what I give now I shall take back in half an hour,' he writes.[34] This inability is lamentable, but not ultimately devastating because one's sacrifice is taken up into the accepted sacrifice of Christ, which is truly beyond taking back. It is faith in this sacrifice that empowers one to make what effort one can, to return to the task of living with the will of God even after one has repeatedly failed. It is the knowledge that one's own activity is received into Christ's that gives one the ability to progress in charity toward God and others even a little bit – and the confidence to return to God with the openness of sonship when one does not. 'All prayer and all obedience is one with the Eucharist, for it is a participation in Christ's dying love. Our self-giving would not be in Christ, nor real in itself, if we could never recollect and say "Ah, but he died."'[35]

The Eucharist gives form to the faithful's belief in their inclusion in Christ's sacrifice, Farrer says. 'For, if our difficulty is one of imagination, that we cannot imagine and feel and live our identification with Christ, is it not one purpose of the sacrament to make such identification visible and palpable?'[36] This account of the function of the Eucharist is consistent with Farrer's well-known insistence on the centrality of the imagination in apprehending the divine, his 'metaphysics of the imagination', as Douglas Hedley calls it.[37] As Farrer argues in *The Glass of Vision*, our knowledge of God runs through images without remainder. Revelation takes place by means of the making and remaking of images, their inspiration and refinement over time, and ultimately their interpretation by Christ. The bread and the wine of the Eucharist are a central example of this process for Farrer.[38]

Does their use by Christ to communicate himself to his followers make them immune to criticism? Some have worried that Farrer gives undue authority to the imagery found in Scripture or is too narrow in identifying the images that can be revelatory.[39] That may be true. Farrer says that those who would seek a more effective sacramentalism should throw themselves into observance of the sacraments as we have them, and grasp the substance beneath the forms.[40] More significantly, though, he would say that the faithful's apprehension of the divine is only one function of the visible image of the elements – and a decidedly secondary one at that. Far more significant is its role as the means by which the divine grasps the faithful, by which God fills and uses them.[41] The outward symbols of bread and wine remain the same, but those who participate in them are gradually transformed. In that sense, the Eucharist bears a certain critical power within itself, precluding the possibility of its being used to dominate or exclude others. It is an image that is repeatedly broken open and poured out, one that is eaten and disappears, one that demands the same openness of those who participate in it. It is an image that reminds the faithful that they never get farther than their need, reminds them of their status as receivers of a will that they have demonstrated that they cannot keep for long. Week after week, by slow degrees, the faithful learn this about themselves, learn to come back for this bread, to desire it once more, 'until their hunger is their mind'.[42] This hunger is always met with the bread of Christ, fed and renewed in this way. And Christ is the one who gives himself entirely away.

Notes

1 See David Hein, 'Farrer on Friendship, Sainthood, and the Will of God', in *Captured by the Crucified: The Practical Theology of Austin Farrer*, ed. David Hein and Edward H. Henderson, New York, T & T Clark, 2004, p. 140.

2 Farrer, *Faith and Speculation*, London, Adam & Charles Black, 1967, p. 111.

3 For recent work on this theme in Farrer's work, see Robert MacSwain, *Solved By Sacrifice: Austin Farrer, Fideism, and the Evidence of Faith*, Walpole, MA, Peeters, 2013.

4 Farrer, *Said or Sung*, London, The Faith Press, 1960, p. 157.

5 Farrer, *Faith and Speculation*, p. 35.

6 Farrer, *The Crown of the Year: Weekly Paragraphs for the Holy Sacrament*, Westminster, Dacre Press, 1952, p. 58.

7 Philip Curtis, *A Hawk Among Sparrows: A Biography of Austin Farrer*, Eugene, OR, Wipf & Stock, 1985, p.7.

8 Farrer, *Said or Sung*, p. 120.

9 Farrer, *The Brink of Mystery*, London, SPCK, 1976, pp. 70–3.

10 See, for example, Farrer, *Said or Sung*, p. 30.

11 Farrer, *The Crown of the Year*, pp. 65–6.

12 See, for example, Farrer, *Said or Sung*, pp. 119–24.

13 Farrer, *The Crown of the Year*, p. 66.

14 Ibid., p. 70.

15 Ibid., p. 71.

16 See Charles C. Hefling, Jnr, *Jacob's Ladder: Theology and Spirituality in the Thought of Austin Farrer*, Cambridge, MA, Cowley, 1979, p. 5.

17 Farrer, *The End of Man*, Grand Rapids, MI, Eerdmans, 1973, p. 22.

18 For a helpful discussion of this, see Edward H. Henderson, 'The God Who Undertakes Us' in *Captured by the Crucified*, pp. 66–99.

19 Farrer, *The Crown of the Year*, p. 17.

20 Farrer, *Said or Sung*, p. 129.

21 Farrer, *The Brink of Mystery*, pp. 1–5.

22 Farrer, *Said or Sung*, p. 30.

23 Farrer, *The Crown of the Year*, p. 29.

24 Ibid., p. 8.

25 Farrer, *Said or Sung*, p. 114.

26 Farrer, *The End of Man*, p. 64.

27 Farrer, *Saving Belief*, New York, Morehouse-Barlow, 1964, pp. 129–30.

28 Farrer, *The Crown of the Year*, p. 21.

29 Farrer, *Said or Sung*, p. 106.

30 Farrer, *The Crown of the Year*, p. 36.

31 Farrer, *Said or Sung*, p. 74.

32 Ibid., p. 147.

33 Farrer, *The End of Man*, p. 60.

34 Farrer, *Lord I Believe: Suggestions for Turning the Creed Into Prayer*, Cambridge, MA, Cowley, 1989, p. 40; see also, *Said or Sung*, p. 158.

35 Ibid., p. 49.

36 Farrer, *The Brink of Mystery*, p. 4.

37 Douglas Hedley, 'Austin Farrer's Shaping Spirit of Imagination', in *The Human Person in God's World: Studies to Commemorate the Austin Farrer Centenary*, ed. Brian Hebblethwaite and Douglas Hedley, London, SCM Press, 2006, p. 129.

38 Farrer, *The Glass of Vision*, Westminster, Dacre Press, 1948, p. 42. On this, see David Hein, *Farrer on Friendship, Sainthood, and the Will of God*, p. 138.

39 For a helpful discussion of this, see Stephen Platten, 'Diaphanous Thought: Spirituality and Theology in the Work of Austin Farrer', in *Anglican Theology Review* LXIX:1, pp. 44–5.

40 Farrer, *The End of Man*, p. 104. It is worth noting that Farrer says whereas the sacraments of the church are 'covenanted mercies', the number of uncovenanted mercies is infinite. See *Saving Belief*, p. 132.

41 Farrer, *The Crown of the Year*, p. 12.

42 Ibid., p. 23.

Farrer and the Future

A Prophetic Influence:
Concluding Reflections

STEPHEN PLATTEN

Anthony Kenny, the distinguished philosopher and former Master of Balliol, has written:

> I went to Oxford as a graduate student in 1957, just before Farrer published *The Freedom of the Will*. I admired the book, but found it little help in writing my own doctoral thesis on the will, because of its unwillingness to engage with mainstream analytic philosophy. I believed that Farrer was quite the equal of Ryle, Austin and Ayer, but because of its idiosyncratic vocabulary and conceptual structure it failed to have the influence it deserved.[1]

Kenny had encountered Farrer's work while studying for his Licentiate degree at the Gregorian University in Rome; indeed he wrote his required short dissertation on Farrer's *Finite and Infinite*.[2] The above paragraph is part of a tribute to Farrer among a selection of brief vignettes on those with whom Kenny has engaged in his academic and public life. It is interesting, inasmuch as it picks up themes common to many reflections upon Farrer and his scholarship. His intellectual brilliance is foremost but then the difficulty with some of his texts is there too, and notably with the two books mentioned by Kenny. Alongside this, however, are recorded countless notes of gratitude for the clarity and originality of so much of his theological writing, from philosophical theology to biblical studies, from his sermons to his studies on the spiritual life. Many of these are also anchored in the practicalities of living a Christian life, and in the moral instincts and principles which underlie such a life. There is an earthy homeliness, alongside intellectual challenge, in so much of Farrer's work, as comments on his sermons so often reflect.

Starting to study theology seriously in 1972, I sadly missed the opportunity of meeting with Austin Farrer, but so many of his pupils and disciples encouraged any budding student of theology to engage with his work. Leslie Houlden, his successor as Fellow and Chaplain of Trinity College, Oxford and certainly a disciple in the realm of New Testament studies, and indeed more widely, was just one such a key influence on me, alongside Basil

Mitchell as a philosophical theologian and John Austin Baker as priest, New Testament scholar and noted preacher. With such encouragement I decided to focus, in an optional paper for the then Oxford Certificate in Theology, on the relationship between spirituality and theology in Farrer's writings.[3] In the course of my research many assisted, including Hugo Dyson (one of those who with J. R. R. Tolkien accompanied C. S. Lewis on Addison's Walk at Magdalen College, Oxford whereby he moved gradually toward Christian belief). Some of Farrer's sometime lodgers offered reflections as did each of his sisters, with whom I met. His sister Eleanor noted in a letter to me:

> You will find me a very different person from my sister, who like Austin, was blessed with such a reliable mind and brain ... He and I were very close, and it will be a pleasure to try to give you some further insight into what made Austin what he became.[4]

Indeed this is just what she did, as did Austin's other sister, Joyce, in a separate meeting. Both referred to the importance of family life, of his rootedness in the everyday alongside his scholarship. His father's influence had been positive; he too, as an ordained minister, had been a scholar within his own Baptist tradition.

I gained further evidence of his down-to-earth enjoyment of the everyday when I was Bishop of Wakefield. Taking the initiative to install a modest plaque to Austin's memory in All Saints, Dewsbury (now Dewsbury Minster), I was engaged in conversation with one of our priests. Her mother had not only known Austin, but she had been an 'early flame' of Austin's, during his time as curate in the parish. The daughter still retained a small collection of gifts that Austin had given her mother during their brief romantic friendship. These varied appreciations from those who were close to him give some indication of how the scholar and priest were integrated entirely in his personal life, from his youth onwards. They offer too some insight into the breadth and range of his contribution to Christian theology and spirituality which is spelt out in so many ways in this collection.

* * *

The essays collected here bring together a wide range of scholars from both sides of the Atlantic, many well-established and some from more recent generations, approaching Farrer with a particular freshness. The areas covered are equally diverse and indicate the remarkable capacity of Farrer to straddle different theological disciplines while at the same time displaying an extraordinarily impressive integrity within his thought. Alongside this, as already hinted, is the sharp contrast between some of his complex early philosophical writings and his later, less opaque work. This too has been addressed within these essays. This has also helped clarify the means by which Farrer wrote with such remarkable integrity across his wide-ranging scholarship. Paul De Hart's analysis of *Finite and Infinite*, for example, will be of great value to those engaging with Farrer's philosophical thought, which achieved a far greater clarity in his later more systematic essay, 'Saving Belief',[5] for example, and in his very late philosophical essay 'Faith and Speculation',[6] which included the Deems Lectures from 1964. The significance of that book was indeed captured brilliantly in a review published just a year before Farrer's death. Hugh Dickinson writes:

> Many readers are now familiar with the dazzle of Dr Farrer's trapeze acts. It is difficult not to be amazed and delighted with the virtuosity with which he divides his argument between two swinging components of his own mind, launches them through the void to join hands in some spectacular gyration in mid-air with perfect mutuality of wit and style, and then returns them to their perches without a hair out of place, but leaving the reader breathless and often slightly puzzled to decide exactly what has happened.[7]

Dickinson indicates how Farrer has here used the wit, rhetoric and articulation that he displays in his sermons to rehearse the key arguments in his philosophical theology. Dickinson concludes his review:

> The difficulties which modern radical theologians find in this belief reflect the shallowness of their meditation on the mysterious relationship between the infinite Creator and his finite creatures. It is a mark of the quality of this book that the reader is forced to reflect again on his (sic) own relationship to God and is moved to try to do something to make it closer.[8]

Here we see a further instance of Farrer's integration of his scholarly theological reflection, and this time relating to his engagement with the spiritual life. It is an echo of what the reader discovers in *Lord, I Believe*,[9] *The Triple Victory*,[10] in the sermons and also in *The Crown of the Year*.[11]

The nature of this counter-trend or, indeed, even counter-suggestive approach is illustrated clearly in Leigh Vicens' reflections on Farrer's theodicy. Here, in the case of both natural and moral evil, Farrer is concerned about what God is doing in the face of these challenging elements within creation. Alongside this, as elsewhere in Farrer's scholarship, we find ourselves engaging with a sceptical mind interestingly and fruitfully combined with a devout temperament. John Barton indicates how this put Farrer at odds with the 'higher criticism' (as it was known at the time) – that is, historical and form criticism. Farrer's literary and typological approach prefigured the increasing impact of redaction criticism, which became increasingly focussed on the 'creative' work of the evangelists and indeed other biblical writers. Mark Goodacre makes a similar point, as he examines the reception of Farrer's essay 'On Dispensing with Q', both by its admirers and its critics. Indeed, some critics were simply incapable of embracing an openness to the evangelists' 'creativity' which the almost midrashic approach within Farrer's essay implies. Here, a more midrashic element requires, of both scholar and reader, a greater historical uncertainty. Nonetheless, Farrer's temperament never allows such scholarship to leave behind the co-creative working together of the divine and the human, the infinite and the finite in bringing inspired images to bear, which carry through the process of inspiration, in what became known as 'double agency'.

Despite Farrer's devotion, he was still more than prepared to be fierce in debate, often using a sort of imagined debate in his own mind, characterized above in Dickinson's review. Richard Harries, for example, points to his fairly sharp rejection of penal substitution theories of the atonement. Some lectures of Farrer, delivered two years before his death in the USA, were rediscovered at Keble College, Oxford in 2019, ironically the fiftieth anniversary of Farrer's death, and are now published;[12] they too see him consistently attacking the Bultmann school's firm adherence to demythologization and their concurrent engagement with existential philosophy. Anthony Kenny, further on in the reflection with which we began, recounts his contribution to the viva voce examination of Dennis Nineham for an Oxford DD. The examination focussed on Nineham's commentary on St Mark's Gospel. Kenny recalls the public examination which, because of the eminence of the individuals involved, gained a significant audience. Kenny attended the examination and notes that it was:

> ... a tournament between three of the senior theologians (Farrer, Nineham and Henry Chadwick) of the Church of England. Chadwick questioned Nineham in a gently urbane manner – but some of Farrer's questioning could only be described as savage. Though himself a venturesome interpreter of St Mark, he made it clear that he thought the commentary conceded too much to higher criticism of the Gospel. However, the examiners awarded the degree.[13]

Alongside this intellectual jousting, however, are countless reports of his pastoral heart and concern for individuals, both pupils and all who came his way. Students could find him daunting – even terrifying in his intellectual capacity. None of this, however, should suggest that he lacked personal warmth or real care. In this case, of course, Farrer was in his element professionally, at the heart of Oxford's rarefied intellectual culture. Indeed, it is frequently argued that at the time Farrer had less impact on theology more widely because of the sheer fact of his life-long career within that same university. Jane Shaw argues that it was this very factor which coloured Farrer's sermons too, and effectively gave them both their distinctive character and their impact intellectually and spiritually –

ironically, over the years, to a much wider audience than that for which they had originally been prepared. Of course, this cut both ways. Adrian Hastings argues that Farrer was 'a little too idiosyncratically enigmatic, too closely confined to Oxford's ways and idioms, to have a resulting national influence'.[14]

In recent years, however, despite periods when his work has been undervalued, as we point out in our introduction, Farrer has more recently been described as both a 'genius' and also the most creative theologian born of Anglicanism in the twentieth century. Alongside all else, he is seen as an apologist for Christian belief, at the most scholarly level. In an interesting critical appraisal of Farrer, Jeremy Morris differentiates between those who see their task as accommodating with secular philosophy – what Hans Frei describes as 'mediating theologians' – and apologists working at a rather different level. Morris is quite clear that the 'mediating apologists' is not the group within which Farrer could be classed as a member and so he writes of Farrer:

> ... for him, God's action is primary and natural accounts of human and physical interaction are framed by, rather than framing, the Christian account of God's relations with his creatures. Although Farrer's argument cannot itself furnish rational criteria which may then be applied outside the experience of the individual to demonstrate or justify belief in God's existence, nevertheless it does protect the believer's own experience of God from the denials of modernity, and so may provide an essential preliminary ingredient for other kinds of argument to the same end.[15]

So Farrer was undoubtedly an apologist, as indeed was Berdyaev as we see from Gregory Platten's contribution. Farrer's apologetics, however, are not offered at the expense of the fundamental Christian message. Once again this is clear in the way that he attacks the reductionist tendencies of the Bultmann school, both in the lectures recently published, referred to above, but also in other contributions at the time.[16]

* * *

Throughout the essays in this volume there have been references to themes upon which Farrer was ahead of his time, prefiguring later developments and so prophetic in his intellectual agenda. Richard Harries posits this as one of the reasons why – both at the time and in the decades that followed – his remarkable contribution was not more influential. Margaret Yee points to significant leaps in Farrer's own development of philosophical theology. Then, almost the entire force of Robert MacSwain's essay is on the manner in which he anticipated what is described as 'Reformed epistemology', and, notably, in Farrer's engagement with his pupil Diogenes Allen. Indeed, the question is posed in a most challenging way: 'Why are Farrer and Allen not better recognized for their trailblazing accomplishments in religious epistemology?' MacSwain's answer is equally direct: 'My brief answer is that they were both so far ahead of their time that their work fell on the proverbial rocky soil.'[17] Goodacre also uses the term 'prophetic' for Farrer's scholarship, not only in the essay on Q, but also when referring to Farrer's other writings on Mark, Matthew and the Apocalypse, that is, the Revelation to St John the Divine. Jenn Strawbridge offers interesting insights to Farrer's understanding of the writings of Paul.

The broader sense of the prophetic on a number of issues is uncannily revealed in the recently published lectures already referred to. In the first of these, 'Something has Died on Us: Can it be God?',[18] we find ourselves caught up into the heart of the controversial debate of the 1960s which led, perhaps most extremely, to the so-called 'Death of God Theology', now little more than an historical entry in dictionaries of theology. Thomas Altizer, Paul van Buren and William Hamilton's work in this area is now largely forgotten, but Farrer's essays were engaging with these trends in 1966 when the heat of the debate was most intense. In Britain, John Robinson's *Honest to God*[19] had also been published in 1963.

Although the manner of the debate has shifted over the years, both in the 1980s, following the publication of Don Cupitt's *Taking Leave of God*,[20] and much more recently with the rash of publications by the 'New Atheists', similar themes have been rehearsed. Farrer's lecture undermines the essential arguments set out in these waves of extreme scepticism, even well before they had been rehearsed. Cupitt's writings might be seen as further examples of what was described earlier by Hans Frei as 'mediating theology'. This was certainly not Farrer's style.

Then, in a second essay,[21] which asks if Christian doctrine is 'reformable', there is a prefiguring of the rather different controversy which surrounded what became known as the discipline of 'doctrinal criticism'. Maurice Wiles, John Hick and others initiated a lively debate which began in some senses as long ago as the mid-nineteenth century, in John Henry Newman's *Essay on the Development of Christian Doctrine*. By the 1980s, however, the argument had effectively advanced in the direction of theories of doctrinal *evolution*.[22] It is interesting how, not long after Farrer's death, Wiles engaged in energetic debate with other theologians in the pages of the journal *Theology*, specifically in relation to Farrer's theology. The main focus here was admittedly that of 'double agency', but issues relating to the reformability of doctrine were not far below the surface.

Farrer was himself open to doctrinal reformability and indeed was as disparaging of propositionalism in doctrine as he was in relation to such an approach to Scripture. At the same time the trend toward re-expressing Christian belief in existentialist categories came within the sights of Farrer's philosophical armoury. It was not only Bultmann's programme of demythologization which Farrer disdained, but also the subsequent existentialist 'remythologization' encountered in Bultmann, Macquarrie, Jaspers and others to which Farrer took exception. It is interesting to note how far the high tide of existentialism has now ebbed, not only in theological, but also in wider philosophical circles. Farrer did indeed prefigure these shifts in philosophical thought.

His final lecture in this series of four, delivered to at least two different audiences in the USA, responds to the question of how far social structure bows to Christian morals and vice versa.[23] The moral implications of the Christian gospel are never far below the surface in so much of Farrer's writing, be it philosophical, homiletic or spiritual. Jeffrey Vogel makes this point powerfully in his essay on eucharistic theology as encountered in Farrer's writings. Rarely is there set out a systematic eucharistic theology, but the essence of Farrer's understanding is there frequently in his sermons and similar ascetic essays. So, at one point he writes:

> When we leave the altar we do not cease to put faith in the Christ of the sacrament, but continue in our prayers to ask for our smouldering faith to be blown into a flame. All prayer and obedience is one within the Eucharist, for it is a participation in Christ's dying love.[24]

There is one slightly extended reflection on the sacrament forming the final piece in *The Crown of the Year*.[25] In another of these short pieces, often described at the time as 'Farrergraphs', we read:

> But as the Holy Spirit grows in us, it is not he but we who grow. He does not grow up and leave us behind, we grow up into him. He becomes the spring and substance of our mind and heart. He is the never failing fountain of which Jesus spoke to the Samaritans. We break up the stony rubbish of our life again and again, to find and release the well of living water.[26]

The Eucharist is thus part of the staple diet which nourishes our spiritual and moral lives.

Interestingly enough, the title of his final lecture in this set has resonances with more recent developments. John Milbank's book *Theology and Social Theory*[27] picked up a similar theme in what became the key monograph in establishing the 'radical orthodox' movement. Farrer would have had sympathy with much of Milbank's critique and even his Aristotelian starting point, although his approach differs quite sharply. Effectively here we see Farrer pointing toward the essence of a 'virtue ethic', thus anticipating the work of Alasdair MacIntyre and those who have followed him. So, in this rather different aspect of his thought, Farrer once again points forward. He writes:

> Moral minds are minds that see with God, and of course no one can suppose that God in measuring what is good goes by rule. God is not a

God of disorder and so no doubt there is an analogy, a rational analogy between God's several actions and intentions.[28]

Later he writes, more directly, and with more than a nod in the direction of virtue ethics:

Morality, as Aristotle wisely said, goes by habit and you cannot have a habit about anything but by the operation of a rule. You cannot have a habit about how to treat unique situations uniquely.[29]

Morality is learned and shapes character, and is not, as the existentialists and situation ethicists tended to suggest, unique on every occasion, despite, of course, the importance of context.

* * *

Having reflected on the various ways in which Farrer's legacy was prophetic and a precursor of what would follow, what agenda might this leave for us half a century after his death?

Perhaps we might begin with a further question about Farrer's own formation. We have seen something of the religious background to his own personal life and of the rather compact world of his professional life. But despite these formative backgrounds, none of us is otherwise entirely self-made nor sui generis with regard to the broader tradition. Which influences might have impinged upon Farrer? We have seen something of his Aristotelian roots but what of the key developments which shaped his later writing. It would be a creative contribution toward both scholarship and to a deeper understanding of Farrer's own development if further discoveries could be made to see something of the early modern and then contemporary influences which brought him to his mature thought. In the light of this question, Leslie Houlden recounted an interesting vignette of conversation. On an occasion during the 1960s a colleague asked Austin Farrer if he had read Edwyn Bevan's monograph, *Symbolism and Belief*.[30] Rather perversely Farrer responded: 'I prefer to write books ...' and then left the conversation in mid-air. But influenced he must have been and this might be a fertile area for research.

Then, in terms of other themes for further research, there are a number which have arisen throughout this volume. Undoubtedly, the significance of analogy and the importance of images must stand clearly in the foreground. *The Glass of Vision*,[31] arguably his most creative single volume, continues to exert its impact. Although critics have pointed to critical areas in his argument, there have been no significantly damaging challenges to this approach, in relation both to the inspiration of Scripture and also doctrinal development. Rather remarkably, his homiletic work is effectively an outflow from this aspect of his theological insight; Morwenna Ludlow very effectively points to the possibilities here in her essay comparing Farrer's approach to that of the work of Gregory of Nazianzus.

Then, following from the debates as 'double agency', there is the key theme of co-creation which also manifests itself in a number of these essays. If Christianity is a living tradition, then we should expect it to display a creative relationship within the finite and infinite compass. In his writing, of course, this is effectively where Farrer began and, indeed, in *Faith and Speculation* it is the point of focus for his final published work of his own lifetime. Rowan Williams' most recent major study moves this discussion forward significantly.[32] In this case, Farrer not only prefigures Williams' work but effectively stimulates further theological engagement, thus moving forward Williams' own account.

A further recurrent theme is that of the integrity of Farrer's oeuvre. The wide sweep of his interests, from biblical scholarship to philosophical theology and then including ascetic and homiletic creativity, stands in a long tradition within Anglican scholarship, beginning with Richard Hooker, developed by the Caroline Divines and continued in the twentieth-century rebirth of Anglican moral theology. Farrer's work spans the entire spectrum and indicates that, despite increased fragmentation through specialization, an integrated theology is both possible and essential to the coherence of Christian belief.

Finally, and issuing from all these, is that emphasis which is clear from his philosophical theology in particular, in the integration of theory and practice. Farrer's determination to remain devout and at the same time properly sceptical was itself one of the contributors to his creativity. But is also makes clear that a lived Christianity is essential for a continuing, developing and thus living tradition. The essays here are far from exhaustive of what Austin Farrer still has to offer; they stimulate us to ask what might be the next chapter in his legacy.

Notes

1 Anthony Kenny, *Brief Encounters: Notes from a Philosopher's Diary*, London, SPCK, 2018, p. 40.

2 Austin Farrer, *Finite and Infinite*, London, Dacre Press, 1943.

3 Stephen Platten, 'Diaphanous Thought: Spirituality and Theology in the Work of Austin Farrer', *Anglican Theological Review*, vol. LXIX, no. 1, Jan. 1987, pp. 30–50.

4 Personal letter to author.

5 Austin Farrer, *Saving Belief*, London, Hodder & Stoughton, 1967.

6 Austin Farrer, *Faith and Speculation*, London, A & C Black, 1967.

7 Hugh Dickinson, 'God in Action', review of Austin Farrer's *Faith and Speculation* in *The Times Literary Supplement*, 27 August 1967, p. 767.

8 Ibid.

9 Austin Farrer, *Lord I Believe*, London, Faith Press, 1958.

10 Austin Farrer, *The Triple Victory*, London, Faith Press, 1965.

11 Austin Farrer, *The Crown of the Year*, London, Dacre Press, 1952.

12 Markus Bockmuehl and Stephen Platten (eds), *Austin Farrer: Oxford Warden, Scholar, Preacher*, London, SCM Press, 2020, pp. 134ff.

13 Kenny, *Brief Encounters*, pp. 40–1.

14 Adrian Hastings, *A History of English Christianity 1920–1985*, London, SCM Press, 1991, p. 492.

15 J. N. Morris, 'Religious Experience in the Philosophical Theology of Austin Farrer', *Journal of Theological Studies*, NS, Oxford University Press, vol. 45, Oct. 1994, p. 592. Here Morris adverts to the work of Richard Swinburne and Basil Mitchell.

16 Cf. here Bockmuehl and Platten, *Austin Farrer*, especially pp. 134ff. and also Austin Farrer, 1961, 'An English Appreciation', in *Kerygma and Myth: A Theological Debate*, ed. H. W. Bartsch and R. H. Fuller, New York, Harper and Row, pp. 212–23.

17 Robert MacSwain in this volume.

18 In Bockmuehl and Platten, *Austin Farrer*, pp. 103–18.

19 John Robinson, *Honest to God*, London, SCM Press, 1963.

20 Don Cupitt, *Taking Leave of God*, London, SCM Press, 1980.

21 In Bockmuehl and Platten, *Austin Farrer*, pp. 119–33.

22 Perhaps the clearest statement of such an approach is seen in Maurice Wiles, *The Remaking of Christian Doctrine*, London, SCM Press, 1974; these had been delivered as the Hulsean Lectures 1974 in Cambridge.

23 Bockmuehl and Platten, *Austin Farrer*, pp. 151–68.

24 Austin Farrer, *Lord, I Believe: Suggestions for Turning the Creed into Prayer*, London, Faith Press, 1955, p. 49.

25 Austin Farrer, *The Crown of the Year*, London, Dacre Press, 1952, pp. 63ff.

26 Ibid., p. 36.

27 John Milbank, *Theology and Social Theory*, Oxford, Wiley-Blackwell, 1990.

28 Bockmuehl and Platten, *Austin Farrer*, p. 155.

29 Ibid., p. 156.

30 Edwyn Bevan, *Symbolism and Belief*, London, George Allen and Unwin, 1962, but based on the 1933–34 Gifford Lectures.

31 *The Glass of Vision*, Westminster, Dacre Press, 1948.

32 Rowan Williams, *Christ the Heart of Creation*, London, Bloomsbury, 2018.

Bibliography of Works by or Related to Austin Farrer

Primary Farrer sources (A) are arranged in chronological order of publication; secondary Farrer sources (B) in alphabetical order by author. Some of Farrer's books in (A.1) have been subsequently reprinted by other publishers. Some of his essays in (A.3) have been reprinted in various of the collections listed in (A.2). None of Farrer's sermons, encyclopaedia articles or posthumously-published essays are listed separately here, but may be found in the cited collection. This is based on the Bibliography in Robert MacSwain, *Solved by Sacrifice: Austin Farrer, Fideism and the Evidence of Faith* (pp. 251–68). For earlier bibliographies see 'A Chronological List of Farrer's Published Writings' in Charles Conti's *Metaphysical Personalism* (pp. 277–87), and for a 'Bibliography of Writings about Austin Farrer with Other Research Aids' see Hein and Henderson (eds), *Captured by the Crucified* (pp. 197–208). Some further additions have been provided by Professor Mark Goodacre.

A.1. Primary Sources: Books Published in Farrer's Lifetime

Finite and Infinite: A Philosophical Essay (Westminster: Dacre Press, 1943); Second Edition with a revised Preface, 1959.

The Glass of Vision: The Bampton Lectures of 1948 (Westminster: Dacre Press, 1948). Reprinted in a critical edition as *Scripture, Metaphysics, and Poetry: Austin Farrer's* The Glass of Vision *with Critical Commentary*, ed. Robert MacSwain (London and New York: Routledge, 2016 – originally published in 2013 by Ashgate).

A Rebirth of Images: The Making of St John's Apocalypse (Westminster: Dacre Press, 1949).

A Study in St Mark (Westminster: Dacre Press, 1951).

The Crown of the Year: Weekly Paragraphs for the Holy Sacrament (Westminster: Dacre Press, 1952).

St Matthew and St Mark (Westminster: Dacre Press, 1954); Second Edition, 1966.

The Freedom of the Will: The Gifford Lectures delivered in the University of Edinburgh, 1957 (London: Adam and Charles Black, 1958); Second Edition, including a 'Summary of the Argument' (New York: Scribners, 1960).

Lord I Believe: Suggestions for Turning the Creed into Prayer, Beacon Books Number 10 (London: The Church Union, 1955); Second Edition, Revised and Enlarged (London: SPCK, 1962).

Said or Sung: An Arrangement of Homily and Verse (London: The Faith Press, 1960). Published in the United States as *A Faith of Our Own*, with a preface by C. S. Lewis (Cleveland, OH and New York: World Publishing Company).

Love Almighty and Ills Unlimited: An Essay on Providence and Evil, Containing the Nathaniel Taylor Lectures for 1961 (New York: Doubleday, 1961 / London: Collins, 1962).

The Revelation of St John the Divine: A Commentary on the English Text (Oxford: Oxford University Press, 1964).

Saving Belief: A Discussion of Essentials (London: Hodder and Stoughton, 1964).

The Triple Victory: Christ's Temptations According to St Matthew (London: The Faith Press, 1965).

A Science of God? (London: Geoffrey Bles, 1966). Published in the United States as *God is Not Dead* (New York: Morehouse-Barlow, 1966).

Faith and Speculation: An Essay in Philosophical Theology, containing the Deems Lectures for 1964 (London: Adam and Charles Black, 1967).

A.2. Primary Sources: Posthumous Collections of Sermons and Essays

A Celebration of Faith, edited by Leslie Houlden (London: Hodder and Stoughton, 1970), containing 'Austin Marsden Farrer', a memorial address by Basil Mitchell.

Reflective Faith: Essays in Philosophical Theology, edited by Charles C. Conti, foreword by John Hick (London: SPCK, 1972).

The End of Man, edited by Charles C. Conti, introduction by John Austin Baker (London: SPCK, 1973).

The Brink of Mystery, edited by Charles C. Conti, foreword by J. L. Houlden (London: SPCK, 1976).

Interpretation and Belief, edited by Charles C. Conti, foreword by E. L. Mascall (London: SPCK, 1976).

The Essential Sermons, edited and introduced by Leslie Houlden (London: SPCK, 1991).

Words for Life: Forty Meditations Previously Unpublished, edited by Charles Conti and Leslie Houlden, preface by Charles Conti, introduction by Leslie Houlden (London: SPCK, 1993).

The Truth-Seeking Heart: Austin Farrer and His Writings, edited and introduced by Ann Loades and Robert MacSwain (Norwich: Canterbury Press, 2006).

See also *The One Genius: Readings Through the Year with Austin Farrer*, edited by Richard Harries (London: SPCK, 1987).

A.3. Primary Sources: Essays Published in Farrer's Lifetime

'A Return to New Testament Christological Categories', *Theology* (Volume XXVI, Number 156, June 1933), 304–18.

'Eucharist and Church in the New Testament', in A. G. Hebert (ed.), *The Parish Communion: A Book of Essays* (London: SPCK, 1937), 74–94.

'Can We Know That God Exists?' (editor's summary of a debate between the Rev. A. M. Farrer and Mr MacNabb), *Socratic Digest* (Volume 2, 1944), 12–13.

'The Extension of St Thomas's Doctrine of Knowledge by Analogy to Modern Philosophical Problems', *The Downside Review* (Volume 65, Number 199, January 1947), 21–32.

'Does God Exist?', *Socratic Digest* (Volume 4, 1947), 27–34.

'On Credulity', *Illuminatio* (Volume 1, Number 3, 1947), 3–9.

'Editor's Introduction' to G. W. Leibniz, *Theodicy: Essays on the Goodness of God, the Freedom of Man, and the Origin of Evil*, edited by A. M. Farrer and translated by E. M. Huggard (London: Routledge and Kegan Paul, 1951), 4–47.

'A Midwinter Daydream', *University: A Journal of Inquiry* (Volume 1, Number 2, Spring 1951), 86–90. Reprinted as 'A Theologian's Point of View' in *Socratic Digest* (Volume 5, 1952), 35–8.

'An English Appreciation', in Hans Werner Bartsch (ed.), *Kerygma and Myth: A Theological Debate*, translated by Reginald H. Fuller (London: SPCK, 1953), 212–23.

'The Trinity in Whom We Live', *Theology* (Volume LVI, Number 399, September 1953), 322–7.

'On Dispensing With Q', in D. E. Nineham (ed.), *Studies in the Gospels: Essays in Memory of R. H. Lightfoot* (Oxford: Blackwell, 1955), 55–88.

'A Starting-Point for the Philosophical Examination of Theological Belief', in Basil Mitchell (ed.), *Faith and Logic: Oxford Essays in Philosophical Theology* (London: George Allen and Unwin, 1957), 9–30.

'Revelation', in Basil Mitchell (ed.), *Faith and Logic: Oxford Essays in Philosophical Theology* (London: George Allen and Unwin, 1957), 84–107.

'The Christian Apologist', in Jocelyn Gibb (ed.), *Light on C. S. Lewis* (London: Geoffrey Bles, 1965), 23–43.

Reply to Dorothy Emmet, Ted Bastin and Margaret Masterman's Review Discussion of Austin Farrer's *A Science of God?*, *Theoria to Theory* (Volume 1, 1966), 72–5.

'Infallibility and Historical Revelation', in Austin Farrer et al., *Infallibility in the Church: An Anglican-Catholic Dialogue* (London: Darton, Longman and Todd, 1968), 9–23.

A.4. Primary Sources: Book Reviews

Review of P. Erich Przywara, 'Polarity', *Theology* (Volume XXXI, Number 186, December 1935), 361–3.

Review of Karl Heim, 'God Transcendent', *The Church Quarterly Review* (Volume CXXII, Number CCXLIV, July–September 1936), 334–7.

Review of Karl Barth, 'The Doctrine of the Word of God and God in Action', *Theology* (Volume XXXIII, Number 198, December 1936), 370–3.

Review of Melville Chaning-Pearce, 'Religion and Reality: An Essay in the Christian Co-Ordination of Contraries', *The Church Quarterly Review* (Volume CXXIV, Number CCXLVIII, July–September 1937), 328–30.

Review of Walter Farrell, OP, 'A Companion to the Summa: Volume II: The Pursuit of Happiness', *Theology* (Volume XXXVIII, Number 224, February 1939), 153–4.

Review of M. C. D'Arcy, SJ, 'Thomas Aquinas: Selected Writings', *Theology* (Volume XXXIX, Number 232, October 1939), 319–20.

Review of Paul Ortegat, 'Philosophie de la Religion', *Journal of Theological Studies* OS (Volume XL, Number 1, 1939), 100–1.

Review of A. C. Bradley, 'Ideals of Religion', *Theology* (Volume XL, Number 240, June 1940), 461–3.

Review of C. J. Shebbeare, 'The Problem of the Future Life', *Journal of Theological Studies* OS (Volume XLI, Number 163–164, 1940), 343–4.

Review of W. M. Urban, 'Language and Reality: The Philosophy of Language and the Principals of Symbolism', *The Church Quarterly Review* (Volume CXXXI, Number CCLXII, January–March 1941), 277–80.

Review of George Santayana, 'The Realm of Spirit', *Theology* (Volume XLII, Number 248, February 1941), 123–5.

Review of W. T. Stace, 'The Nature of the World: An Essay in Phenomenalist Metaphysics', *Journal of Theological Studies* OS (Volume XLII, Number 1, 1941), 108–10.

Review of Norman Kemp Smith, 'The Philosophy of David Hume', *Journal of Theological Studies* OS (Volume XLIII, Numbers 171–172, 1942), 229–32.

Review of C. C. J. Webb, 'Religious Experience', *Theology* (Volume XLIX, Number 307, January 1946), 23–4.

Review of J. Ramsey McCallum, 'Abelard's Christian Theology', *Journal of Theological Studies* NS (Volume I, Part 2, 1950), 221.

Review of B. C. Butler, *The Originality of St Matthew* (Cambridge: Cambridge University Press, 1951), *Journal of Theological Studies* 3 (1952): 102–6.

Review of John Hick, 'Faith and Knowledge: A Modern Introduction to the Problems of Religious Knowledge', *Journal of Theological Studies* NS (Volume IX, Part 2, 1958), 410.

Review of Josef Pieper, 'Introduction to Thomas Aquinas', *Journal of Theological Studies* NS (Volume XV, Part 1, 1964), 202.

Review of Ian T. Ramsey, 'Models and Mystery', *Journal of Theological Studies* NS (Volume XV, Part 2, 1964), 489–90.

Review of Axel Hägerström, 'Philosophy and Religion', *Journal of Theological Studies* NS (Volume XVI, Part 2, 1965), 561–3.

Review of M. J. Charlesworth, 'St Anselm's Proslogion', *Journal of Theological Studies* NS (Volume XVII, Part 2, 1966), 502.

Review of Henk Van Luijk, 'Philosophie du fait Chrétien', *Journal of Theological Studies* NS (Volume XVII, Part 2, 1966), 553.

Review of P. F. Strawson, 'The Bounds of Sense: An Essay on Kant's Critique of Pure Reason', *Journal of Theological Studies* NS (Volume XIX, Part 1, 1968), 420–1.

Review of Thomas J. J. Altizer, 'The Gospel of Christian Atheism', *Journal of Theological Studies* NS (Volume XIX, Part 1, 1968), 422–3.

Review of A. H. Armstrong (ed.), 'The Cambridge History of Latin, Greek, and Early Mediaeval Philosophy', *Religious Studies* (Volume 4, Numbers 1 and 2, 1969), 287–8.

A.5. Primary Sources: Letters

A collection of Farrer's correspondence and family papers is held in the Bodleian Libraries, University of Oxford. Most of the correspondence with his parents (although just from Farrer's side) has been catalogued and foliated in MS. Eng. Lett. c. 270 and d. 272. Other letters from Farrer may be found elsewhere in the collection. Most of the family papers, which include correspondence, are uncatalogued and are kept in 12 boxes.

A.6. Primary Sources: Collaborative Work

Catholicity: A Study of the Conflict of Christian Traditions in the West, being a Report presented to His Grace the Archbishop of Canterbury, with a foreword by the Archbishop of Canterbury (Westminster: Dacre Press, 1947).

A.7. Primary Sources: Unfinished Book Manuscript

Farrer was working on a manuscript at his death, *St Mark's Material*. Of 80 typescript and handwritten pages, the first eight were published posthumously in Charles Conti (ed.), *Interpretation and Belief* (London: SPCK, 1976), 14–22. The rest are unpublished. The manuscript is currently in the possession of Mark Goodacre.

B.1. Secondary Sources: Single-Authored Books On or Related to Farrer

Conti, Charles, *Metaphysical Personalism: An Analysis of Austin Farrer's Theistic Metaphysics* (Oxford: Clarendon Press, 1995).

Curtis, Philip, *A Hawk Among Sparrows: A Biography of Austin Farrer* (London: SPCK, 1985).

Eaton, Jeffrey C., *The Logic of Theism: An Analysis of the Thought of Austin Farrer* (Lanham, MD: University Press of America, 1980).

Hebblethwaite, Brian, *The Philosophical Theology of Austin Farrer* (Leuven: Peeters, 2007).

Hefling, Jr, Charles C., *Jacob's Ladder: Theology and Spirituality in the Thought of Austin Farrer* (Cambridge, MA: Cowley Publications, 1979).

Kennedy, Darren M., *Providence and Personalism: Karl Barth in Conversation with Austin Farrer, John Macmurray and Vincent Brümmer* (Bern: Peter Lang, 2011).

MacSwain, Robert, *Solved by Sacrifice: Austin Farrer, Fideism, and the Evidence of Faith* (Leuven: Peeters, 2013).

Proudfoot, Wayne, *God and the Self: Three Types of Philosophy of Religion* (Lewisburg, PA: Bucknell University Press / London: Associated University Presses, 1976).

Slocum, Robert Boak, *Light in a Burning Glass: A Systematic Presentation of Austin Farrer's Theology* (Columbia, SC: University of South Carolina Press, 2007).

Titley, Robert, *A Poetic Discontent: Austin Farrer and the Gospel of Mark* (London and New York: T & T Clark International, 2010).

B.2. Secondary Sources: Essay Collections On or Related to Farrer

Bockmuehl, Marcus and Platten, Stephen (eds) with Nevsky Everett, *Austin Farrer: Oxford Warden, Scholar, Preacher* (London: SCM Press, 2020).

Eaton, Jeffrey C. and Ann Loades (eds), *For God and Clarity: New Essays in Honor of Austin Farrer* (Allison Park, PA: Pickwick Publications, 1983).

Hedley, Douglas and Brian Hebblethwaite (eds), *The Human Person in God's World: Studies to Commemorate the Austin Farrer Centenary* (London: SCM Press, 2006).

Hebblethwaite, Brian and Edward Henderson (eds), *Divine Action: Studies Inspired by the Philosophical Theology of Austin Farrer* (Edinburgh: T & T Clark, 1990).

Hein, David and Edward Hugh Henderson (eds), *Captured by the Crucified: The Practical Theology of Austin Farrer* (New York and London: T & T Clark International, 2004).

Loades, Ann and Michael McLain (eds), *Hermeneutics, the Bible and Literary Criticism* (London: Macmillan/New York: St. Martin's Press, 1992).

McLain, F. Michael and W. Mark Richardson (eds), *Human and Divine Agency: Anglican, Catholic, and Lutheran Perspectives* (Lanham, MD: University Press of America, 1999).

Poirier, John C. and Jeffrey Peterson (eds), *Marcan Priority Without Q: Explorations in the Farrer Hypothesis* (London: Bloomsbury T & T Clark, 2015).

B.3. Secondary Sources: Articles and Book Reviews On or Related to Farrer

Allen, Diogenes, 'Faith and the Recognition of God's Activity', in Brian Hebblethwaite and Edward Henderson (eds), *Divine Action: Studies Inspired by the Philosophical Theology of Austin Farrer* (Edinburgh: T & T Clark, 1990), 197–210.

——, 'Farrer's Spirituality', in David Hein and Edward Hugh Henderson (eds), *Captured by the Crucified: The Practical Theology of Austin Farrer* (New York and London: T & T Clark International, 2004), 47–65.

Alston, William, 'How to Think About Divine Action: Twenty-five Years of Travail for Biblical Language', in Brian Hebblethwaite and Edward Henderson (eds), *Divine Action: Studies Inspired by the Philosophical Theology of Austin Farrer* (Edinburgh: T & T Clark, 1990), 51–70.

Anon, 'Obituary: Rev. A. M. Farrer,' *The Times*, 30 December 1968.

Baker, John Austin, 'Introduction' in Austin Farrer, *The End of Man*, edited by Charles C. Conti, introduced by John Austin Baker (London: SPCK, 1973), ix–xii.

Barrett, C. K., Review of *St Matthew and St Mark*, *Journal of Theological Studies* 7/1 (1956): 107–10.

Beckett, Lucy, 'Not a Theory, but a Life', Review of Ann Loades and Robert MacSwain (eds), *The Truth-Seeking Heart: Austin Farrer and His Writings* and Douglas Hedley and Brian Hebblethwaite (eds), 'The Human Person in God's World: Studies to Commemorate the Austin Farrer Centenary', *Times Literary Supplement* (Number 5444, 3 August 2007), 23–4.

Blakesley, John, 'Pictures in the Fire? Austin Farrer's Biblical Criticism and John's Gospel – a Comment', *Journal of Literature and Theology* (Volume 1, Number 2, September 1987), 184–90.

Blyth Martin, W. H., 'The Indispensability of Q', *Theology* 59 (1956): 182–8.

Boycott, W. A., Review of Austin Farrer, 'A Science of God?', *Theology* (Volume LXIX, 1966), 184–5.

Brown, Colin, Review of Robert Boak Slocum, 'Light in a Burning-Glass: A Systematic Presentation of Austin Farrer's Theology', and Ann Loades and Robert MacSwain (eds), 'The Truth-Seeking Heart: Austin Farrer and His Writings', *Anglican and Episcopal History* (Volume 76, Number 4, December 2007), 578–81.

Brown, David, 'God and Symbolic Action', in Brian Hebblethwaite and Edward Henderson (eds), *Divine Action: Studies Inspired by the Philosophical Theology of Austin Farrer* (Edinburgh: T & T Clark, 1990), 103–22. Reprinted in *Scripture, Metaphysics, and Poetry: Austin Farrer's The Glass of Vision with Critical Commentary*, ed. Robert MacSwain (London and New York: Routledge, 2016).

——, 'The Role of Images in Theological Reflection', in Douglas Hedley and Brian Hebblethwaite (eds), *The Human Person in God's World: Studies to Commemorate the Austin Farrer Centenary* (London: SCM Press, 2006), 85–105.

——, Review of David Hein and Edward Hugh Henderson (eds), *Captured by the Crucified: The Practical Theology of Austin Farrer*, *Anglican Theological Review* Volume 91, Number 4, Fall 2009), 652–4.

Brown, Stuart, 'Farrer, Austin Marsden,' in Stuart Brown, Diané Collinson, and Robert Wilkinson (eds), *Biographical Dictionary of Twentieth-Century Philosophers* (London and New York: Routledge, 1996), 226–7.

Brümmer, Vincent, 'Farrer, Wiles and the Causal Joint', *Modern Theology* (Volume 8, Number 1, January 1992), 1–14.

Buckley, James J. and William McF. Wilson, 'A Dialogue with Barth and Farrer on Theological Method', *The Heythrop Journal* (Volume XXVI, Number 3, July 1985), 274–93.

Burrell, David, 'Divine Practical Knowing: How an Eternal God Acts in Time', in Brian Hebblethwaite and Edward Henderson (eds), *Divine Action: Studies Inspired by the Philosophical Theology of Austin Farrer* (Edinburgh: T & T Clark, 1990), 93–102.

——, 'Divine Action and Human Freedom in the Context of Creation', in Thomas F. Tracy (ed.), *The God Who Acts: Philosophical and Theological Explorations* (University Park, PA: The Pennsylvania University Press, 1994), 103–9.

Chapman, C. T., Review of Austin Farrer, 'The Freedom of the Will', *Church Quarterly Review* (Volume CLXI, 1960), 107–8.

Conti, Charles, 'Editor's Preface', in Austin Farrer, *Reflective Faith: Essays in Philosophical Theology*, ed. Charles C. Conti, foreword by John Hick (London: SPCK, 1972), vii–xii.

——, 'Editor's Preface', in *The Brink of Mystery*, ed. Charles C. Conti, foreword by J. L. Houlden (London: SPCK, 1976), vii–viii.

——, 'Editor's Introduction', in *Interpretation and Belief*, ed. Charles C. Conti, foreword by E. L. Mascall (London: SPCK, 1976), vii–xii.

——, 'Austin Farrer and the Analogy of Other Minds', in *For God and Clarity: New Essays in Honor of Austin Farrer*, ed. Jeffrey C. Eaton and Ann Loades (Allison Park, PA: Pickwick Publications, 1983), 51–91.

——, 'Farrer's Christian Humanism', *Modern Theology* (Volume 7, Number 5, October 1991), 403–34.

——, 'Preface', in Austin Farrer, *Words for Life: Forty Meditations Previously Unpublished*, ed. Charles Conti and Leslie Houlden, preface by Charles Conti, introduction by Leslie Houlden (London: SPCK, 1993), vii–ix.

——, 'Farrer, Austin Marsden (1904–68)', in *The Dictionary of Twentieth-Century British Philosophers*, ed. Stuart Brown (Bristol: Thoemmes Continuum, 2005), 277–8.

Creery, Walter E., Review of Austin Farrer, 'Reflective Faith', *Theology Today* (Volume 30, Number 3, October 1973), 298–301.

Crombie, I. M. (revised), 'Farrer, Austin Marsden (1904–1968),' in *Oxford Dictionary of National Biography: Volume 19*, ed. H. C. G. Matthew and Brian Harrison (Oxford: Oxford University Press, 2004), 121–3.

Curtis, Philip, 'The Rational Theology of Doctor Farrer', *Theology* (Volume LXXIII, Number 600, June 1970), 249–56.

——, 'The Biblical Work of Doctor Farrer', *Theology* (Volume LXXIII, Number 601, July 1970), 292–301.

Dalferth, Ingolf, '"Esse Est Operari": The Anti-Scholastic Theologies of Farrer and Luther', *Modern Theology* (Volume 1, Number 3, April 1985), 183–210.

——, 'The Stuff of Revelation: Austin Farrer's Doctrine of Inspired Images', in *Hermeneutics, the Bible and Literary Criticism,* ed. Ann Loades and Michael McLain (New York: St. Martin's Press, 1992), 71–95. Reprinted in *Scripture, Metaphysics, and Poetry: Austin Farrer's The Glass of Vision with Critical Commentary,* ed. Robert MacSwain (London and New York: Routledge, 2016).

Davey, F. N., Review of *A Study in St Mark, Journal of Theological Studies* 3/2 (October 1952): 239–42.

Davie, Ian, 'Inverse Analogy', *Downside Review* (Volume 113, Number 392, July 1985), 196–202.

Davies, J. G., Joint Review of Karl Heim, 'The World: Its Creation and Consummation', Austin Farrer, 'Love Almighty and Ills Unlimited', and Harry Johnson, 'The Humanity of the Saviour', *The Expository Times* (Volume 73, October 1961–September 1962), 296–7.

——, Joint Review of Daniel Jenkins, 'The Christian Belief in God', Austin Farrer, 'Saving Belief', Eric C. Rust, 'Towards a Theological Understanding of History', and H. A. Hodges, 'Death and Life Have Contended', *The Expository Times* (Volume 75, October 1963–September 1964), 231.

——, de Burge, W. G., Review of Austin Farrer, 'Finite and Infinite', *Mind* (Volume LII, Number 208, October 1943), 344–51.

Dupré, Louis, 'Themes in Contemporary Philosophy of Religion', *New Scholasticism* (Volume 43, 1969), 577–601.

Duncan, Steven M., 'Experience and Agency', in *Human and Divine Agency: Anglican, Catholic, and Lutheran Perspectives,* ed. F. Michael McLain and W. Mark Richardson (Lanham, MD: University Press of America, 1999), 149–61.

Eaton, Jeffrey C., 'Three Necessary Conditions for Thinking Theistically', in *For God and Clarity: New Essays in Honor of Austin Farrer,* ed. Jeffrey C. Eaton and Ann Loades (Allison Park, PA: Pickwick Publications, 1983), 151–61.

——, 'The Problem of Miracles and the Paradox of Double Agency', *Modern Theology* (Volume 1, Number 3, April 1985), 211–22.

——, 'Divine Action and Human Liberation', in *Divine Action: Studies Inspired by the Philosophical Theology of Austin Farrer,* ed. Brian Hebblethwaite and Edward Henderson (Edinburgh: T & T Clark, 1990), 211–29.

Eaton, Jeffrey C. and Ann Loades, 'Austin Marsden Farrer (1904–1968)', in *For God and Clarity: New Essays in Honor of Austin Farrer,* ed. Jeffrey C. Eaton and Ann Loades (Allison Park, PA: Pickwick Publications, 1983), xi–xiii.

Edwards, O. C. and David Hein, 'Farrer's Preaching: "Some Taste of the Things We Describe"', in *Captured by the Crucified: The Practical Theology of Austin Farrer,* ed. David Hein and Edward Hugh Henderson (New York and London: T & T Clark International, 2004), 173–95.

Emmet, Dorothy, Ted Bastin and Margaret Masterman, Review Discussion of Austin Farrer's 'A Science of God?', *Theoria to Theory* (Volume 1, 1966), 55–71.

Ferré, Frederick, Review of Austin Farrer, 'Faith and Speculation', *Theology Today* (Volume 25, Number 2, July 1968), 269.

——, Review of Charles Conti, 'Metaphysical Personalism', *Process Studies* (Volume 28, Numbers 1–2, Spring–Summer 1999), 141–3.

Forsman, Roger, '"Apprehension" in Finite and Infinite', in *For God and Clarity: New Essays in Honor of Austin Farrer*, ed. Jeffrey C. Eaton and Ann Loades (Allison Park, PA: Pickwick Publications, 1983), 111–30.

——, '"Double Agency" and Identifying Reference to God', in *Divine Action: Studies Inspired by the Philosophical Theology of Austin Farrer*, ed. Brian Hebblethwaite and Edward Henderson (Edinburgh: T & T Clark, 1990), 123–42.

——, 'Revelation and Understanding: A Defence of Tradition', in *Hermeneutics, the Bible and Literary Criticism*, ed. Ann Loades and Michael McLain (New York: St Martin's Press, 1992), 46–68.

Fox, Adam, Review of 'Austin Farrer, Love Almighty and Ills Unlimited', *Church Quarterly Review* (Volume CLXIII, 1962), 500–1.

Galilee, David and Brian Hebblethwaite, 'Farrer's Concept of Double Agency: A Reply', *Theology* (Volume LXXXV, Number 703, January 1982), 7–10.

Gill, Jerry H., 'Divine Action as Mediated', *Harvard Theological Review* (Volume 80, Number 3, 1987), 269–378.

Glasse, John, 'Doing Theology Metaphysically: Austin Farrer', *Harvard Theological Review* (Volume 59, Number 4, October 1966), 319–50.

Goulder, Michael, 'The Fram Abandoned', in Michael Goulder and John Hick, *Why Believe in God?* (London: SCM Press, 1983), 1–30.

——, 'Farrer on Q', *Theology* 83 (1980): 190–5.

——, 'Farrer the Biblical Scholar', in Philip Curtis, *A Hawk Among Sparrows: A Biography of Austin Farrer* (London: SPCK, 1985), 192–212.

Greer, Rowan, 'Foreword', in *Captured by the Crucified: The Practical Theology of Austin Farrer*, ed. David Hein and Edward Hugh Henderson (New York and London: T & T Clark International, 2004), ix–xi.

Gundry, D. W., 'The Philosophy of Religion, the Banner of a Sect', *Scottish Journal of Theology* (Volume 10, 1957), 113–21.

Hanson, Philip J., 'Austin Farrer and Jacques Ellul', *Cross Currents* (Volume XXXV, Number 1, Spring 1985), 81–3.

Harries, Richard, 'Introduction' to *The One Genius: Readings Through the Year with Austin Farrer*, ed. Richard Harries (London: SPCK, 1987), ix–xvi.

——, '"We Know On Our Knees": Intellectual, Imaginative, and Spiritual Unity in the Theology of Austin Farrer', in *Divine Action: Studies Inspired by the Philosophical Theology of Austin Farrer*, ed. Brian Hebblethwaite and Edward Henderson (Edinburgh: T & T Clark, 1990), 21–33.

——, 'The Commemoration Sermon', in *The Human Person in God's World: Studies to Commemorate the Austin Farrer Centenary*, ed. Douglas Hedley and Brian Hebblethwaite (London: SCM Press, 2006), 135–40.

Hartt, Julian, 'Dialectic, Analysis, and Empirical Generalization in Theology', *Crozer Quarterly* (Volume XXIX, Number 1, January 1952), 1–17.

——, 'Austin Farrer as Philosophical Theologian: A Retrospective and Appreciation', in *For God and Clarity: New Essays in Honor of Austin Farrer*, ed. Jeffrey C. Eaton and Ann Loades (Allison Park, PA: Pickwick Publications, 1983), 1–22.

——, Review of Charles Conti, 'Metaphysical Personalism', *Religious Studies* (Volume 32, 1996), 525–8.

Haugh, Hans, 'The Sin of Reading: Austin Farrer, Helen Gardner and Frank Kermode on the Poetry of St Mark', in *Hermeneutics, the Bible and Literary*

Criticism, ed. Ann Loades and Michael McLain (New York: St. Martin's Press, 1992), 113–28. Reprinted in *Scripture, Metaphysics, and Poetry: Austin Farrer's The Glass of Vision with Critical Commentary*, ed. Robert MacSwain (London and New York: Routledge, 2016).

Hebblethwaite, Brian, 'Austin Farrer's Concept of Divine Providence', *Theology* (Volume LXXIII, Number 606, December 1970), 541–51.

——, 'Providence and Divine Action', *Religious Studies* (Volume 14, 1978), 223–36.

——, 'The Experiential Verification of Religious Belief in the Theology of Austin Farrer', in *For God and Clarity: New Essays in Honor of Austin Farrer*, ed. Jeffrey C. Eaton and Ann Loades (Allison Park, PA: Pickwick Publications, 1983), 163–76.

——, 'Freedom, Evil and Farrer', *New Blackfriars* (Volume 66, Number 778, April 1985), 178–87.

——, 'The Doctrine of the Incarnation in the Thought of Austin Farrer' in Brian Hebblethwaite, *The Incarnation: Collected Essays in Christology* (Cambridge: Cambridge University Press, 1987), 112–25. Originally published in *New Fire* (Volume 4, Number 33, 1977), 460–8.

——, 'The Communication of Divine Revelation' in *Reason and the Christian Religion: Essays in Honour of Richard Swinburne*, ed. Alan G. Padgett (Oxford: Clarendon Press, 1994), 143–59.

——, 'The Believer's Reasons', in *Spirituality and Theology: Essays in Honor of Diogenes Allen*, ed. Eric O. Springsted (Louisville, KY: Westminster / John Knox Press, 1998), 37–48.

——, 'Finite and Infinite Freedom in Farrer and von Balthasar', in *Human and Divine Agency: Anglican, Catholic, and Lutheran Perspectives*, ed. F. Michael McLain and W. Mark Richardson (Lanham, MD: University Press of America, 1999), 83–96.

——, 'Farrer, Austin Marsden', in *The Oxford Dictionary of the Christian Church*, ed. F. L. Cross and E. A. Livingstone, Third Edition Revised (Oxford: Oxford University Press, 2005), 602.

——, 'God and the World as Known to Science', in *The Human Person in God's World: Studies to Commemorate the Austin Farrer Centenary*, ed. Douglas Hedley and Brian Hebblethwaite (London: SCM Press, 2006), 65–84.

——, 'Ann Loades and Austin Farrer', in *Exchanges of Grace: Essays in Honour of Ann Loades*, ed. Natalie K. Watson and Stephen Burns (London: SCM Press, 2008), 130–41.

——, 'Austin Farrer (1904–68)', in *The Blackwell Companion to the Theologians*, Volume 2, ed. Ian S. Markham (Chichester: Wiley-Blackwell, 2009), 257–62.

Hebblethwaite, Brian and Edward Henderson, 'Introduction' to *Divine Action: Studies Inspired by the Philosophical Theology of Austin Farrer*, ed. Brian Hebblethwaite and Edward Henderson (Edinburgh: T & T Clark, 1990), 1–20.

Hedley, Douglas, 'Austin Farrer's Shaping Spirit of Imagination', in *The Human Person in God's World: Studies to Commemorate the Austin Farrer Centenary*, ed. Douglas Hedley and Brian Hebblethwaite (London: SCM Press, 2006), 106–34. Reprinted in *Scripture, Metaphysics, and Poetry: Austin Farrer's The Glass of Vision with Critical Commentary*, ed. Robert MacSwain (London and New York: Routledge, 2016).

Hedley, Douglas and Brian Hebblethwaite, 'Preface and Acknowledgements' to *The Human Person in God's World: Studies to Commemorate the Austin Farrer Centenary*, ed. Douglas Hedley and Brian Hebblethwaite (London: SCM Press, 2006), vii.

Hefling, Charles C., Jr, 'Farrer, Austin M.', in *The Westminster Dictionary of Christian Spirituality*, ed. Gordon S. Wakefield (Philadelphia: The Westminster Press, 1983), 146–7.

———, 'Origen *Redivivus*: Farrer's Scriptural Divinity', in *For God and Clarity: New Essays in Honor of Austin Farrer*, ed. Jeffrey C. Eaton and Ann Loades (Allison Park, PA: Pickwick Publications, 1983), 35–50.

———, 'Farrer's Scriptural Divinity', in *Captured by the Crucified: The Practical Theology of Austin Farrer*, ed. David Hein and Edward Hugh Henderson (New York and London: T & T Clark International, 2004), 149–72.

———, Review of Brian Hebblethwaite, *The Philosophical Theology of Austin Farrer*, *Reviews in Religion and Theology* (Volume 16, Issue 1, January 2009), 123–5.

Hein, David, 'Farrer on Friendship, Sainthood, and the Will of God', in *Captured by the Crucified: The Practical Theology of Austin Farrer*, ed. David Hein and Edward Hugh Henderson (New York and London: T & T Clark International, 2004), 119–48.

———, 'Austin Farrer on Justification and Sanctification', *The Anglican Digest* (Volume 49, Number 1, Lent 2007), 51–4.

Hein, David and Edward Hugh Henderson, 'Acknowledgements', in *Captured by the Crucified: The Practical Theology of Austin Farrer*, ed. David Hein and Edward Hugh Henderson (New York and London: T & T Clark International, 2004), xiii–xvii.

———, 'Introduction', in *Captured by the Crucified: The Practical Theology of Austin Farrer*, ed. David Hein and Edward Hugh Henderson (New York and London: T & T Clark International, 2004), 1–13.

Henderson, Edward, 'Knowing the World: The Process View of Austin Farrer', *Philosophy Today* (Volume 12, 1968), 204–14.

———, 'Knowing Persons and Knowing God', *The Thomist* (Volume 46, 1982), 394–422.

———, 'Valuing in Knowing God: An Interpretation of Austin Farrer's Religious Epistemology', *Modern Theology* (Volume 1, Number 3, April 1985), 165–82.

———, 'Austin Farrer and D. Z. Phillips on Lived Faith, Prayer, and Divine Reality', *Modern Theology* (Volume 1, Number 3, April 1985), 223–43.

———, 'The Supremely Free Agent', in *Human and Divine Agency: Anglican, Catholic, and Lutheran Perspectives*, ed. F. Michael McLain and W. Mark Richardson (Lanham, MD: University Press of America, 1999), 97–119.

———, 'How to Be a Christian Philosopher in the Postmodern World', in *Spirituality and Theology: Essays in Honor of Diogenes Allen*, ed. Eric O. Springsted (Louisville, KY: Westminster / John Knox Press, 1998), 63–86.

———, 'The God Who Undertakes Us', in *Captured by the Crucified: The Practical Theology of Austin Farrer*, ed. David Hein and Edward Hugh Henderson (New York and London: T & T Clark International, 2004), 66–99.

———, 'Incarnation and Double Agency', in *Truth, Religious Dialogue, and Dynamic Orthodoxy: Essays in Honour of Brian Hebblethwaite*, ed. Julius J. Lipner (London: SCM Press, 2005), 154–64.

——, 'Double Agency and the Relations of Persons to God,' in *The Human Person in God's World: Studies to Commemorate the Austin Farrer Centenary*, ed. Douglas Hedley and Brian Hebblethwaite (London: SCM Press, 2006), 38–64.

Hick, John, Review of Austin Farrer, 'The Freedom of the Will', *Theology Today* (Volume 17, Number 2, July 1960), 268–70.

——, Review of Austin Farrer, 'Faith and Speculation', *Theology* (Volume LXX, Number 570, December 1967), 557–8.

——, 'Foreword' in Austin Farrer, *Reflective Faith: Essays in Philosophical Theology*, ed. Charles C. Conti (London: SPCK, 1972), xiii–xv.

Hobbs, Edward, 'A Quarter Century without Q', *Perkins School of Theology Journal* 33/4 (1980): 10–19.

Horne, B. L., 'Austin Farrer's Metaphysics' (Review of Charles Conti, 'Metaphysical Personalism'), *The Expository Times* (Volume 108, Number 5, 1997), 153–4.

Houlden, Leslie, 'Foreword' in Austin Farrer, *The Brink of Mystery*, ed. Charles C. Conti, foreword by Leslie Houlden (London: SPCK, 1976), ix–x.

——, 'Introduction' in Austin Farrer, *The Essential Sermons*, ed. and introduced by Leslie Houlden (London: SPCK, 1991), ix–x.

——, 'Introduction: Farrer the Preacher' in Austin Farrer, *Words for Life: Forty Meditations Previously Unpublished*, ed. Charles Conti and Leslie Houlden, preface by Charles Conti, introduction by Leslie Houlden (London: SPCK, 1993), xi–xiii.

Howatch, Susan, 'Author's Note' in *Absolute Truths* (New York: Fawcett Crest / Ballantine Publishing, 1994), 622–4.

——, 'Introduction' to Austin Farrer, *Saving Belief: A Discussion of Essentials*, Library of Anglican Spirituality, ed. and with an introduction by Susan Howatch (London: Mowbray / Harrisburg, PA: Morehouse, 1994), vii–xi.

Huston, Hollis W., 'The "Q Parties" at Oxford', *The Journal of Bible and Religion* 25/2 (April 1957): 123–8.

Jasper, David, 'General Editor's Preface', in *Hermeneutics, the Bible and Literary Criticism*, ed. Ann Loades and Michael McLain (New York: St. Martin's Press, 1992), vii.

Jones, Bernard, Review of Austin Farrer, 'The Freedom of the Will', *The Expository Times* (Volume 75, October 1963–September 1964), 170–1.

Kenny, Anthony, 'Introduction' in *The Unknown God: Agnostic Essays* (London and New York: Continuum, 2004), 1–6.

——, 'The Problem of Evil and the Argument from Design' in Anthony Kenny, *The Unknown God: Agnostic Essays* (London and New York: Continuum, 2004), 81–100. Originally published in *Archivo di Filosofia* (Volume 56, 1988), 545–55.

King, Robert H., 'The Agent's World: Farrer's Contribution to Cosmology', in *For God and Clarity: New Essays in Honor of Austin Farrer*, ed. Jeffrey C. Eaton and Ann Loades (Allison Park, PA: Pickwick Publications, 1983), 23–34.

Koons, Robert C., 'Dual Agency: A Thomistic Account of Providence and Human Freedom', *Philosophia Christi* (Series 2, Volume 4, Number 2, 2002), 397–410.

Lewis, C. S., 'Preface' to Austin Farrer, *A Faith of Our Own* (Cleveland, OH and New York: The World Publishing Company, 1960). American edition of *Said or Sung*.

Lewis, H. D., Review of Basil Mitchell (ed.), 'Faith and Logic', *Journal of Theological Studies* NS (Volume X, 1959), 202–5.

Lewis, John Underwood, 'Austin Farrer's Notion of "Conscience as an Appetite for Moral Truth": its Metaphysical Foundation and Importance to Contemporary Moral Philosophy', in *For God and Clarity: New Essays in Honor of Austin Farrer*, ed. Jeffrey C. Eaton and Ann Loades (Allison Park, PA: Pickwick Publications, 1983), 131–50.

Loades, Ann, 'Austin Farrer on Love Almighty', in *For God and Clarity: New Essays in Honor of Austin Farrer*, ed. Jeffrey C. Eaton and Ann Loades (Allison Park, PA: Pickwick Publications, 1983), 93–109.

——, 'Farrer, Austin Marsden,' in *The SPCK Handbook of Anglican Theologians*, ed. Alister E. McGrath (London: SPCK, 1998), 120–3.

——, 'The Vitality of Tradition: Austin Farrer and Friends', in *Captured by the Crucified: The Practical Theology of Austin Farrer*, ed. David Hein and Edward Hugh Henderson (New York and London: T & T Clark International, 2004), 15–46.

——, Review of Robert Boak Slocum, 'Light in a Burning Glass: A Systematic Presentation of Austin Farrer's Theology', *Theology* (Volume, CXII, Number 868, July/August 2009), 281–2.

Loades, Ann and Michael McLain, 'Foreword' to *Hermeneutics, the Bible and Literary Criticism*, ed. Ann Loades and Michael McLain (New York: St Martin's Press, 1992), viii–ix.

Loughlin, Gerard, 'Making it Plain: Austin Farrer and the Inspiration of Scripture', in *Hermeneutics, the Bible and Literary Criticism*, ed. Ann Loades and Michael McLain (New York: St Martin's Press, 1992), 96–112. Reprinted in *Scripture, Metaphysics, and Poetry: Austin Farrer's The Glass of Vision with Critical Commentary*, ed. Robert MacSwain (London and New York: Routledge, 2016).

MacSwain, Robert, Review of 'Captured by the Crucified: The Practical Theology of Austin Farrer', ed. David Hein and Edward Hugh Henderson, *Studies in Christian Ethics* (Volume 18, Number 3, 2005), 154–7.

——, 'Above, Beside, Within: The Anglican Theology of Austin Farrer', *Journal of Anglican Studies* (Volume 4, Number 1, June 2006), 33–57.

——, Review of 'The Human Person in God's World: Studies to Commemorate the Austin Farrer Centenary', ed. Douglas Hedley and Brian Hebblethwaite, *International Journal of Systematic Theology* (Volume 9, Number 4, October 2007), 471–3.

——, Review of Robert Boak Slocum, 'Light in a Burning Glass: A Systematic Presentation of Austin Farrer's Theology', *Anglican Theological Review* (Volume 89, Number 4, Fall 2007), 682–3.

——, 'A Fertile Friendship: C. S. Lewis and Austin Farrer', *The Chronicle of the Oxford University C. S. Lewis Society* (Volume 5, Issue 2, Trinity Term / May 2008), 22–45.

——, 'Imperfect Lives and Perfect Love: Austin Farrer, Stanley Hauerwas, and the Reach of Divine Redemption', in *Exchanges of Grace: Essays in Honour of Ann Loades*, ed. Natalie K. Watson and Stephen Burns (London: SCM Press, 2008), 142–54.

——, Review of Brian Hebblethwaite, 'The Philosophical Theology of Austin Farrer', *International Journal of Systematic Theology* (Volume 11, Number 3, July 2009), 365–7.

——, 'Learning to Pray with Austin Farrer', *Sewanee Theological Review* (Volume 52, Number 4, Michaelmas 2009), pp. 409–21.

———, Review of Austin Farrer, 'A Science of God?', second edition with a new foreword by Margaret Yee, *Anglican Theological Review* (Volume 92, Number 3, Summer 2010), 564–6.

———, 'Centenary Perspectives on Austin Farrer: A Review Article', *Philosophy Compass* (Volume 5, Issue 9, September 2010), 820–29, published online at: http://onlinelibrary.wiley.com/doi/10.1111/j.1747-9991.2010.00322.x/abstract.

———, 'Farrer, Austin Marsden' in *A Dictionary of Philosophy of Religion*, ed. Charles Taliaferro and Elsa J. Marty (London and New York: Continuum, 2010), 86–7. Revised entry, 101–02, in the Second Edition, 2018.

———, 'Documentation and Correspondence Related to Austin Farrer's Baptism in the Church of England on 14 May 1924', *Anglican and Episcopal History* (Volume 81, Number 3, September 2012), 241–76.

———, Review of Robert Titley, 'A Poetic Discontent: Austin Farrer and the Gospel of Mark', *Anglican Theological Review* (Volume 94, Number 3, Summer 2012), 579–83.

———, Review of Darren M. Kennedy, 'Providence and Personalism: Karl Barth in Conversation with Austin Farrer, John Macmurray and Vincent Brümmer', *Sewanee Theological Review* (Volume 56, Number 1, Christmas 2012), 94–6.

———, "Introduction: 'The Form of Divine Truth in the Human Mind'," in *Scripture, Metaphysics, and Poetry: Austin Farrer's The Glass of Vision with Critical Commentary*, ed. Robert MacSwain (London and New York: Routledge, 2016), 1–8.

———, "Austin Farrer", in *Twentieth-Century Anglican Theologians*, ed. Stephen Burns, Bryan Cones and James Tengatenga (Wiley-Blackwell, forthcoming 2020).

———, "Farrer, Austin Marsden", in *Dictionary of Christian Apologists and Their Critics*, ed. R. Douglas Geivett and Robert B. Stewart (Wiley-Blackwell, forthcoming 2020).

Mascall, E. L., 'Austin Marsden Farrer (1904–1968)', in *Proceedings of the British Academy*, Volume LIV, 1968 (London: Oxford University Press, 1970), 435–42.

———, 'On Dispensing with Q' (Poem), in *Pi in the High* (London: The Faith Press, 1959), 48.

———, Review of Austin Farrer, 'Reflective Faith', *Religious Studies* (Volume 9, Number 2, June 1973), 241–4.

———, 'Foreword' in *Interpretation and Belief*, ed. Charles C. Conti, foreword by E. L. Mascall (London: SPCK, 1976), xiii–xiv.

Mathew, Gervase, OP, Review of Austin Farrer, 'Finite and Infinite', *Blackfriars* (Volume XXV, Number 286, January 1944), 33–4.

McIntosh, Mark A., 'Essential Reading', *Anglican Theological Review* (Volume 83, Number 1, Winter 2001), 189–90.

McLain, F. Michael, 'Austin Farrer's Revision of the Cosmological Argument', *The Downside Review* (Volume 88, Number 292, July 1970), 270–9.

———, 'Narrative Interpretation and the Problem of Double Agency', in *Divine Action: Studies Inspired by the Philosophical Theology of Austin Farrer*, ed. Brian Hebblethwaite and Edward Henderson (Edinburgh: T & T Clark, 1990), 143–72.

———, 'Introduction' to *Human and Divine Agency: Anglican, Catholic, and Lutheran Perspectives*, ed. F. Michael McLain and W. Mark Richardson (Lanham, MD: University Press of America, 1999), vi–x.

Miller, Sarah, '"With My Utmost Art": The Inspiration of George Herbert's Poetry and the Limits of Austin Farrer's Vision,' in *Anglican Theological Review* (Volume 98, Number 3, Summer 2016), 513–31.

Mitchell, Basil, 'Austin Marsden Farrer', in Austin Farrer, *A Celebration of Faith*, edited by Leslie Houlden (London: Hodder and Stoughton, 1970), 13–16.

——, 'Austin Farrer', in *The Anglican Spirit*, ed. P. G. Wignall (Cuddesdon, Oxfordshire: Ripon College, Cuddesdon, 1982), 41–4.

——, 'Austin Farrer: The Philosopher', *New Fire* (Volume 7, Number 57, Winter 1983), 452–6.

——, 'Two Approaches to the Philosophy of Religion', in *For God and Clarity: New Essays in Honor of Austin Farrer*, ed. Jeffrey C. Eaton and Ann Loades (Allison Park, PA: Pickwick Publications, 1983), 117–90.

——, 'War and Friendship', in *Philosophers Who Believe: The Spiritual Journeys of 11 Leading Thinkers*, ed. Kelly James Clark (Downers Grove, IL: InterVarsity Press, 1993), 23–44.

——, 'Introduction' to *The Human Person in God's World: Studies to Commemorate the Austin Farrer Centenary*, ed. Douglas Hedley and Brian Hebblethwaite (London: SCM Press, 2006), 1–13.

Morris, J. N., 'Religious Experience in the Philosophical Theology of Austin Farrer', *The Journal of Theological Studies* NS (Volume 45, Part 2, October 1994), 569–92.

——, Review of Charles Conti, 'Metaphysical Personalism: An Analysis of Austin Farrer's Theistic Metaphysics', *Journal of Theological Studies* (Volume 47, Part 2, 1996), 792–6.

——, '"An Infallible Fact-Factory Going Full Blast": Austin Farrer, Marian Doctrine, and the Travails of Anglo-Catholicism', in *The Church and Mary: Papers Read at the 2001 Summer Meeting and the 2002 Winter Meeting of the Ecclesiastical History Society, Studies in Church History 39*, ed. R. N. Swanson (Woodbridge, Suffolk: Boydell Press, 2004), 358–67.

Murphy, Nancey, 'Downward Causation and The Freedom of the Will', in *The Human Person in God's World: Studies to Commemorate the Austin Farrer Centenary*, ed. Douglas Hedley and Brian Hebblethwaite (London: SCM Press, 2006), 14–37.

Norris, Richard A., Jr, 'Essential Reading', *Anglican Theological Review* (Volume 82, Number 3, Summer 2000), 631–4.

Ogden, Schubert M., '*Must* God Be Really Related to Creatures?', *Process Studies* (Volume 20, Number 1, Spring 1991), 54–6.

Oliver, Simon, 'The Theodicy of Austin Farrer', *The Heythrop Journal* (Volume XXXIX, Number 3, July 1998), 280–97.

——, Review of Brian Hebblethwaite, 'The Philosophical Theology of Austin Farrer', *The Chronicle of the Oxford University C. S. Lewis Society* (Volume 6, Issue 3, Michaelmas Term / October 2009), 42–4.

Olson, Ken, 'Unpicking on the Farrer Theory' in *Questioning Q*, ed. Mark Goodacre and Nicholas Perrin (London: SPCK, 2004), 127–50.

Owen, H. P., Review of Austin Farrer, 'Faith and Speculation', *The Journal of Theological Studies* (Volume XIX, Part 2, October 1968), 699–702.

Packer, J. I., 'Farrer, Austin Marsden', in *New Dictionary of Theology*, ed. Sinclair B. Ferguson and David F. Wright (Leicester, UK / Downers Grove, IL: InterVarsity Press, 1988), 253.

Peterson, Jeffrey, 'A Pioneer Narrative Critic and His Synoptic Hypothesis: Austin Farrer and Gospel Interpretation', in *Society of Biblical Literature Seminar Papers 2000*, *Society of Biblical Literature Seminar Paper Series* 39 (Atlanta: Society of Biblical Literature, 2000), 651–72.

Platten, Stephen, 'Diaphanous Thought: Spirituality and Theology in the Work of Austin Farrer', *Anglican Theological Review* (Volume 69, Number 1, January 1987), 30–50.

Ramsey, I. T., Review of Austin Farrer, 'The Freedom of the Will', *Journal of Theological Studies*, NS (Volume X, 1959), 456–9.

Ramsey, Michael, 'Foreword' to *The One Genius: Readings Through the Year with Austin Farrer* (London: SPCK, 1987), vii.

Richardson, W. Mark, 'A Look at Austin Farrer's Theory of Agency', in *Human and Divine Agency: Anglican, Catholic, and Lutheran Perspectives*, ed. F. Michael McLain and W. Mark Richardson (Lanham, MD: University Press of America, 1999), 121–48.

Root, Howard, Joint Review C. A. Campbell, 'On Selfhood and Godhood' and Basil Mitchell (ed.), 'Faith and Logic', *Theology* (Volume LXII, Number 463, January 1959), 36–8.

Sarot, Marcel, 'Farrer, Austin Marsden (1904–68)', in *The Dictionary of Historical Theology*, ed. Trevor Hart (Carlisle, UK and Waynesboro, GA: Paternoster Press/Grand Rapids, MI and Cambridge, UK: William B. Eerdmans Publishing Company, 2000), 209–10.

Slocum, Robert B., 'Light in a Burning-Glass: The Theological Witness of Austin Farrer', *Anglican Theological Review* (Volume 85, Number 2, Spring 2003), 365–73.

———, 'Farrer in the Pulpit: A Systematic Introduction to His Sermons', *Anglican Theological Review* (Volume 86, Number 3, Summer 2004), 493–503.

Smart, Ninian, 'Revelation and Reasons', *Scottish Journal of Theology* (Volume 11, 1958), 352–61.

———, Review of Austin Farrer, 'Faith and Speculation', *The Philosophical Quarterly* (Volume 20, Number 78, January 1970), 93.

Stahl, John T., 'Austin Farrer on C. S. Lewis as "The Christian Apologist"', *Christian Scholars' Review* (Volume 4, Number 3, 1975), 231–7.

Strawson, P. F., Review of Austin Farrer, 'The Freedom of the Will', *Mind* (Volume LXIX, Number 275, 1960), 416–18.

Taliaferro, Charles, Review of 'Divine Action: Studies Inspired by the Philosophical Theology of Austin Farrer', ed. Brian Hebblethwaite and Edward Henderson, *Faith and Philosophy* (Volume 10, Number 1, January 1993), 119–23.

———, Review of Charles Conti, 'Metaphysical Personalism: An Analysis of Austin Farrer's Theistic Metaphysics', in *Journal of Religion* (Volume 78, Number 1, January 1998), 143–4.

Taylor, A. E., Review of Austin Farrer, 'Finite and Infinite', *Journal of Theological Studies* OS (Volume XLV, Number 179–180, 1944), 237–47.

TeSelle, Eugene, 'Divine Action: The Doctrinal Tradition', in *Divine Action: Studies Inspired by the Philosophical Theology of Austin Farrer*, ed. Brian Hebblethwaite and Edward Henderson (Edinburgh: T & T Clark, 1990), 71–91.

Thomas, Owen C., 'Recent Thought on Divine Agency', in *Divine Action: Studies Inspired by the Philosophical Theology of Austin Farrer*, ed. Brian Hebblethwaite and Edward Henderson (Edinburgh: T & T Clark, 1990), 35–50.

Tortorelli, Kevin, 'Some Contributions of Balthasar and Farrer on the Subject of the Analogy of Being', *The Downside Review* (Volume 107, July 1989), 183–90.

Tracy, Thomas F., 'Narrative Theology and the Acts of God', in *Divine Action: Studies Inspired by the Philosophical Theology of Austin Farrer*, ed. Brian Hebblethwaite and Edward Henderson (Edinburgh: T & T Clark, 1990), 173–96.

———, 'Divine Action, Created Causes, and Human Freedom', in *The God Who Acts: Philosophical and Theological Explorations*, ed. Thomas F. Tracy (University Park, PA: The Pennsylvania University Press, 1994), 77–102.

Turner, Vincent, SJ, 'Mr Austin Farrer's Metaphysics of Theism', *Theology* (Volume XLVII, Number 287, May 1944), 99–104.

Vaughn, J. Barry, 'Resurrection and Grace: The Sermons of Austin Farrer', *Preaching* (Volume 9, Number 5, 1994), 61–3.

Vogel, Arthur A., 'Essential Reading', *Anglican Theological Review* (Volume 81, Number 4, Fall 1999), 767–8.

Vogel, Jeffrey, Review of *The Human Person in God's World: Studies to Commemorate the Austin Farrer Centenary*, ed. Douglas Hedley and Brian Hebblethwaite, and *The Truth-Seeking Heart: Austin Farrer and His Writings*, ed. Ann Loades and Robert MacSwain, *Anglican Theological Review* (Volume 90, Number 3, Summer 2008), 660–3.

———, 'A Little While in the Son of God: Austin Farrer on the Trinitarian Nature of Prayer', *Scottish Journal of Theology* (Volume 64, Issue 04, November 2011), 410–24.

———, 'A Self-effacing Gardener: The Unity of God's Activity in Nature and Grace in the Theology of Austin Farrer', *Christian Scholar's Review* (Volume 45, Issue 3, 2016): 229–47.

Ward, Keith, Review of Austin Farrer, 'Faith and Speculation', *Scottish Journal of Theology* (Volume 21, 1968), 224–5.

Williams, Thomas, 'Farrer, Austin Marsden (1904–68)', in *The Routledge Encyclopedia of Philosophy. Volume 3: Descartes to Gender and Science*, General Editor: Edward Craig (London: Routledge, 1998), 560–1.

Wiles, Maurice, 'Farrer's Concept of Double Agency', *Theology* (Volume LXXXIV, Number 700, July 1981), 243–9.

———, 'Continuing the Discussion', *Theology* (Volume LXXXV, Number 703, January 1982), 10–13.

Wilson, M. P., 'Austin Farrer and the Paradox of Christology', *Scottish Journal of Theology* (Volume 35, Number 2, April 1982), 145–63.

———, 'St John, the Trinity, and the Language of the Spirit', *Scottish Journal of Theology* (Volume 41, Number 4, December 1988), 471–83.

Wilson, William M., 'A Different Method, a Different Case: The Theological Program of Julian Hartt and Austin Farrer', *The Thomist* (Volume 53, Number 2, 1989), 599–633.

Wilson, William McF. and Julian N. Hartt, 'Farrer's Theodicy', in *Captured by the Crucified: The Practical Theology of Austin Farrer*, ed. David Hein and Edward Hugh Henderson (New York and London: T & T Clark International, 2004), 100–18.

Woods, G. F., Review of Austin Farrer, 'Love Almighty and Ills Unlimited', *Theology* (Volume LXVI, 1963), 375–7.

Author Index

Subject Index